EDUCATIONAL AND SOCIAL UPLIFT OF BACKWARD CLASSES

About the Authors

S.P. Agrawal (*b.* 1929) was Director, National Social Science Documentation Centre, ICSSR, and Member Secretary, Indian Association of Social Science Institutions. He was also the Vice- Chairman of the Asia and Pacific Information Network in Social Sciences (APINESS). In 1988 he was awarded the degree of Doctor of Philosophy in Education (*honoris causa*) by International University Foundation. Presently he is Member, Round Table on Research in Reading, IFLA, and Member, International Committee for Social Science Information and Documentation. He is also Member of Hindi Advisory Committee. Ministry of Energy, Department of Coal. He has written extensively on various aspects of education as well as of library and information science. His numerous raido broadcastes on *Gandhian* have been widely appreciated.

J.C. Aggarwal (*b.* 1928) has authored singly/jointly more than 100 books on various aspects of social science subjects. His recent publications include *Lok Sabha and Vidhan Sabha Elections in India* 1989 and 1990, (1990) *Information India,* 1980-90 *Global View* (1990), *Documentation Encyclopaedia of UNESCO and Education* (1990), *Education in India : Comparative Study of States and Union Territories* (1990), *Educational Reforms in India : World Perspective* (1990); *Curriculum Reforms in India : World Overview* (1990), *A Handbook of Teaching Aptitude* (1990), *A Handbook of Subject Competency* (1990), *Elementary Education in India and Teacher Functions : A comparative Study of Elementary Education in 172 countries* (1990), *Elementary Educational Psychology* (1990), *Emerging Problems of Elementary Education* (1990), *Educational Research - An Introduction (1990), Development of Modern Education and Planning* (1990), *Theory and Principles of Education (1990) and Seven Indian Educationists* (1990).

Shri Aggarwal retired as Deputy Director of Education/Executive Director, Delhi Bureau of Textbooks, Delhi Administration.

Concepts in Communication Informatics & Librarianship-26

General Editor: **S.P. Agrawal**

EDUCATIONAL AND SOCIAL UPLIFT OF BACKWARD CLASSES

At What Cost and How?

Mandal Commission and After

Part I

Constitutional Provisions, Observations in Education Commission, New Education Policy and Review Committee on NPE (1990), Commitment in various Election Manifestoes, Government Policy, a Critique by Cross-Section of Society, Listing of Backward Classes and Bibliographical Documentation

S.P. Agrawal
J.C. Aggarwal

CONCEPT PUBLISHING COMPANY PVT. LTD.
NEW DELHI-110059

ISBN : 978-81-7022-339-9

Edition 2020

Published and Printed by

Concept
Since 1974

Concept Publishing Company Pvt. Ltd.
A/15-16, Commercial Block, Mohan Garden,
New Delhi-110059 (INDIA)
T: +91 11 25351460, +91 11 25351794
E : publishing@conceptpub.com, *W* : www.conceptpub.com

Cataloging in Publication Data--Courtesy: D.K. Agencies (P) Ltd. <docinfo@dkagencies.com>

Agrawal, S. P., 1929- author.
Educational and social uplift of backward classes : at what cost and how? : Mandal Commission and after / S.P. Agrawal, J.C. Aggarwal.
volumes cm. -- (Concepts in communication, informatics & librarianship ; 26)
Reprint. Originally published: 1991.
Includes bibliographical references and index.
Contents: part 1. Constitutional provisions, observations in Education Commission, New Education Policy and Review Committee on NPE (1990), commitment in various election manifestoes, government policy, a critique by cross-section of society, listing of backward classes and bibliographical documentation
ISBN 9788170223399

1. Caste--India. 2. People with social disabilities--Government policy--India. 3. Reverse discrimination--India. 4. India. Backward Classes Commission, 1980. I. Aggarwal, J. C., author. II. Title. III. Series: Concepts in communication informatics & librarianship ; 26.

LCC HT720.A37 2020 | DDC 305.51220954 23

Dedicated

To our younger brothers and sisters who have suffered — some even laid down their lives emotionally — to focus attention on the gravity of the issues involved, for whom our hearts bleed;

To our backward and depressed brethren, who have lived all along almost in sub-human conditions for their no visible fault, for whom the bell tolls;

To anthropologists, historians, social scientists and all research workers, who would analyse events and draw conclusions, for whom we have toiled to be objective; and

To political workers and legislators of all shades whom we pray and expect to take judicious decisions based on all relevant information for the uplift of one and all — UNTO THE LAST.

General Editor's Introduction

THE PRIME Minister Shri Vishwanath Pratap Singh announced on August 7, 1990, in both the Houses of the Parliament, the National Front Government's decision to give 27 per cent job reservation to Socially and Educationally Backward Classes, (SEBCs) in the Central Government and Public Sector Undertakings. This raised the reservation of jobs for various classes to 49.5 per cent since there was already a reservation of 15 per cent for the Scheduled Castes and 7.5 per cent for the Scheduled Tribes. The 27 per cent reservations are said to be in pursuance of the recommendations of the Second Backward Classes Commission, under the Chairmanship of the late Shri B.P. Mandal. The Commission was appointed on January 1, 1979 and it submitted its report on December 31, 1980.

On August 17, 1990, the Union Government issued a Memorandum reserving 27 per cent of the vacancies in Civil Posts and Services for SEBCs. This reservation also applies to Public Sector Undertakings and financial institutions.

The country witnesses widespread agitation against the reservation policy.

The need of the hour is to break the barriers that divide the nation.

While there is a general consensus regarding the promotion of welfare of the weaker sections of the society, there are differences over the measures to be adopted for the achievement of this task.

Only time will tell if the reservation policy is an harbinger of prosperity or a cause of disunity. Nevertheless, there is an urgent need to avoid populist decisions for the ultimate good of the people.

As observed very emphatically by the Education Commission (1964-66), **The education of the backward classes in general and the tribal people in particular is a major programme of equalisation and of social and national integration. No expenditure is too great for the purpose.**

In the following pages an attempt has been made to throw light on the reservation policy within the Fundamental Rights and Directive Principles of State Policy as outlined in the Constitution of India, to provide adequate material on the recommendations of the Mandal Commission and to evaluate the impact of the reservation policy as seen by the cross-section of society.

A chapter on the commitment of the major political parties as reflected in their Election Manifestoes (1989-90) has also been included for ready reference.

It is hoped that the book will prove to be a handy reference tool for diverse sections of society – Policy Makers, Political Party Workers, Reservationists and the Anti-reservationists, to be able to view the whole issue in an objective perspective.

S.P. AGRAWAL

Contents

APPENDICES

1

Fundamental Rights and Directive Principles of State Policy

THE CONSTITUTION OF INDIA

PREAMBLE

WE THE people of India, having solemnly resolved to constitute India into a [1][**Sovereign Socialist Secular Democratic Republic**] and to secure to all its citizens:

Justice, social, economic and political;
Liberty of thought, expression, belief, faith and worship;
Equality of status and of opportunity;

and to promote among them all

Fraternity assuring the dignity of the individual and the [2][unity and integrity of the Nation]

In our Constituent Assembly this twenty-sixth day of November, 1949, do **Hereby Adopt, Enact and Give to Ourselves this Constitution.**

PART III

FUNDAMENTAL RIGHTS

Right to Equality

14. *Equality before Law*: The State shall not deny to any person

equality before the law or the equal protection of the laws within the territory of India.

15. *Prohibition of Discrimination on Grounds of Religion, Race, Caste, Sex or Place of Birth*

(1) The State shall not discriminate against any citizen on grounds only of religion, race, caste, sex, place of birth or any of them.
(2) No citizen shall, on grounds only of religion, race, caste, sex, place of birth or any of them, be subject to any disability, liability, restriction or condition with regard to—

(*a*) access to shops, public restaurants, hotels and places of public entertainment; or
(*b*) the use of wells, tanks, bathing ghats, roads and places of public resort maintained wholly or partly out of State funds or dedicated to the use of general public.

(3) Nothing in this article shall prevent the State from making any special provision for women and children.
[3][(4) Nothing in this article or in clause (2) of article 29 shall prevent the State from making any special provision for the advancement of any socially and educationally backward classes of citizens or for the Scheduled Castes and the Scheduled Tribes.]

16. *Equality of Opportunity in Matters of Public Employment*

(1) There shall be equality of opportunity for all citizens in matters relating to employment or appointment to any office under the State.
(2) No citizen shall, on grounds only of religion, race, caste, sex, descent, place of birth, residence or any of them, be ineligible for, or discriminated against in respect of, any employment or office under the State.
(3) Nothing in this article shall prevent Parliament from making any law prescribing, in regard to a class or classes of employment or appointment to an office [4][under the Government of, or any local or other authority within, a State or union territory, any requirement as to residence within that state

or Union Territory] prior to such employment or appointment.

(4) Nothing in this article shall prevent the State from making any provision for the reservation of appointments or posts in favour of any backward class of citizens which, in the opinion of the State, is not adequately represented in the services under the State.

(5) Nothing in this article shall affect the operation of any law which provides that the incumbent of an office in connection with the affairs of any religious or denominational institution or any member of the governing body thereof shall be a person professing a particular religion or belonging to a particular denomination.

17. *Abolition of Untouchability* - "Untouchability" is abolished and its practice in any form is forbidden. The enforcement of any disability arising out of "Untouchability" shall be an offence punishable in accordance with law.

PART IV

DIRECTIVE PRINCIPLES OF STATE POLICY

37. *Application of the Principles contained in this Part* - The provisions contained in this Part shall not be enforceable by any court, but the principles therein laid down are nevertheless fundamental in the governance of the country and it shall be the duty of the State to apply these principles in making laws.

38. *State to secure a social order for the promotion of welfare of the people* -

[5][(1)] The State shall strive to promote the welfare of the people by securing and protecting as effectively as it may a social order in which justice, social, economic and political, shall inform all the institutions of the national life.

[6][(2)] The State shall, in particular strive to minimise the inequalities in income, and endeavour to eliminate inequalities in status, facilities and opportunities, not only amongst individuals but also amongst groups of people residing in different areas or engaged in different vocations.]

39. *Certain Principles of Policy to be followed by the State* – The State shall, in particular, direct its policy towards securing–

(a) that the citizen, men and women equally, have the right to an adequate means of livelihood;
(b) that the ownership and control of the material resources of the community are so distributed as best to subserve the common good;
(c) that the operation of the economic system does not result in the concentration of wealth and means of production to the common detriment;
(d) that there is equal pay for equal work for both men and women;
(e) that the health and strength of workers, men and women, and the tender age of children are not abused and that citizens are not forced by economic necessity to enter avocations unsuited to their age or strength;
[7][(f) that children are given opportunities and facilities to develop in a healthy manner and in conditions of freedom and dignity and that childhood and youth are protected against exploitation and against moral and material abandonment.]

[8][39 A. *Equal Justice and Free Legal Aid*– The State shall secure that the operation of the legal system promotes justice, on a basis of equal opportunity, and shall, in particular, provide free legal aid, by suitable legislation or schemes or in any other way, to ensure that opportunities for securing justice are not denied to any citizen by reason of economic or other disabilities.]

41. *Right to Work, to Education and to Public Assistance in Certain Cases*– The State shall, within the limits of its economic capacity and development, make effective provision for securing the right to work, to education and to public assistance in cases of unemployment, old age, sickness and disablement, and in other cases of undeserved want.

44. *Uniform Civil Code for the Citizens*– The State shall endeavour to secure for the citizens a uniform civil code throughout the territory of India.

45. *Provision for Free and Compulsory Education for Children*– The State shall endeavour to provide, within a period of ten years from the commencement of this Constitution, for free and compulsory education for all children until they complete the age of fourteen years.

46. *Promotion of Educational and Economic Interests of Scheduled*

Castes, Scheduled Tribes and Other Weaker Sections– The State shall promote with special care the educational and economic interests of the weaker sections of the people, and in particular, of the Scheduled Castes and the Scheduled Tribes, and shall protect them from social injustice and all forms of exploitation.

338. *Special Officer for Scheduled Castes, Scheduled Tribes, etc.*

(1) There shall be a Special Officer for the Scheduled Castes and Scheduled Tribes to be appointed by the President.
(2) It shall be the duty of the Special Officer to investigate all matters relating to the safeguards provided for the Scheduled Castes and Scheduled Tribes under this Constitution and report to the President upon the working of those safeguards at such intervals as the President may direct and the President shall cause all such reports to be laid before each House of Parliament.
(3) In this article, references to the Scheduled Castes and Scheduled Tribes shall be construed as including references to such other backward classes as the President may, on receipt of the report of a Commission appointed under clause (1) of article 340, by order specify and also to the Anglo-Indian community.

339. *Control of the Union over the Administration of Scheduled Areas and the Welfare of Scheduled Tribes*

(1) The President may at any time and shall, at the expiration of ten years from the commencement of this Constitution by order appoint a Commission to report on the administration of the Scheduled Areas and the welfare of the Scheduled Tribes in the States[9].
The order may define the composition, powers and procedure of the Commission and may contain such incidental or ancillary provisions as the President may consider necessary or desirable.
(2) The executive power of the Union shall extend to the giving of directions to [10][a State] as to the drawing up and execution of schemes specified in the direction to be essential for the welfare of the Scheduled Tribes in the State.

340. *Appointment of a Commission to Investigate the Conditions of Backward Classes*

(1) The President may by order appoint a Commission consisting of such persons as he thinks fit to investigate the conditions of socially and educationally backward classes within the territory of India and the difficulties under which they labour and to make recommendations as to the steps that should be taken by the Union or any State to remove such difficulties and to improve their condition and as to the grants that should be made for the purpose by the Union or any State and the conditions subject to which such grants should be made, and the order appointing such Commission shall define the procedure to be followed by the Commission.

(2) A Commission so appointed shall investigate the matters referred to them and present to the President a report setting out the facts as found by them and making such recommendations as they think proper.

(3) The President shall cause a copy of the report so presented together with memorandum explaining the action taken thereon to be laid before each House of Parliament.

NOTES

1. Subs. by the Constitution (Forty-second Amendment) Act, 1976, s 2. for "SOVEREIGN DEMOCRATIC REPUBLIC" (w.e.f. 3-1-1977).
2. Subs. by s.2. *ibid* for "unity of the Nation" (w.e.f. 3-1-1977).
3. Added by the Constitution (First Amendment) Act, 1951, s. 2.
4. Subs. by the Constitution (Seventh Amendment) Act, 1956, s. 29 and Sch., for "under any State specified in the First Schedule or any local or other authority within its territory, any requirement as to residence within that State".
5. Art. 38 renumbered as cl. (1) thereof by the Constitution (Forty-fourth Amendment) Act, 1978, s. 9. (w.e.f. 20-6-1979).
6. Ins. by s. 9. *ibid.* (w.e.f. 20-6-1979).
7. Subs. by the Constitution (Forty-second Amendment) Act, 1976, s. 7. for cl. (f) (w.e.f. 3-1-1977).
8. Ins. by s. 8, *ibid.* (w.e.f. 3-1-1977).
9. The words and letters "specified in Part A or Part B of the First Schedule" omitted by the Constitution (Seventh Amendment) Act, 1956, s. 29 and Sch.
10. Subs. by s. 29 and Sch., *ibid.*, for "any such State".

2

The First Backward Classes Commission, 1953-55

THE FIRST Backward Classes Commission set up by a Presidential Order under Article 340 of Constitution of India on January 29, 1953, submitted its report on March 30, 1955.

Composition

1. Shri Kakasaheb Kalelkar, M.P., Chairman
2. Shri Narrayan Sadoba Kajrolkar, M.P.
3. Shri Bheekha Bhai, M.P.
4. Shri Shivdayal Singh Chaurasia
5. Shri Rajeshwar Patel, M.P.
6. Shri Abdul Qaiyum Ansari, M.L.A. (Bihar)
7. Shri T. Mariappa, M.L.A. (Mysore)
8. Lala Jagannath
9. Shri Atma Singh Namdhari, M.P.
10. Shri N.R.M. Swamy, M.P.
11. Shri Arunangshu De, Member-Secretary

Terms of Reference

The Backward Classes Commission shall–

(a) determine the criteria to be adopted in considering whether any sections of the people in the territory of India (in addition to the Scheduled Castes and Scheduled Tribes specified by notifications issued under Articles 341 and 342 of the Constitution) should be treated as socially and educationally backward classes; and, in accordance with such criteria, prepare a list of such classes setting out also their approximate numbers and their territorial distribution;

(b) investigate the conditions of all such socially and educationally backward classes and the difficulties under which they labour;

and make recommendations–

(i) as to the steps that should be taken by the Union or any State to remove such difficulties or to improve their condition, and

(ii) as to the grants that should be made for the purpose by the Union or any State and the conditions subject to which such grants should be made;

(c) investigate such other matters as the President may hereafter refer to them; and

(d) present to the President a report setting out the facts as found by them and making such recommendations as they think proper.

The Commission may–

(a) obtain such information as they may consider necessary or relevant for their purpose in such form and such manner as they may think appropriate, from the Central Government, the State Governments and such other authorities, organizations or individuals as may, in the opinion of the Commission, be of assistance to them;

(b) hold their sittings or the sittings of such sub-committees as they may appoint from amongst their own members at such authority of the Chairman and

(c) visit or depute a sub-committee of theirs to visit such parts of the territory of India as they consider necessary or convenient.

Methodology Followed

The Commission issued a Questionnaire comprising 182 questions for eliciting the views of the Governments and the general public on various aspects of its inquiry. It also undertook extensive tour of the country to collect on the spot evidence.

After sifting and sorting the facts collected, the Commission formulated the following criteria identifying socially and educationally backward classes:

(i) Low social position in the traditional caste hierarchy of Hindu society.
(ii) Lack of general educational advancement among the major section of a caste or community.
(iii) Inadequate or no representation in Government service.
(iv) Inadequate representation in the field of trade, commerce and industry.

The Commission also prepared a list of 2399 backward castes or communities for the entire country, and 837 of these were classified as 'most backward'. The Registrar General and Census Commissioner of India assisted the Commission in making population projections of 930 backward castes or communities.

Major Recommendations

The recommendations of the Commission for upliftment of the backward classes are extremely wide-ranging and comprehensive. They cover such fields as Extensive Land Reforms, Reorganisation of Village Economy, Bhoodan Movement, Development of Livestock, Dairy Farming, Cattle Insurance, Bee-keeping, Piggery, Fisheries, Development of Small and Cottage Industries, Rural Housing, Public Health and Rural Water Supply, Adult Literacy, University Education, Representation of Backward Classes in Government service, etc. Some of the noteworthy recommendations of the Commission are:

(i) Undertaking caste-wise enumeration of population in the Census of 1961;
(ii) Relating Social backwardness of a class to its low position in the traditional caste hierarchy of Hindu society;
(iii) Treating all women as a class as "backward";
(iv) Reservation of 70 per cent seats in all technical and professional institutions for qualified students of backward classes;
(v) Minimum reservation of vacancies in all Government services and local bodies for other Backward Classes on the following scale:

Class I	..	25%
Class II	..	33-1/3%
Class III & IV	..	40%

Dissenting Views on Linking Caste with Backwardness

It is of interest to note that the Commission could not present a unanimous report. Five of its Members recorded minutes of dissent. Dr. Anup Singh, Shri Arunangshu De and Shri P. G. Shah were opposed to the view of linking caste with backwardness. They were also opposed to the reservation of posts on the basis of caste. On the other hand, Shri S. D. S. Chaurasia strongly advocated the acceptance of caste as the criterion for backwardness in his 67-page minute of dissent. Shri T. Mariappa's minute of dissent was concerned only with the inclusion of a couple of castes in the list of Other Backward Classes.

Shri Kaka Kalelkar, the Chairman, took a rather equivocal stand on this issue. Though he did not record a formal minute of dissent in his forwarding letter to the President he opposed the acceptance of caste as the basis for backwardness. He also expressed his reservations regarding several other important recommendations made by the Commission.

Government Action on the Report

After a detailed examination of the Commission's Report, the Government laid its copy together with a Memorandum of action taken before each House of the Parliament on September 3, 1956 in compliance with Article 340(3) of the Constitution. In this Memorandum it was observed, "For the purpose of the enquiry specifically contemplated in Article 340 of the Constitution it was necessary to consider whether these other backward sections could be properly classified, and the Commission had to find objective tests and criteria by which such classifications were to be made; they had to find indisputable yardsticks by which social and educational backwardness could be measured. The report of the Commission has not been unanimous on this point, in fact, it reveals considerable divergence of opinion." It was further stated, "The Commission's list contains as many as 2399 communities out of which 930 alone account for an estimated population of 11.5 crores; Scheduled Castes and Tribes will make up another 7 crores" (on the basis of 1951 Census). Regarding the acceptance of caste as criterion for backwardness, it was stated, "It cannot be denied that the caste system is the greatest hindrance in the way of our progress towards an egalitarian society, and the recognition of the specified castes as backward may serve to maintain and even perpetuate the existing distinctions on the basis of caste."

Regarding the recognition of a large number of castes and communities as backward, it was pointed out, "If the entire community, barring a few exceptions has thus to be regarded as backward, the really needy would be swamped by the multitude and hardly receive any special attention or adequate assistance, nor would such dispensation fulfil the conditions laid down in Article 340 of the Constitution."

In view of the above, the Government considered it necessary that "some positive and workable criteria should be devised for the specification of the socially and educationally backward classes" and to undertake further investigation "so that deficiencies that have been noticed in the findings of the Commission are made good. . . ." It was also pointed out in the Memorandum that the Planning Commission had already formulated the development programmes for the removal of backwardness and "the main point to be stressed was whether the special needs of the backward classes could be intensively and effectively served by appropriate shifts of emphasis or by re-arrangement of priorities within the framework of the existing programmes or whether additional programmes needed to be drawn up".

No Discussion in the Parliament

Incidentally, the Commission's report was not discussed by the Parliament.

After presenting the Memorandum to the Parliament, the Government made efforts "to discover some criteria other than caste which could be of practical application in determining the backward classes." The Deputy Registrar General was asked to conduct a pilot survey to see if backwardness could be linked to occupational communities instead of caste. Such a survey was undertaken but it failed to throw up the desired criteria. The matter was also discussed at a conference of State representatives on 7-4-1959 and subsequently reviewed at a meeting of State officers convened by the Ministry of Home Affairs, but no consensus emerged as a result of these efforts.

Criteria for Defining Backwardness

The Central Government ultimately took a decision that no all-India lists of backward classes should be drawn up, nor any reservation made in the Central Government service for any group of backward classes other than the Scheduled Castes and Scheduled Tribes. Consequently, on August 14, 1961, the Ministry of Home Affairs addressed all the State Governments stating, "While the State Governments have the discretion to choose their own criteria for defining backwardness, in the view of the Government of India it would be better **to apply economic,* tests than to go by caste."** Regarding the preparation of lists of backward classes it was observed, "Even if the Central Government were to specify under Article 338(3) certain groups of people as belonging to 'other backward classes', it will still be open to every State Government to draw up its own lists for the purposes of Articles 15 and 16. As therefore, the State Governments may adhere to their own lists, any all-India list drawn up by the Central Government would have no practical utility".

Mandal Commission's Observations

(i) *On Kaka Kalelkar Commission Report*

It is well worth remembering that Kaka Kalelkar Commission Report was the first national level inquiry of its kind after the adoption of the Constitution. Since then ten States have set up fifteen Commissions and their reports provide a wealth of material on this subject. Further, the present Commission has the additional benefit of a plethora of judicial pronouncements by the Supreme Court and several High Courts on the question of extending various types of benefit to backward classes other than the Scheduled Castes and Scheduled Tribes.

But despite making due allowance for its handicaps, it cannot be denied that Kaka Kalelkar Commission Report suffers from grave flaws of methodology and serious internal contradictions. For instance, the Commission was required to determine the criteria for identifying socially and educationally backward classes and, in accordance with such criteria, to prepare a list of such classes. . . . 2399 backward classes were identified by the Kalelkar Commission Report. But it is not clear from the Report as to how the lists of backward classes were derived by the application of that criterion. The Commission's

* stress added

State-wise lists are based on the lists prepared by the Ministry of Education for the grant of scholarships etc. to 'Other Educationally Backward Classes' in 1949. The Ministry of Education, in its turn, had compiled these lists on the basis of the recommendations received from the respective State Governments.

It is seen that Ministry of Education had prepared its list not only without undertaking any special survey for the identification of the backward classes it was meant only for 'Other *Educationally* Backward Classes' and not for 'Socially and Educationally Backward Classes' as contemplated in Article 340 of the Constitution.

Of course, Kaka Kalelkar Commission modified the Education Ministry's original lists in the light of the evidence collected by it. But the fact remains that it broadly adopted the lists of Other Educationally Backward Classes prepared by another Government agency for an entirely different purpose, and treated it as the list of socially and educationally backward classes of India. This was done without undertaking any field survey to check their validity for the purpose of the Commission. Nor were they tested against criteria evolved by the Commission for identifying socially and educationally backward classes.

Kaka Kalelkar Commission recommended different percentages of reservation of seats/vacancies in educational institutions, Government services, etc. for other Backward Classes (OBCs). For instance, it recommended reservation of 40 per cent posts in Class III and Class IV categories, 25 per cent in Class I category and 70 per cent of the seats in professional and technical institutions. But in the absence of any explanation of the rationale for fixing different percentages for different groups of posts etc. the approach appears somewhat arbitrary.

Though the above failings are serious, yet the real weakness of the Report lies in its internal contradictions. Three of the Members were opposed to one of the most crucial recommendations of the Report, that is, the acceptance of caste as a criterion for social backwardness and the reservation of posts in Government services on that basis. The degree of dissidence greatly compromised the force of the Commission's recommendations. But it was the 30-page forwarding letter of Shri Kaka Kalelkar to the President which demolished the very basis of the Report. The following extracts from this letter speak for themselves:

"Beside convinced that the upper castes among the Hindus have to atone for the neglect of which they were guilty towards the 'lower' classes'. I was prepared to recommend to Government that all special help should be given only to the backward classes and even the poor and the deserving among the upper classes may be safely kept out from the benefit of this special help. My eyes were however opened to the dangers of suggesting remedies on the caste basis when I discovered that it is going to have a most unhealthy effect on the Muslim and Christian sections of the nation. . . ."

"This was a rude shock and it drove me to the conclusion that the remedies we suggested were worse than the evil we were out to combat."

"This painful realisation came to me almost towards the end of our labours. I could not stem the current of opinion without the Commission itself and ultimately decided, though reluctantly, to side with the majority with whom I had cooperated throughout in formulating remedies on caste basis. It is only when the Report was being finalised that I started thinking anew and found that backwardness could be tackled on a basis or a number of bases other than that of caste. I only succeeded in raising the suspicion of the majority of my colleagues that I was trying to torpedo the recommendations of the Commission. This was another reason why I signed the Report without even a minute of dissent. . . ."

". . . If such communities have neglected education it is because they had no use for it. Now that they have discovered their mistake it is for them to make the necessary efforts for making up the leeway."

"Till recently, good many Communities were organising caste conferences and collecting funds for granting scholarships to boys and girls of their own community. That was a good lesson in self help and a good number of communities have thus come forward in material well-being. But now all burden is sought to be thrown on the common exchequer and those who have thoughtlessly neglected education in the past are now seeking preferential treatment in Government services. This is anything but fair. . . ."

"I am definitely against reservation in Government Services for any Community for the simple reason that the services are not meant for the servants but they are meant for the service of society as a whole. . . ."

"I believe that in Class I and Class II services, the backward classes will stand to gain, both morally and materially, it they do

> not demand a reservation percentage in the vacancies and simply rely on the fair-mindedness of the administration to use their preference in favour of the backward classes. . . ."

The above extracts form an eloquent testament of Shri Kalelkar's views on backwardness and social justice. It must have caused this gentle Gandhian no end of anguish to refrain from recording a formal note of dissent to a Report which recommended caste as one of the main criteria for determining social backwardness. Despite giving such clear expression to his views, he observed in a latter para of this letter, "Following the analogy of the proverb, viz., 'Use the thorn to remove a thorn', we held that the evils of caste could be removed by measures which could be considered in terms of caste alone". Here, the strain of squaring the circle becomes so palpable that one can only sympathise with Kaka Sahib in his predicament.

A Report so fragmented in its conceptual design carried within itself the logic for its rejection.

(ii) *On Government Action*

Whereas Kaka Kalelkar Commission Report received the closest attention of the Government right up to the highest level, there is one aspect of its examination which merits special attention. Despite referring to various constitutional provisions and accepting the need to give special relief to socially and educationally backward classes, in the overall context the Government thinking was mainly conditioned by the national imperative of reducing economic disparities between different classes of society. This approach is clearly summed up in the letter that Home Ministry addressed to all the State Governments after full examination of the Report. The concluding sentence of this letter reads, "They (Government of India) also consider that while the State Governments have the discretion to choose their own criteria for defining backwardness, in the view of the Government of India *it would be better to apply economic tests than to go by caste.*" (Emphasis added).

As the main thrust of Government's development programmes has always been the removal of mass poverty, this preoccupation with economic criterion in determining backwardness is quite understandable. But howsoever laudable the objective may be, it is not in consonance with the spirit of Article 340 of the Constitution, under which the Commission was set up. Both Articles 15(4) and 340(1) make a pointed reference to "socially and educationally backward classes". Any reference to "economic backwardness" has been advisedly left out of these Articles. Whereas we shall have more to say on this subject in a subsequent chapter, it may be pertinent to point out that in giving primacy to 'economic tests' in determining the type of backwardness referred to in Article 340(1) of the Constitution, the Government has, perhaps inadvertently, paid less than adequate attention to the constitutional requirements in this matter. It may be possible to make out a very plausible case for not accepting caste as a criterion for defining 'social and educational backwardness'. But the substitution of caste by economic tests will amount to ignoring the genesis of social backwardness in the Indian society.

(*Excerpts from Chapter 1 of Mandal Commission's Report*)

3

Mandal Commission at Work

Appointment of the Commission and Submission of the Report

ON THE 20th December 1978, Shri Morarjibhai Desai, the then Prime Minister of India announced on the floor of the Parliament, the decision to appoint Backward Classes Commission under the Chairmanship of Shri B.P. Mandal with four other members. The Commission was appointed by the Janata Government and it received two extensions by the Congress-I Government headed by Smt. Indira Gandhi. Thus, the Commission got three extensions, first for three months from 1st January to 31st March 1980 and two more extensions from 1st April 1980 to 30th September and 1st October to 31st December 1980.

It is of interest to note that the Commission started its work after the inaugural speech of Shri Morarjibhai Desai, Prime Minister of India on 21st March 1979 and ended with the valedictory address by Smt. Indira Gandhi, Prime Minister of India, on 12th December 1980.

Shri B.P. Mandal, the Chairman of the Commission submitted its report on 31st December 1980 to Shri Neelam Sanjiva Reddy, the then President of India.

One of the members, Shri L.R. Naik recorded a minute of dissent.

Notification setting up Backward Classes Commission was issued on 1 January, 1979 and the Report was submitted in December 1980.

While the Commission was formally inaugurated by the then Prime Minister, Shri Morarji Desai, on 21 March, 1979, it became fully operational only in the middle of 1979.

By the time the Commission's work get into full swing, the Parliament was dissolved in August 1979 and States got busy with preparations for the next General elections. By the time these elections were over 9 States Assemblies were dissolved, and the assembly election became the major concern of the administrations of these states.

The above developments had an unsettling effect on the work of the Commission, specially so far as its tour to various States was concerned. The progress of the country-wide socio-educational field survey which commenced in February, 1980 was also seriously hampered. Owing to paucity of time and somewhat disturbed conditions in the 7 North-eastern States, the Commission could not undertake the tour of this region.

The Commission adopted a multilateral approach to the collection of data in connection with its inquiry.

The Commission issued detailed questionnaires to all State Governments, Union territories and the Ministries and Departments of the Government of India.

A large number of members of Sixth and Seventh Lok Sabha, Rajya Sabha, State Legislatures and representatives of a number of voluntary organisations, thousands of social workers and members of the public appeared before the Commission to tender evidence.

The Commission also placed on record its appreciation for the Tata Institute of Social Sciences, Bombay and Indian Law Institute, Delhi for preparing two special reports for the Commission.

Composition and Terms of Reference

In exercise of the powers conferred by Article 340 of the Constitution, the President appointed a Backward Classes Commission to investigate the conditions of socially and educationally backward classes within the territory of India. The composition of the Commission was as follows:

Composition

1.	Shri B.P.Mandal (ex-M.P.)	Chairman
2.	Shri R.R. Bhole, M.P.	Member
3.	Shri Dewan Mohan Lal	Member
4.	Shri L.R. Naik* (ex-M.P.)	Member
5.	Shri K. Subramaniam	Member
6.	Shri S.S. Gill	Secretary

* Shri L.R. Naik was appointed in place of Shri Dina Bandhu Sahu, who resigned from membership of the Commission on November 5, 1979 on health grounds.

Chairman and the members were appointed on part-time basis and worked in an honorary capacity.

Terms of Reference

(i) to determine the criteria for defining the socially and educationally backward classes;
(ii) to recommend steps to be taken for the advancement for the socially and educationally backward classes of citizens so identified;
(iii) to examine the desirability or otherwise of making provision for the reservation of appointments or posts in favour of such backward classes of citizens which are not adequately represented in public services and posts in connection with the affairs of the Union or of any State; and
(iv) present to the President a report setting out of the facts as found by them and making such recommendations as they think proper.

In this connection, the Commission may also examine the recommendations of the Backward Classes Commission appointed earlier and the considerations which stood in the way of the acceptance of its recommendations by Government.

1. The Commission may:

(a) obtain such information as they may consider necessary or relevant for their purpose in such form and such manner as they may think appropriate, from the Central Government, the State Government, the Union Territory Administrations and such other authorities, organisations or individuals as may in the opinion of the Commission, be of assistance to them; and
(b) hold their sittings or the sittings of such sub-committees as they may appoint from the amongst their own members at such times and such places as may be determined by, or under the authority of the Chairman.

2. During the visits of the Commission or of any sub-committee

appointed by them to any State and during any sittings held by the Commission or any such sub-committee in any State, the Commission may co-opt two persons who belong to that State and who are members of the Backward Classes, to be additional members of the Commission or the sub-committee, as the case may be.

4. The Headquarters of the Commission were located at Delhi.

5. The Commission was required to present their Report to the President not later than the 31st December, 1979.*

Methodology Adopted by the Commission

The Commission made use of the following techniques of enquiry:

1. State Government Questionnaire
2. Questionnaire for Central Ministries/Departments
3. Questionnaire for the general public, Voluntary organisations etc.
4. Commission's Tour
5. Evidence of a number of people's representatives, eminent public men, sociologists, journalists, demographers etc.
6. Socio-economic Field Survey
7. Case studies, special reports etc.
8. Analysis of Census Data, Village monographs and Special Reports
9. Study of Legal and Constitutional Issues.

Questionnaires

In April 1979 the Commission issued the following three questionnaires to all the State Governments, Central Ministries/Departments and the General Public

(i) State Government Questionnaire

In this questionnaire State Governments were requested to supply information on their concept of social and educational backwardness, steps taken for the welfare of OBCs, representation of Other Backward Classes in Government services, income levels and social status of

* Later extended in stages up to 31 December, 1980.

manual workers and occupational communities, their educational levels and incidence of drop-outs, etc. Replies were received from all the State Governments and Union Territories.

(ii) Questionnaire for Central Ministries/Departments

In this questionnaire the Central Ministries/Departments and the Public Undertakings working under them were requested to supply information regarding the number and percentage of employees of Other Backward Classes employed in those Organisations. A rough and ready criterion of social and educational backwardness was also given in this questionnaire. In all 30 Ministries and Departments and 31 Attached and Subordinate offices furnished the desired information.

(iii) Questionnaire for the General Public, Voluntary Organisations, etc.

This questionnaire was issued to Members of the general public, social workers, publicmen, caste associations, voluntary organisations, etc., to elicit their views on the criterion for social and educational backwardness, social mobility since Independence, place of caste in the social structure of India, social and civil disabilities suffered by backward classes, etc. This questionnaire was published in leading English and vernacular papers of each State at the time of the Commission's tour and it was also widely distributed in meetings held during the Commission's tour. In all 1872 replies to this questionnaire were received by the Commission from all over the country.

Information collected in response to the above three questionnaires was systematically compiled, collated and analysed and it has been used in the relevant Chapters of this Report.

Commission's Touring

The Commission undertook extensive tours of the country to get first hand information from various communities and sections of the public on the problems of social and educational backwardness. It toured and in the process, it visited 84 district headquarters, 37 villages, attended 171 formal meetings and received 2638 representations from publicmen and voluntary organisations. At each State Headquarters the Commission had discussions with Chief Ministers, Ministers, Members of Parliament, Members of Legislative Assemblies, senior officials, representatives of State and Central Public Undertakings, voluntary social organisations and other prominent publicmen.

Evidence Before the Commission

The Commission invited a number of people's representatives, eminent publicmen, sociologists, journalists, demographers, etc., for tendering evidence on various problems pertaining to the socially and educationally backward classes. In 1979, all Members of the Sixth Lok Sabha were issued invitations in this behalf and quite a large number appeared before the Commission for evidence. Quite a few Rajya Sabha Members also tendered evidence in this connection.

Socio-Educational Field Survey

The Commission constituted a panel of 15 experts under Prof. M.N. Srinivas for preparing the design of a country-wide Socio-Educational Field Survey. The panel met in Delhi from July 16th to 20th, 1979, and, after detailed deliberations, prepared a set of schedules, dummy tables, instructions, etc., for undertaking this Survey.

To make full and proper use of the massive information flowing from the Survey, it was also decided that the whole operation of processing the data should be computerised. It was hoped that the results of this Survey will throw up a set of indicators which constituted the syndrome of social and educational backwardness in the Indian Conditions.

Case-Studies, Special Reports, etc.

North-South Comparison of Backward Classes Welfare

Southern States have a fairly long and peaceful history of giving substantial benefits to Other Backward Classes and these States have done more for their welfare than any other region in India. On the other hand Northern States have been quite slow and hesitant in framing any welfare scheme for Other Backward Classes. In fact very modest reservations made in services and Educational Institutions in Bihar and Uttar Pradesh in the recent years have given rise to wide-spread protests and agitation. As it appeared necessary to have a clear understanding of local factors, social attitudes, prejudices, etc. for this contrast in responses to the same phenomenon, the Commission engaged Tata Institute of Social Sciences, Bombay, to undertake a case-study of four States, *i.e.* Tamil Nadu, Karnataka, Bihar and Uttar Pradesh with this end in view.

Analysis of Census Data, Village Monographs and Special Reports

Caste Indexing 1891/1931

On the basis of 1891 and 1931 Censuses, data were collected and analysed with a view to getting a frame for the linkage of traditional occupations by caste. The main object of this exercise was to get an idea of social mobility amongst various castes during the intervening period of 40 years. Such data were compiled fully for the States of Bihar and Uttar Pradesh and caste index by traditional occupations was prepared for these two States. This study could not be carried beyond 1931, as listing of castes was discontinued in subsequent Census operations.

Village Studies by Anthropological Survey of India, Calcutta

At the Commission's request, the Anthropological Survey of India, Calcutta, made available its village studies pertaining to Andhra Pradesh, Bihar, Karnataka, Madhya Pradesh, Maharashtra, Punjab, Tamil Nadu, Tripura and Uttar Pradesh. From these studies the Commission could cull useful information about the socio-economic conditions of rural population of these States.

A large number of survey reports and monographs prepared by the Indian Council of Social Sciences Research, New Delhi, Labour Bureau (Ministry of Labour), National Labour Institute, Institute of Economic Growth, New Delhi, Centre for the Study of Developing Societies, New Delhi, Indian Social Institute, New Delhi, etc., provided the Commission with a mine of useful information on the conditions and problems of socially and educationally backward classes.

Legal and Constitutional Issues

During the last 20 years Supreme Court and various High Courts had decided a number cases regarding the reservation of posts in Government Services, allocation of seats in Educational Institutions and giving of various other benefits to Other Backward Classes by several States. As very important Constitutional and Legal issues had been discussed in these judgments, it was necessary for the Commission to take due cognisance of these judicial pronouncements in formulating its recommendations for the identification of Backward Classes and suggesting measures for their upliftment. In view of this, the Commission engaged Law Institute of India, New Delhi, to prepare a comprehensive Report on this subject.

Summary of Mandal Commission Report

Chapter I — The First Backward Classes Commission

THE FIRST Backward Classes Commission was set up on January 29, 1953 and it submitted its report on March 31, 1955. On the basis of criteria evolved by it, the Commission listed 2,399 castes as socially and educationally backward. It recommended various welfare measures for OBCs including reservation in Government services and educational institutions.

The Central Government did not accept the recommendations of the Commission on the ground that it had not applied any objective tests for identifying Backward Classes. Five out of the 11 Members of the Commission had given notes of dissent. The Government felt that the Commission had classified a very large section of the population as backward and if special assistance had to be extended to all these people, "the really needy will be swapped by the multitude". The Government was also opposed to the adoption of caste as one of the criterion for backwardness and preferred the application of economic tests.

As Article 340 of the Constitution speaks of "socially and educationally backward classes", the application of 'economic tests' for their identification seems to be misconceived.

Chapter II — Status of OBCs in some States

It is for nearly 100 years that Provincial Governments in India have been implementing special programmes for the welfare of depressed and backward classes. Madras Government took the lead by framing Grant-in-Aid Code in 1885 to regulate financial aid to educational institutions for backward classes students. Mysore State was the next to follow and, by now, all the Southern States are implementing fairly comprehensive programmes for OBCs. As on date 16 States and two Union Territories are providing special assistance of varying degrees to Other Backward Classes. Ten State Governments are doing so on the basis of recommendations made by Backward Classes Commission specially set up by them in this behalf and the others are doing in an *ad hoc* manner.

Special concessions like reservation of jobs in Government employment and seats in educational institutions; financial assistance; subsidised educational facilities, etc. are being given by several State Governments to OBCs. Southern States have done much more work in this connection as compared to the rest of the country. Karnataka has reserved 48 per cent of all Government jobs for OBC candidates in addition to 18 per cent for SCs and STs. In the case of Tamil Nadu, these figures stand 50 per cent and 18 per cent respectively.

Chapter III — Methodology and Data Base

One serious defect noticed by the Government in the report of first Backward Classes Commission was that it had not formulated any objective criterion for classifying Other Backward Classes. The need for field surveys and formulation of objective tests has also been repeatedly emphasised by the Supreme Court in several cases. In view of this, the Commission has taken special care to tap a number of independent sources for the collection of primary data. Some of the important measures taken in this connection were: seminar of sociologists on social backwardness; issue of three sets of questionnaires to State Governments, Central Government and the public; extensive touring of the country by the Commission, taking evidence of legislators, eminent publicmen, sociologists, etc.; undertaking a country-wide socio-educational survey; preparation of reports on some important issues by specialised agencies; analysis of census data, etc.

By adopting this multilateral approach the Commission was able to cast its net far and wide and prepared a very firm and dependable database for its Report.

Chapter IV — Social Backwardness and Caste

Castes are the building bricks of the Hindu social structure. They have kept Hindu society divided in a hierarchical order for centuries. This has resulted in a close linkage between the caste ranking of a person and his social, educational and economic status.

This manner of stratification of society gave the higher castes deep-rooted vested interests in the perpetuation of the system. The priestly castes evolved an elaborate and subtle scheme of scripture, ritual and mythology and perpetuate their supremacy and, hold the lower castes in bondage for ages. Most of our Shastras uphold the four-fold Varna system and, because of this religious sanction, caste system has lasted longer than most other social institutions based on inequality and inequity.

In view of the permanent stratification of society in hierarchical caste order, members of lower castes have always suffered from discrimination in all walks of life and this has resulted in their social, educational and economic backwardness. In India, therefore, the low ritual caste status of a person has a direct bearing on his social backwardness.

Chapter V — Social Dynamics of Castes

Caste system has been able to survive over the centuries because of its inherent resilience and its ability to adjust itself to the ever changing social reality. The traditional view of caste system, as contained in Chapter IV, is based more on Hindu Shastras than the actual state of social reality. Moreover, caste restrictions have loosened considerably as a result of the rule of law introduced by the British, urbanisation, industrialisation, spread of mass education and, above all, the introduction of adult franchise after Independence. But all the above changes mark only shift of emphasis and not any material alteration in the basic structure of caste.

It is generally agreed that whereas certain caste taboos have weakened as a result of the above changes, the importance of casteism in Indian politics is on the increase. This perhaps, was inevitable. Caste system provided the political leadership with readymade channels of communication and mobilisation and, in view of this, the importance of caste was bound to increase in Indian politics. As Rajni Kothari has observed, "those in India who complain of 'casteism' in politics are really looking for a sort of politics which has no basis in society."

The pace of social mobility is no doubt increasing and some traditional features of caste system have inevitably weakened. But what caste has lost on the ritual front, it has more than gained on the political front. In view of this it will be unrealistic to assume that the institution of caste will wither away in the foreseeable future.

Chapter VI — Social Justice, Merit and Privilege

Equality before the law is a basic Fundamental Right guaranteed under Article 14 of the Constitution. But the principle of 'equality' is a double edged weapon. It places the strong and the handicapped on the same footing in the race of life. It is a dictum of social justice that there is equality only among equals. To treat unequals as equals is to perpetuate inequality. The humaneness of a society is determined by the degree of protection it provides to its weaker, handicapped and less gifted members.

'Equality of opportunity' and 'equality of treatment' places the weak and the strong on par and to that extent, it amounts to denial of social justice. In fact, it is 'equality of results' which is the acid test of society's egalitarian pretentions. In a highly unequal society like ours, it is only by giving special protection and privileges to the under-privileged section of society that we can enable the weak to resist exploitation by the strong.

It was in view of these considerations that our Constitution makers made special provisions under Articles 15(4), 16(4) and 46 etc. to protect the interests of SCs, STs and OBCs. Some people consider provisions like reservation of posts for backward classes, etc., as a violation of their Fundamental Right and denial of meritorious person's legitimate due. In fact, 'merit' itself is largely a product of favourable environmental privileges and higher rating in an examination does not necessarily reflect higher intrinsic worth of the examinee. Children of socially and educationally backward parents coming from rural background cannot compete on an equal footing with children from well to do homes. In view of this 'merit' and 'equality' should be viewed in proper perspective and the element of privilege should be duly recognised and discounted for when 'unequals' are made to run the same rate.

Chapter VII — Social Justice, Constitution and the Law

The element of conflict between the Fundamental Rights and the Directive Principles of State Policy has been the subject-matter of numerous Parliamentary debates and judicial pronouncements. In pursuance of Articles 15(4) and 16(4) a number of State Governments made reservations in Government services and educational institutions for OBCs and several petitions were filed before the High Courts and the Supreme Court against such orders. Gradually a sizeable body of case law has grown on the subject and a gist of it is given below.

Caste is an important factor in the identification of Other Backward Classes among Hindu communities. Backwardness must be both social and educational and not either social or educational. Caste is also a class of citizens and if the caste as a whole is socially and educationally backward, reservation can be made in favour of such a caste on the ground that it is a socially and educationally backward class of citizens within the meaning of Article 15(4). The further division of backward classes into 'backward' and 'most backward' is not warranted by Article 15(5). The aggregate reservation of posts under Article 15(4) should be less that 50 per cent. Objective criterion should be evolved on the basis of field survey, etc., for identifying OBCs.

Chapter VIII — North South Comparison of OBC Welfare

Southern States have done much more for the welfare of Other Backward Classes than Northern States. Moreover, in the South the whole operation was conducted quite smoothly whereas in the North even modest welfare measures for OBCs have given rise to sharp resistance. The Commission approached Tata Institute of Social Sciences, Bombay, to prepare a comparative study of the 4 States of Tamil Nadu, Karnataka, Bihar and Uttar Pradesh, so as to have better appreciation of this phenomenon.

Tata Institute Study formulated a number of hypotheses in this regard. They are: Reservation scheme had a much longer history in the South; forward castes were more divided among themselves in the South; OBCs were not getting along very well with SCs/STs in the North and thus divided the backward classes movement; backward classes were more politicised in the South; reservation scheme was introduced too suddenly in the North; the capacity of backward classes to retaliate depends upon their numbers, political consciousness, dominance and perceived lack of alternative opportunities; more rapid expansion of tertiary sector gave opening to forward castes in the South which was not available to the same extent in the North, etc.

Tata Institute Study supports the above hypotheses by citing a number of examples and historical developments in the 4 States under consideration.

Chapter IX — Evidence by Central and State Governments

Two sets of questionnaires were circulated to all State Governments, Union Territories and Ministries and Departments of Central Government for eliciting information on various aspects of our inquiry. These questionnaires were designed to obtain a comparative picture of status of backward classes in various States, steps taken for their welfare, views of various Government agencies on the question of social and educational backwardness and any useful suggestions regarding the Commission's terms of reference.

Most of the State Governments favoured caste as an important criterion for determining social and educational backwardness. Some States preferred economic criterion and some a combination of caste and means-test. Eighteen State Governments and Union Territories have taken special steps for the welfare of Other Backward Classes, though there is wide variation in the quantum of assistance provided by them. For instance, reservation in Government services for OBCs ranges from 50 per cent in the case of Karnataka and Tamil Nadu and 5 per cent in Punjab and nil in the case of Rajasthan, Orissa, Delhi, etc. Representation of OBCs in local bodies, State Public Service Commissions, High Courts, etc., is also negligible. Social discrimination is still practised against OBCs. There are a number of castes and communities which are treated as untouchables though they have not been included in the list of Scheduled Castes. All the State Governments which have launched programmes for the welfare of backward classes have to fund the same from their own resources as no separate Plan allocation is made by the Centre for this purpose.

Most States have reported loss of employment by village artisans owing to the introduction of machines, change in consumption patterns, etc.

From the information supplied by the Central Government Ministries and Departments it is seen that Other Backward Classes constitute 12.55 per cent of the total number of Government employees, whereas their aggregate population is 52 per cent. Their representation in Class I jobs is only 4.69 per cent, i.e., less than 1/10th of their proportion to the country's total population.

Chapter X — Evidence by the Public

Nearly 2/3 of the respondents to our questionnaire from General Public felt that no material changes have taken place in the country's caste structure since Independence. Regarding criterion for identifying backwardness, nearly 3/4th of the respondents favoured caste. More than 3/4th of the respondents also complained of various disabilities suffered by backward classes and many felt that no concrete steps have been taken to remove them. They wanted job reservation quotas to be enhanced and more educational concessions to be given to the children of OBC. Ameliorative measures suggested for OBCs were: reservation in Government employment and educational institutions; grant of interest free loans, free distribution of agricultural land and house sites; etc.

In their evidence before the Commission, Members of Sixth and Seventh Lok Sabha also expressed views similar to those summarised above. Some MPs warned against malicious propaganda being carried on by vested interests to create conflict between OBCs and SCs and STs. Some stated that the Commission should adopt those criterion for determining backwardness which have been tested before the Courts. They also suggested that the lists of OBCs prepared by State Governments and accepted by the courts should be adopted by the Commission *in toto*.

During the Commission's tour to various States, a large number of representations were received for including particular castes in the list of OBCs. Most of the other respondents expressed similar views on the criterion for identifying backward classes and measures to be taken for their upliftment as already indicated above.

Chapter XI—Socio-educational Field Survey—Criteria for Backwardness

A country-wide socio-educational survey covering 405 out of 407 Districts was conducted with the help of Bureau of Economics and Statistics of various States from February to June, 1980. Voluminous data gathered from the Survey were computerised and 31 primary tables were generated from these data in respect of each State and Union Territory. On the basis of these tables, 11 Indicators or Criteria for social and educational backwardness were derived and they were grouped under 3 broad heads, i.e., Social, Educational and Economic.

In view of their relative importance, 3 points were assigned to each one of the Social Indicators, 2 to Educational Indicators and 1 to Economic Indicators. This added up to a total score of 22 points. All these 11 indicators were applied to each one of the castes covered by the Survey in each State. Castes obtaining a minimum scope of 11 points on this scale were listed as socially and educationally backward.

Chapter XII — Identification of OBCs

A large number of castes were identified as backward in each State as a result of the Socio-Educational Survey. As this Survey covered only 2 villages and one urban block per District, a large number of castes were naturally left out. Moreover, in some cases, the size of the sample was so small that the results were not dependable.

In view of this, two supplementary approaches were adopted to prepare complete lists of OBCs for each State. First, State-wise list of the 11 groups of primitive tribes, exterior castes, criminal tribes, etc. contained in the Registrar General of India's compilation of 1961 were culled and included in the Commission's lists of OBCs. This was done as the social and educational status of these castes and communities was more or less akin to Scheduled Castes and Scheduled Tribes. Secondly, based on the public evidence and personal knowledge of the Members of the Commission, State-wise list of those OBCs were drawn up which could not be covered by the socio-educational survey.

It was as a result of this three pronged approach that State lists of OBCs were prepared.

From the results of the field survey it was seen that some of the well-known OBCs which were also included in the lists of backward classes notified by various State Governments were not ranked as 'backward' in the survey. This is unavoidable in any sociological survey based on Statistical methods. Such aberrations were corrected in the light of the other field evidence available with the Commission.

The set of eleven Indicators (criteria), being caste-based, could not be applied to non-Hindu Communities. In view of this, a separate set of 3 criterion was evolved for the identification of non-Hindu backward communities.

On the basis of the available census data, the population of Hindu and non-Hindu OBCs was estimated to be 52 per cent of the total population of India. This is in addition to the population of Scheduled Castes and Scheduled Tribes which amounts to 22.5 per cent.

Chapter XIII–Recommendations

Reservation of SCs and STs is in proportion to their population, i.e., 22.5 per cent. But as there is a legal obligation to keep reservations under Articles 15(4) and 16(4) of the Constitution below 50 per cent, the Commission recommends a reservation of 27 per cent for OBCs. This reservation should apply to all Government services as well as technical and professional institutions, both in the Centre and the States.

Special educational facilities designed at upgrading the cultural environment of the students should be created in a phased manner in selected areas containing high concentration of OBCs. Special emphasis should be placed on vocational training. Separate coaching facilities should be provided in technical and professional institutions to OBC students to enable them to catch up with students from open quota.

Special programmes for upgrading the skills of village artisans should be prepared and subsidised loans from financial institutions granted to them for setting up small scale industries. To promote the participation of OBCs in the industrial and business life of the country, a separate network of financial and technical institutions should be created by all State Governments.

Under the existing scheme of production-relations, Backward Classes comprising mainly small land-holders, tenants, agricultural labour, village artisans, etc., are heavily dependent on the rich peasantry for their sustenance. In view of this, OBCs continue to remain in mental and material bondage of the dominant castes and classes. Unless these production-relations are redically altered through structural changes and progressive land reforms implemented rigorously all over the country, OBCs will never become truely independent. In view of this, highest priority should be given to radical land reforms by all the States.

At present no central assistance is available to any State for implementing any welfare measures for other Backward Classes. Several State Governments expressed their helplessness in undertaking more purposeful development programmes for backward classes in view of lack of resources. It is, therefore, recommended that welfare programmes specially designed for OBC should be financed by the Central Government in the same manner and to the same extent as done in the case of SCs and STs.

5

Historical Survey

Social Backwardness and Caste

AS CASTE conditioned and controlled every aspect of an individual's life, it led to the creation of a society in which there was no 'rank disequilibrium'. In other words, the lower castes were backward not only socially, but also educationally, politically and economically. On the other hand, the higher castes were advanced in all these spheres. The basic cause of this phenomenon was the higher or lower rank of a particular caste in the ritual hierarchy. **(4.29)**

In fact the role of caste status was so pervasive in society that the idea and administration of justice were completely coloured by it. Used as we are today to the concept of the 'Rule of law', it will be interesting to compare this view with the perception of law in the earlier Hindu society where a man's worth was directly related to his status in the caste hierarchy. **(4.30)**

"For Englishmen, the law, if it is to be universal, impersonal and impartial, ought to be blind, an idea graphically illustrated by the representation of justice as a classically clad, blindfolded women holding balanced scales. For Hindu law, the reverse was true; the differences among men in society were central to their legal identity, rights and obligations".* [1] **(4.31)**

The fact that despite having lived under the rule of law during the British regime and made it the corner-stone of our Constitution, in actual practice our law still makes a lot of allowance for a person's status, is an interesting example of the historical hang-over from the

---

* 'The Modernity of Tradition' by Lloyd I. Rudolph and Susane Hoeber Rudolph (Orient Longmans Ltd., New Delhi, 1967).

earlier times. **(4.32)**

In view of the foregoing will it be too much to say that in the traditional Indian society social backwardness was a direct consequence of caste status and, further, that various other types of backwardness flowed directly from this crippling handicap? **(4.33)**

Social Dynamics of Caste

The above account should serve as a warning against any hasty conclusion about the weakening of caste as the basis of social organisation of the Hindu society. The pace of social mobility is no doubt increasing and some traditional features of the caste system have inevitably weakened. But what caste has lost on the ritual front, it has more than gained on the political front. This has also led to some adjustments in the power equation between the high and low castes and thereby accentuated social tensions. Whether these tensions rent the social fabric or the country is able to resolve them by internal adjustments will depend on how understandingly the ruling high castes handle the legitimate aspirations and demands of the historically suppressed and backward classes. **(5.17)**

Social Justice, Merit and Privilege

In this connection, Shri Justice K. Subba Rao has observed:

> ". . . unless adventitious aids are given to the under-privileged people, it would be impossible to suggest that they have equal opportunities with the more advanced people. This is the reason and the justification for the demand of social justice that the under-privileged citizens of the country should be given a preferential treatment in order to give them an equal opportunity with other more advanced sections of the community."* **(6.14)**

In this connection nothing generates so much heat and genuine indignation as the concept of 'merit'. Whereas no body objects to the grant of special educational facilities and various other concessions to the backward classes, the provision of a reserved quota in educational institutions or services for members of Scheduled Castes, Scheduled

* Social Justice and Law by Shri Justice K. Subba Rao National, New Delhi.

Tribes or Other Backward Classes provokes sharp reaction. The advocates of 'merit' find it very unfair when a depressed class student securing 45 per cent marks gets admission to a medical college in preference to a student from the general quota obtaining 70 per cent marks. The resentment is much greater when a lower ranked backward class competitor is selected in preference to a much higher ranked general quota counterpart to an All India Service. **(6.15)**

This sort of reaction is based on two considerations: First, it hurts a person's sense of fair play to see that a more 'meritorious' candidate has been left out in preference to a less 'meritorious' person on purely extraneous grounds. Secondly, it is argued, that by selecting candidates with lower 'merit' against reserved quota vacancies, the nation is being deprived of the services of the best talent that is available to it. **(6.16)**

This line of argument, though plausible on the face of it, suffers from a serious fallacy regarding the nature of 'merit'. We shall try to illustrate this point by a homely example. Mohan comes from a fairly well-off middle-class family and both his parents are well educated. He attends one of the good public schools in the city which provides a wide range of extra-curricular activities. At home, he has a separate room to himself and he is assisted in his studies by both the parents. There is a television and a radio set in the house and his father also subscribes to a number of magazines. In the choice of his studies and, finally, his career, he is continuously guided by his parents and his teachers. Most of his friends are of similar background and he is fully aware of the nature of the highly competitive world in which he will have to carve a suitable place for himself. Some of his relations are fairly influential people and he can bank on the right sort of recommendation or push at the right moment. **(6.17)**

On the other hand, Lallu is a village boy and his backward class parents occupy a low social position in the village caste hierarchy. His father owns a 4-acre plot of agricultural land. Both his parents are illiterate and his family of 8 lives huddled in a two-room hut. Whereas a primary school is located in his village, for his high school he had to walk a distance of nearly three kilometres both ways. Keen on pursuing higher studies, he persuaded his parents to send him to an uncle at the Tehsil headquarters. He never received any guidance regarding the course of studies to be followed or the career to be chosen. Most of his friends did not study beyond middle-school level. He was never exposed to any stimulating cultural environment and he completed his college education without much encouragement from any quarter. Owing to his rural background, he has a rustic appearance. Despite his college education, his pronunciation is poor, his manners awkward and he lacks self-confidence. **(6.18)**

Assuming that Mohan and Lallu had the same level of intelligence at the time of their birth, it is obvious that owing to vast differences in social, cultural and environmental factors, the former will beat the latter by lengths in any competitive field. Even if Lallu's intelligence quotient was much higher as compared to Mohan, chances are that the former will lag far behind the latter in any competition where selection is made on the basis of 'merit'. **(6.19)**

Let us suppose that both of them sit for the All India Services examination and Mohan secures 50 per cent more marks than Lallu. Does it mean that Mohan's merit is 50 per cent higher than that of Lallu or, that, he will be 50 per cent more efficient than that village boy. Is it possible to determine that, in view of their respective native intelligence, how these boys would have faired in case they had exchanged places? If merit also includes grit, determination, ability to fight odds, etc. should not the marks obtained by Mohan and Lallu be suitably moderated in view of the privileges enjoyed by the former and the handicaps suffered by the latter? **(6.20)**

In fact, what we call 'merit' in an elitist society is an amalgam of native endowments and environmental privileges. Mohan and Lallu are not 'equals' in any fair sense of the term and it will be unfair to judge them by the same yard stick. The conscience of a civilized society and the dictates of social justice demand that 'merit' and 'equality' are not turned into a fetish and the element of privilege is duly recognised and discounted for when 'unequals' are made to run the same race. **(6.21)**

Social Justice, Constitution and the Law

We may close this Chapter with an observation by Shri Justice K. Subba Rao on the import of Article 16(4) of the Constitution in *General Manager Southern Railway* v. *Rangachari.** Supreme Court held that Article 16(4) was in the nature of a proviso or exception to Article 16(1) and it could not be so interpreted as to nullify or destroy the main provision. "No provision of the Constitution or of any enactment can be so construed as to destroy a provision contemporaneously enacted therein . . .". In his dissenting judgment,

* A.I.R. 1962 S.C. 36

Justice Subba Rao observed that Article 16(4) was not an exception to Article 16(1). "The expression 'nothing in this Article' is a legislative device to express its intention in a most emphatic way that the power conferred therein is not limited in any way by the main provision but falls outside it. It has not really carved out an exception, but has preserved a power untrammelled by the other provisions of the Article." **(7.45)**

Though the observation was made in a dissenting judgment, yet it merits serious consideration while examining the implication of Article 16(4) of the Constitution for extending special benefits to Other Backward Classes. **(7.46)**

North-South Comparison of Other Backward Classes Welfare

The reasons for much stronger reaction in the North than South to reservations, etc., for Other Backward Classes may be summarised as below:

(1) Tamil Nadu and Karnataka had a long history of Backward Classes movements and various measures for their welfare were taken in a phased manner. In Uttar Pradesh and Bihar such measures did not mark the culmination of a mass movement.

(2) In the South "the forward communities have been divided either by the classification schemes or politically or both . . . In Bihar the U.P. and G.Os. have not divided the forward castes."

(3) In the South, clashes between Scheduled Castes and the Backward peasant castes have been rather mild. In the North these cleavages have been much sharper, often resulting in acts of violence. This has further weakened the backward classes solidarity in the North.

(4) In the non-Sanskritic South, the basic Varna cleavage was between Brahmins and non-Brahmins and Brahmins constituted only about 3 per cent of the population. In the Sanskritic North, there was no sharp cleavage between the forward castes and together they constituted nearly 20 per cent of the population. In view of this the higher castes in U.P. and Bihar were in a stronger position to mobilise opposition to backward class movement.

(5) Owing to the longer history and better organisation of Other Backward Castes in the South, they were able to acquire

considerable political clout. Despite the lead given by the Yadavas and other peasant castes, a unified and strong OBC movement has not emerged in the North so far.

(6) The traditions of semi-feudalism in Uttar Pradesh and Bihar have enabled the forward castes to keep tight control over smaller backward castes and prevent them from joining the mainstream of backward classes movement. This is not so in the South.

(7) "The economies of Tamil Nadu and Karnataka have been expanding relatively faster. The private tertiary sector appears to be growing. It can shelter many forward caste youths. Also, they are prepared to migrate outside the State. The private tertiary sectors in Bihar and U.P. are stagnant. The forward caste youths in these two States have to depend heavily on Government jobs. Driven to desperation they have reacted violently." **(8.45)**

Criteria for Defining Backwardness

Nearly 78 per cent of the respondents were of the view that caste should be accepted as a criterion for identifying backwardness. However, 28 per cent favoured the acceptance of caste as the sole criterion. Nearly 70 per cent were in favour of evolving multiple criterion based on social status, political influence, educational attainments, economic level, employment status, etc. Others favoured the inclusion of place of habitation and financial position also in the list of criterion. **(10.4)**

Regarding non-Hindu religious groups, 62 per cent were of the view that the criterion should be based on economic status, employment, educational level, pursuit of traditional occupations associated with low social status, etc. Nearly 18 per cent were of the opinion that caste was a fact of life among non-Hindus also and it should be accepted as one of the criterion for backwardness. **(10.5)**

OBCs List of State Governments

Nearly 82 per cent of the respondents who belonged to States which have notified lists of OBCs were aware of this fact. However 62 per cent were not satisfied with the lists thus notified for one reason or the other. It was pointed out that many advanced castes have been included in the lists and several backward classes left out. Some people also felt that those lists were not based on objective tests. **(10.6)**

Nearly 82 per cent of the replies showed that special facilities have been given to socially and educationally backward classes. Nearly 52 per cent testified that educational facilities as well as reservation in jobs have been extended to backward classes. **(10.7)**

Jobs Reservations

In the States where jobs have been reserved under Government employment and public sector undertakings for OBCs, nearly 75 per cent of the respondents showed awareness of this fact, but 65 per cent expressed dissatisfaction with the quantum of reservation. **(10.8)**

Regarding the steps to be taken to enhance the intake of Other Backward Class candidates in services, 45 per cent suggested increase in the percentage of reservation. Nearly 17 per cent asked for caste-wise reservation of jobs and seats in educational institutions. Free educational facilities, relaxation of maximum age limit, special coaching facilities for OBC candidates appearing in competitive examination, etc. were some of the other measures suggested in this behalf. **(10.9)**

Disabilities suffered by OBCs

Nearly 78 per cent of the respondents stated that various types of disabilities like free access to public utilities, social discrimination, lack of educational opportunities, habitation in segregated and neglected areas, etc. were some instances of such disabilities. Only nine per cent of the replies indicated that OBCs were not subjected to any discrimination or disability. **(10.10)**

Regarding steps taken by the respective State Governments to remove these disabilities, nearly 43 per cent were of the view that no concrete steps have been taken so far. On the other hand, 17 per cent felt that some steps have been taken in this direction, but one-third of these persons felt that the steps taken were neither adequate nor effective. Others acknowledged that measures like expansion of educational and employment opportunities provision of housing facilities, etc. have helped to mitigate the hardships of OBCs. **(10.11)**

Access to Employment/Education

Nearly 82 per cent of the respondents felt that OBCs have to face a number of hurdles in securing employment or admission to institutions of higher education. Increase in the percentage of reservation, relaxation of upper age limit, creation of a separate Ministry or a Commission to protect the rights of OBCs were some of the remedial measures suggested by them. **(10.12)**

Indebtedness

According to 71 per cent of the respondents, majority of the members of OBCs were in debt. This high incidence of indebtedness was attributed to illiteracy, poverty, social customs, etc. **(10.13)**

Literacy

For the promotion of literacy for the OBCs, nearly 40 per cent of the respondents recommended that free and compulsory education for the children of backward classes was necessary. Nearly 12 per cent wanted special adult education programmes for OBCs. Provision of employment to the educated among OBCs, assistance for higher education and vocational training, setting up of more educational institutions, provision of free books and school uniforms, as also free board and lodging and other educational facilities on par with the SC/ST students were some of the other measures recommended for the promotion of literacy among OBCs. **(10.14)**

Steps to Ameliorate Hardships

For improving the lot of OBCs, nearly 25 per cent suggested the grant of low or interest-free loans, 10 per cent were in favour of free distribution of agricultural land and house sites, 31 per cent wanted reservation in educational institutions and employment, and 26 per cent suggested combination of all the facilities mentioned above. **(10.15)**

Dominant Castes

Nearly 50 per cent of the respondents defined dominant castes as those which indulged in social, economic or political exploitation. About 74 per cent held the view that the three upper Varnas constituted the dominant castes. As regards the factor leading to dominance of a caste in the country-side, it was attributed to educational, economic or political status or a combination of more than one of these factors. Nearly 35 per cent of the replies indicated that relations between dominant castes and OBCs were strained. **(10.16)**

Role of Voluntary Organisations

Nearly 72 per cent of the respondents were aware of the existence of voluntary organisations and thought that they work for the welfare of their respective castes or classes. As regards the impact of their activities, 17 per cent stated that these organisations helped only members of their own castes. Nearly 35 per cent were of the view that some sort of educational, economic, political and social benefits have accrued as a result of the activities of these organisations, but another 20 per cent felt that their impact has been nominal. **(10.17)**

Shift in the Occupational Patterns

Regarding shift in occupational patterns, nearly 45 per cent of the respondents felt that significant changes have taken place in the last three decades. Nearly 14 per cent stated that these changes have been for the worse and a large number of people have been rendered jobless as a result of industrialisation, social change, etc. Above 35 per cent of the respondents were of the view that these changes have been for the better. **(10.18)**

Economic Criteria

Regarding validity of economic criterion for the identification of backwardness nearly 36 per cent of the respondents were not in its favour, but 28 per cent thought that backwardness was directly linked with poverty. **(10.19)**

Evidence of Members of Parliament

Shri R.P. Gaekwad said that lack of education was the main handicap of backward classes and all facilities should be provided for their educational advancement. But he did not see any justification for reserving jobs for them. Shri N.K. Shejawalkar was also of the view that it will not be proper to make reservation in services for OBCs. Shri Bapusaheb Parulekar stated that the goal of the nation was to establish a casteless and classless society and this goal should not be lost sight of while framing criterion for listing OBCs. **(10.35)**

Prof. Madhu Dandavate stated that conversion from one faith to another did not change the socio-economic status of a person. It was, therefore, desirable that converts from Scheduled Castes to Buddhism. Christianity, etc. should be treated as Scheduled Castes. But until this change was brought about by legislation, all such converts should be listed as OBCs. He also felt that economically backward classes should be treated as a separate entity from socially and educationally backward classes. As an example of blind priestly prejudice against low castes, he cited the incident when Lord Mountbatten had invited Dr. B. R. Ambedkar, a member of his Executive Council to accompany him to a visit to Jagannath Puri temple. Whereas the local priests happily welcomed Mountbatten to enter the temple, they refused permission to Dr. Ambedkar. **(10.36)**

Shri Mubarak felt that in view of the special location and problems of Jammu and Kashmir, all-India model of caste-based society was not applicable to that State. He felt that geographical location and complete isolation of certain areas should form the basis for determining backwardness for Jammu and Kashmir. **(10.37)**

Shri Jyotirmoy Bosu pointed that caste was a legacy of the feudal system and viewing the social scene from the casteist angle was no longer relevant for West Bengal. He also stated that his party would express its considered views on various issues before the Commission after examining the matter more thoroughly. **(10.38)**

Shrimati Gita Mukerjee stated that caste based discrimination was a thing of the past in West Bengal. Old occupational patterns had undergone changes and there was no single caste following any single hereditary occupation. She was in favour of giving special assistance to economically weaker sections of society. **(10.39)**

Broadly speaking, two types of evidence were tendered before the Commission. First, a large number of publicmen and caste association argued their case for the inclusion of a particular caste in the list of Other Backward Classes. Some of them, whose caste was already notified as backward by the State concerned, wanted it to be included in the list of Scheduled Castes or Scheduled Tribes. Nearly 3/4th of the respondents appearing before the Commission belonged to this category. Their representations have been separately examined and the results of this examination have been incorporated in the State-wise lists of OBCs prepared by the Commission. Secondly, there were associations or persons which discussed the question of social and educational backwardness in more general terms and offered various suggestions on the terms of reference of the Commission. **(10.41)**

An over-whelming proportion of respondents appearing before the Commission contended that caste should be the basis for determining social and educational backwardness. They were in favour of giving liberal concessions to OBCs so as to off-set their historical handicaps which they had suffered for centuries as a result of their low caste status. Some of the important measures were: reservation in Government services and educational institutions; relaxation in minimum qualifying marks and upper age limit for admission to various courses, etc.; other educational concessions like free books, uniforms and special coaching facilities; allotment of house-sites; grant of liberal loans at low rates of interest; assistance in setting up small-scale industries, etc. **(10.42)**

A number of respondents argued that the reservations for OBCs should be in proportion to their population, as it was only just and fair that in a democratic set-up they are adequately represented in public services. Some of them also maintained that there should be reservations for OBCs in Parliament and Legislative Assemblies, as Other Backward Classes will be in a position to assert their rights only after they have acquired sufficient political clout. A number of associations and persons suggested that Public Service Commissions, Selection Boards and all other recruiting agencies should have adequate representation of OBCs so that backward class candidates could get a fair and sympathetic treatment from these bodies. It was repeatedly emphasised that with a view to ensuring proper protection and fair treatment at the hands of law-enforcement agencies, the bulk of the police force should be recruited from the weaker sections of society. This sort of policy would not only instil confidence in the underprivileged and backward classes, but also ensure that the law enforcement agency is more sensitive and understanding towards the problems of these defenceless people. **(10.43)**

The following table gives a summary of the over-all employment position:

Category of Employees	Total number of employees	Percentage of SC/ST	Percentage of OBCs
Class I	1,74,043	5.68	4.69
Class II	9,12,786	18.81	10.63
Class III & IV	4,84,646	24.40	24.40
All Classes	15,71,475	18.71	12.55

(9.48)

Two things become clear from the above table. First, the percentage of SC/ST employees and, much more so, that of Other Backward Classes, is much below the percentage of their total population in the country. Whereas the aggregate employment for SC/ST comes to 18.71 per cent against their total population of 22.5 per cent, the employment of OBCs works out to 12.55 per cent against their estimated population of 52 per cent. Secondly, the representation of SC/ST and OBC employees in Class I services is much smaller even when compared to the overall employment percentages of these classes. For instance for Scheduled Castes and Scheduled Tribes employees, this figure comes to 5.68 per cent and for OBCs it is 4.69 per cent only. In other words, the representation of OBC employees in Class I Services of the Government of India is not even 1/10 of their proportion to total population. **(9.49)**

6

Indicators of Identification of Backwardness

IN THE Indian situation where vast majority of the people are illiterate, poor or backward, one has to be very careful in setting deviations from the norms as in our conditions, norms themselves are very low. For example, Per Capita Consumer Expenditure for 1977-78 at current prices was Rs. 991 per annum. For the same period, the poverty line for urban area was at Rs. 900 per annum for the rural areas at Rs. 780. It will be seen that this poverty line is quite close to the Per Capita Consumer Expenditure of an average Indian. Now following the dictum of *Balaji's* case, if 50 per cent deviation from the average Per Capita Consumer Expenditure was to be accepted to identify 'economically backward' classes, their income level will have to be 50 per cent below the Per Capita Consumer Expenditure i.e. less than Rs. 495.5 per year. This figure is so much below the poverty line both in urban and rural areas that most of the people may die of starvation before they qualify for such a distinction ! **(11.21)**

In view of the above, 'Indicators for Backwardness' were tested against various cut-off points. For doing so, about a dozen castes well-known for their social and educational backwardness were selected from amongst the castes covered by our survey in a particular State. These were treated as 'Control' and validation checks were carried out by testing them against 'indicators' at various cut-off points. For instance, one of the 'indicators' for social backwardness is the rate of students drop-outs in the age group 5-15 years as compared to the State average. As a result of the above tests, it was seen that in educationally backward castes this rate is at least 25 per cent above the State average. Further, it was also noticed that this deviation of 25 per cent from the State average in the case of most of the 'Indicators' gave satisfactory results. In view of this, wherever an 'Indicator' was based on deviation from the State average, it was fixed at 25 per cent, because a deviation of 50 per cent was seen to give wholly unsatisfactory results and, at times, to create anomalous situations. (11.22)

Indicators (Criteria) for Social and Educational Backwardness

As a result of the above exercise, the Commission evolved eleven 'Indicators' or 'Criteria' for determining social and educational backwardness. These 11 "Indicators' were grouped under three broad heads, i.e., Social, Educational and Economic. They are :

A. *Social*

(i) Castes/Classes considered as socially backward by others.
(ii) Castes/Classes which mainly depend on manual labour for their livelihood.
(iii) Castes/Classes where at least 25 per cent females and 10 per cent males above the State average get married at an age below 17 years in rural areas and at least 10 per cent females and 5 per cent males do so in urban areas.
(iv) Castes/Classes where participation of females in work is at least 25 per cent above the State average.

B. *Educational*

(v) Castes/Classes where the number of children in the age group of 5-15 years who never attained school is at least 25 per cent above the State average.
(vi) Castes/Classes where the rate of students drop-out in the age group of 5-15 years is at least 25 per cent above the State average.
(vii) Castes/Classes amongst whom the proportion of matriculates is at least 25 per cent below the State average.

C. *Economic*

(viii) Castes/Classes where the average value of family assets is at least 25 per cent below the State average.
(ix) Castes/Classes where the number of families living in *Kuccha* houses is at least 25 per cent above the State average.

(x) Castes/Classes where the source of drinking water is beyond half a kilometre for more than 50 per cent of the households.

(xi) Castes/Classes where the number of households having taken consumption loan is at least 25 per cent above the State average. **(11.23)**

As the above three groups are not of equal importance for our purpose, separate weightage was given to 'Indicators' in each group. All the Social 'Indicators' were given a weightage of 3 points each, Educational 'Indicators' a weightage of 2 points each and Economic 'Indicators' a weightage of one point each. Economic indicators, in addition to social and Educational Indicators, were considered important as they directly flowed from social and educational backwardness. This also helped to highlight the fact that socially and educationally backward classes are economically backward also. **(11.24)**

It will be seen that from the values given to each Indicator, the total score adds up to 22. All these 11 Indicators were applied to all the castes covered by the survey of a particular State. As a result of this application, all castes which had a score of 50 per cent (i.e., 11 points) or above were listed as socially and educationally backward and the rest were treated as 'advanced'. (It is a sheer coincidence that the number of the indicators and minimum points score for backwardness, both happen to be eleven). Further, in case the number of households covered by the survey for any particular caste were below 20, it was left out of consideration, as the sample was considered too small for any dependable inference. **(11.25)**

The above system of listing castes as socially and educationally backward on the basis of their score may appear somewhat arbitrary. On the face of it, this is a tenable viewpoint. On the other hand, the points scored by a particular caste under the above system actually reflect the number of indicators of backwardness which it satisfies. Secondly, this method has the great merit of objectivity, as point system allows no subjective assessment. Thirdly, this method was found to be highly dependable in practice. For instance, as a result of its application, most of the well-known socially and educationally backward castes were identified as backward. **(11.26)**

In the end it may be emphasised that this survey has no pretensions to being a piece of academic research. It has been conducted by the administration machinery of the Government and used as a rough and ready tool for evolving a set of simple criterion for identifying social and educational backwardness. Throughout this survey our approach has been conditioned by practical considerations, realities of field conditions, constraints of resources and trained manpower and paucity of time. All these factors obviously militate against the requirements of a technically sophisticated and academically satisfying operations. **(11.27)**

Identification of O.B.Cs.

The Commission adopted a multiple approach for the preparation of comprehensive lists of Other Backward Classes for all the States and Union Territories. The main sources examined for the preparation of these lists were :

(i) Socio-educational field survey;
(ii) Census Report of 1961 (particularly for the identification of primitive tribes, aboriginal tribes, hill tribes, forest tribes and indigenous tribes);
(iii) Personal knowledge gained through extensive touring of the country and receipt of voluminous public evidences as described in Chapter X of this Report; and
(iv) Lists of OBCs notified by various State Governments. **(12.17)**

It may also be stated that in some cases, the findings based on socio-educational field survey happened to be inconsistent with the living social reality. For example, the social status of Kasera caste in Bihar, Dhobi in Gujarat, Agasa in Karnataka, Kumbhar in Rajasthan, Badager in Tamil Nadu, etc. is known to be very low. Yet these castes scored below 11 points and, thus, qualified for ranking as forward. Such aberrations are bound to occur in any sociological survey which is based on statistical methods owing to lopsidedness of the sample covered. The only corrective to these aberrations is the intimate personal knowledge of local conditions and the use of massive public evidence produced before the Commission. The results of the field survey have been carefully scrutinised and such aberrations rectified as far as possible. **(12.9)**

Whereas the Commission has tried to make the State-wise lists of OBCs as comprehensive as possible, it is quite likely that several synonyms of the castes listed as backward have been left out. Certain castes are known by a number of synonyms which vary from one region to the other and their complete coverage is almost impossible. In view of this the Commission recommends that if a particular caste has been listed as backward then all its synonyms whether mentioned in the State lists or not should also be treated as backward. **(12.10)**

O.B.Cs. Among Non-Hindu Communities

There is no doubt that social and educational backwardness among non-Hindu communities is more or less of the same order as among Hindu Communities. Through caste system is peculiar to Hindu society yet, in actual practice, it also pervades the non-Hindu communities in India in varying degrees. There are two main reasons for this phenomenon : first, caste system is a great conditioner of the mind and leaves an indelible mark on a person's social consciousness and cultural mores. Consequently, even after conversion, the ex-Hindus carried with them there deeply ingrained ideas of social hierarchy and stratification. This resulted in the Hindu converts inadvertently acting as Trojan horses of caste system among highly equalitarian religions such as Islam, Christianity, Sikhism, etc. Secondly, non-Hindu minorities living in predominantly Hindu India could not escape from its dominant social and cultural influences. Thus, both from within and without, caste amongst non-Hindu communities received continuous sustenance and stimulus. **(12.11)**

". . . Sayyads and Sheikhs are the priestly castes like the Brahmins and the Mughals and Pathans, famous for their chivalry, are equal to the Kshatryas. . . . There are occupational castes who are considered lower castes in the hierarchy. . . . Thus castes are hereditary names based on their occupation and there is basic tendency among them to practise endogamy. . . . They are descendents of the members of the Hindu clean castes who have been converted to Islam either in groups from different castes or as whole castes".* **(12.12)**

On the same point Dr. Imtiaz Ahmed observes, "There is a notion of hierarchy among the Muslims, through it is hard to say how far the criterion of the ranking among them can be said to conform to the Hindu model. . . . It is clear that castes exists as a basis of social relations amongst them (Muslims) but its form has been greatly

* Caste Among Non-Hindus in India, edited by Dr. Harijinder Singh, National, 1977.

weakened and modified as its differ from the Hindu model in certain details."*

Similar is the situation among Indian Christians. ". . . Christians in Kerala are divided into various denominations on the basis of beliefs and rituals and into various ethnic groups on the basis of their caste background . . . even after conversion, the lower caste converts were continued to be treated as Harijans by all sections of the society including the Syrian Christians, even though with conversion the former ceased to be Harijans and untouchables. . . . In the presence of rich Syrian Christians and Harijans Christians had to remove their head-dress while speaking with their Syrian Christian master. They had to keep their mouth closed with their hands. . . . It was found that the Syrian and Pulaya members of the same Church conduct religious rituals separately in separate buildings. . . . Thus lower caste converts to a very egalitarian religion like Christianity, ever anxious to expand its membership, even after generations were not able to efface the effect of their caste background."** **(12.14)**

About Sikhs, the Hindu caste model is almost literally replicated and fact is too well-known to need any elaboration. **(12.15)**

But despite the prevalence of caste system among non-Hindu communities in varying degrees, the fact of the matter is that all these religious are totally egalitarian in their outlook, they proclaim absolute equality of all their co-religionists and any social differentiation based on caste is anathema to them. In view of this, caste cannot be made the basis for identifying socially and educationally backward classes among non-Hindu communities. We, therefore shall have to evolve some other rough and ready criterion for identifying non-Hindu OBCs. **(12.16)**

On the face of it, the criterion of poverty appears to be the most plausible, but it is full of pitfalls. For instance, even a highly respected and well-educated Sayyad or Syrian Christian may be poor. Thus he will not satisfy the constitutional provision of 'social and educational backwardness'. Secondly, economic criterion is very difficult to apply. A person who is poor today may be well of tomorrow and *vice versa*. Moreover, verification of economic status is very tricky. **(12.17)**

* Caste and Social Stratification among Muslims in India edited by Dr. Imtiaz Ahmed. Manohar Publications, 1978.

** K.C. Alexander in 'Caste among Non-Hindus in India, edited by Dr. Harinder Singh.

After giving a good deal of thought to these difficulties the Commission has evolved the following rough and ready criterion for identifying non-Hindu OBCs :

(i) All untouchables converted to any non-Hindu religion; and
(ii) Such occupational communities which are known by the name of their traditional hereditary occupation and whose Hindu counterparts have been included in the list of Hindu OBCs. (*Examples* : Dhobi, Teli, Dheemar, Nai, Gujar, Kumhar, Lohar, Darji, Badhai, etc.) **(12.18)**

Estimated Population of OBCs

Systematic caste-wise enumeration of population was introduced by the Registrar General of India in 1881 and discontinued in 1931. In view of this, figure of caste-wise population beyond 1931 are not available. But assuming that the *inter se* rate of growth of population of various castes, communities and religious groups over the last half a century has remained more or less the same, it is possible to work out the percentage that all these groups constitute of the total population of the country. **(12.19)**

Working on the above basis the Commission culled out caste/community-wise population figures from the census records of 1931 and, then grouped them into broad caste-clusters and religious groups. These collectivities were subsequently aggregated under five major heads, i.e. (i) Scheduled Castes and Scheduled Tribes; (ii) Non-Hindu Communities, religious groups, etc., (iii) Forward Hindu Castes and Communities. (iv) Backward Hindu Castes and Communities; and (v) Backward Non-Hindu Communities. Results of this exercise are contained in the table and a look at it will indicate the broad classification adopted by the Commission. **(12.20)**

The population of Hindu OBCs could be derived by subtracting from the total population of Hindu, the population of Scheduled Castes, Scheduled Tribes and that of forward Hindu castes and communities and it work out to 52 per cent. But the same approach could not be adopted in respect of non-Hindu OBCs. Assuming that roughly the proportion of OBCs amongst non-Hindu was of the same order as amongst the Hindu, population of non-Hindu OBCs was also taken as 52 per cent of the actual proportion of their population of 16.7 per cent, or 8.40 per cent. Thus the total population of Hindu and non-Hindu

OBCs naturally added up to nearly 52 per cent (43.70% + 8.40%) of the country's population. **(12.21)**

From the forgoing it will be seen that excluding Scheduled Castes and Scheduled Tribes, Other Backward Classes constitute nearly 52 per cent of the Indian population.

7

Recommendations of Mandal Commission

Need for Structural Changes

IT MAY appear that the upliftment of Other Backward Classes (OBCs) is part of the larger national problem of the removal of mass poverty. This is only partially correct. The deprivation of OBCs is a very special case of the larger national issue: here the basic question is that of social and educational backwardness and poverty is only a direct consequence of these two crippling caste-based handicaps. As these handicaps are embedded in our social structure, their removal will require far-reaching structural changes. No less important will be changes in the perception of the problems of OBCs by the ruling classes of the country. **(13.1)**

Attitude of the Elite to Reservations

One such change in the attitude of the ruling elite pertains to the provision of reservation in Government services and educational institutions for the candidates of Other Backward Classes. It is generally argued that looking to the large population of OBCs (52%), recruitment of a few thousand OBCs every year against reserved vacancies is not going to produce any perceptible impact on their general condition. On the other hand, the induction of a large proportion of employees against reserved vacancies will considerably impair the quality and efficiency of the Government services. It is also stated that the benefits of such reservations will be skimmed off by those sections of OBCs which are already well off and the really backward sections will be left high and dry. Another argument advanced against this approach is that the policy of large scale reservations will cause great heart burning to those meritorious candidates whose entry into services will be barred as a result thereof. **(13.2)**

All the above arguments are based on fairly sound reasoning. But there are also the arguments advanced by the ruling elite which is keen on preserving its privileges. Therefore, like all such reasoning, it is based on partisan approach. By the same token, while illuminating some immediate areas of concern it tends to ignore much larger issues of national importance. **(13.3)**

A Feeling of Participation

It is not at all our contention, that by offering a few thousand jobs to OBC candidates we shall be able to make 52 per cent of the Indian population as forward. But we must recognise that an essential part of the battle against social backwardness is to be fought in the minds of the backward people. In India Government service has always been looked upon as a symbol of prestige and power. By increasing the representation of OBCs in Government services, we give them an immediate feeling of participation in the governance of this country. When a backward class candidate becomes a Collector or a Superintendent of Police, the material benefits accruing from his position are limited to the members of his family only. But the psychological spin off of this phenomenon is tremendous; the entire community of that backward class candidates feels socially elevated. Even when no tangible benefits flow to the community at large, the feeling that now it has its "own man" in the "corridors of power" acts as morale booster. **(13.4)**

In a democratic set-up every individual and community has a legitimate right and aspiration to participate in ruling this country. Any situation which results in a near-denial of this right to nearly 52 per cent of the country's population needs to be urgently rectified. **(13.5)**

Quality of Government Services

Apprehensions regarding drop in the quality of Government services owing to large scale induction of S.C./S.T. and O.B.C. candidates against reserved posts may be justified only up to a point. But is it possible to maintain that all candidates selected on merit turn out to be honest, efficient, hard-working and dedicated? At present, top echelons of all the Government services are manned predominantly by open competition candidates and if the performance of our bureaucracy is any indication, it has not exactly covered itself with glory. Of course, this does not imply that candidates selected against reserved posts will do better. Chances are that owing to their social and cultural handicaps they may be generally a shade less competent. But, on the other hand, they will have the great advantage of possessing first hand knowledge of the sufferings and problems of the backward sections of society. This is not a small asset for field workers and policy-makers even at the highest level. **(13.6)**

Introduction of Egalitarianism

It is not doubt true that the major benefits of reservation and other welfare measures for Other Backward Classes will be cornered by the more advanced sections of the backward communities. But is not this a universal phenomenon? All reformist remedies have to contend with a slow recovery along the hierarchical gradient; there are no quantum jumps in social reform. Moreover, human nature being what it is, a "new class" ultimately does emerge even in classless societies. The chief merit of reservation is not that it will introduce egalitarianism amongst OBCs when the rest of the Indian society is seized by all sorts of inequalities. But reservation will certainly erode the hold of higher castes on the services and enable OBCs in general to have a sense of participation in running the affairs of their country. **(13.7)**

No Heart-burning

It is certainly true that reservation for OBCs will cause a lot of heart burning to others. But should the mere fact of this heart burning be allowed to operate as a moral-veto against social reform. A lot of heart burning was caused to the British when they left India. It burns the hearts of all whites when the black protest against apartheid in South Africa. When the higher castes constituting less than 20 per cent of the country's population subjected the rest to all manner of social injustice, it must have caused a lot of heart burning to the lower castes. But now that the lower castes are asking for a modest share of the national cake of power and prestige, a chorus of alarm is being raised on the plea that this will cause heart burning to the ruling elite. Of all the spacious arguments advanced against reservation for backward classes, there is none which beats this one about 'heart-burning' in sheer sophistry.

(13.8)

In fact the Hindu society has always operated a very rigorous scheme of reservation, which was internalised through caste system. Eklavya lost his thumb and Shambhuk his neck for their breach of caste rules of reservation. The present furore against reservations for OBCs is not aimed at the principle itself, but against the new class of beneficiaries, as they are now clamouring for a share of the opportunities which were all along monopolised by the higher castes. **(13.9)**

Quantum and Scheme of Reservations

Scheduled Castes and Scheduled Tribes constitute 22.5 per cent of the country's population. Accordingly, a *pro-rata* reservation of 22.5 per cent has been made for them in all services and public sector undertakings under the Central Government. In the States also, reservation of SCs and STs is directly proportional to their population in each State. **(13.10)**

The population of OBCs, both Hindu and non-Hindu, is around 52 per cent of the total population of India. Accordingly, 52 per cent of all posts under the Central Government should be reserved for them. But this provision may go against the law laid down in a number of Supreme Court judgments wherein it has been held that the total quantum of reservation under Articles 15(4) and 16(4) of the Constitution should be below 50 per cent. In view of this the proposed reservation for OBCs would have to be pegged at a figure which, when added to 22.5 per cent for SCs and STs, remains below 50 per cent. In view of this legal constraint, the Commission is obliged to recommend a reservation of 27 per cent only, even though their population is almost twice this figure. **(13.11)**

States which have already introduced reservation for OBCs exceeding 27 per cent will remain unaffected by this recommendation. **(13.12)**

Overall Scheme of Reservation

With the above general recommendation regarding the quantum of reservation, the Commission proposes the following over-all scheme of reservation for OBCs:

(1) Candidates belonging to OBCs recruited on the basis of merit in

an open competition should not be adjusted against their reservation quota of 27 per cent.

(2) The above reservation should also be made applicable to promotion quota at all levels.

(3) Reserved quota remaining unfilled should be carried forward for a period of three years and dereserved thereafter.

(4) Relaxation in the upper age limit for direct recruitment should be extended to the candidates of OBCs in the same manner as done in the case of SCs and STs.

(5) A roster system for each category of posts should be adopted by the concerned authorities in the same manner as presently done in respect of SC and ST candidates. **(13.13)**

The above scheme of reservation in its *toto* should also be made applicable to all recruitment to public sector undertakings both under the Central and State Governments, as also to nationalised banks. **(13.14)**

Reservation in Public Sector

All private sector undertakings which have received financial assistance from the Government in one form or the other should also be obliged to recruit personnel on the aforesaid basis. **(13.15)**

Higher Educational Institutions

All universities and affiliated colleges should also be covered by the above scheme of reservation. **(13.16)**

Statutory Provisions

To give proper effect to these recommendations, it is imperative that adequate statutory provisions are made by the Government to amend the existing enactments, rules, procedures, etc., to the extent they are not in consonance with the same. **(13.17)**

Concessions in Education

Our educational system is elitist in character, results in a high degree of wastage and is least suited to the requirements of an over-populated and developing country. It is a legacy of the British rule which was severely criticised during the independence struggle, and yet, it has not undergone any structural changes. Though it is least suited to be needs of backward classes, yet, they are forced to run the rat-race with others as no options are available to them. As 'educational reform' was not within the terms of reference of this Commission, we are also forced to trend the beaten track and suggest only the palliative measure within the existing framework. **(13.18)**

Various, State Governments are giving a number of educational concessions to Other Backward Class students like exemption of tuition fees, free supply of books and clothes, mid-day meals, special hostel facilities, stipends, etc. These concessions are all right as far as they go. But they do not go far enough. What is required is, perhaps, not so much as the provision of additional funds as the framing of integrated schemes for creating the proper environment and incentives for serious and purposeful studies. **(13.19)**

It is well known that most backward class children are irregular and indifferent students and their drop-out rate is very high. There are two main reasons for this. First, these children are brought up in a climate of extreme social and cultural deprivation and, consequently, a proper motivation for schooling is generally lacking. Secondly, most of these children come from very poor homes and their parents are forced to press them into doing small chores from a very young age. **(13.20)**

Cultural Environment

Upgrading the cultural environment is a very slow process. Transferring these children to an artificially upgraded environment is beyond the present resources of the country. In view of this it is recommended that this problem may be tackled on a limited and selective basis on two fronts. **(13.21)**

First, an intensive and time bound programme for adult education should be launched in selected pockets with high concentration of OBC population. This is a basic motivational approach, as only proper motivated parents will take serious interest in educating their children. Secondly, residential schools should be set up in these areas for backward class students to provide a climate specially conducive to serious studies. All facilities in these schools including board and lodging, will have to be provided free of cost to attract students from poor and backward homes, separate Government Hostels for OBC students with the above facilities will be another step in the right direction. **(13.22)**

A beginning on both these fronts will have to be made on a limited scale and selective basis. But the scope of these activities should be expanded as fast as the resources permit. Adult education programme and residential schools started on a selective basis will operate as growing-points of conciousness for the entire community and their multiplier effect is bound to be substantial. Whereas several States are extended a number of *ad hoc* concessions to backward class students, few serious attempts have been made to integrate these facilities into a comprehensive scheme for a qualitative upgradation of educational environment available to OBC students. **(13.23)**

Vocational Training

After all, education is the best catalyst of change and educating the backward classes is the surest way to improve their self image and raise their social status. As OBCs cannot afford the high wastage rates of our-educational system, it is very important that their education is highly biased in favour of vocational training. After all reservation in services will absorb only a very small percentage of the educated backward classes and the rest should be suitably equipped with vocational skills to enable them to get a return on having invested several years in education. **(13.24)**

It is also obvious that even if all the above facilities are given to OBC students, they will not be able to compete on an equal footing with others in securing admission to technical and professional institutions. In view of this it is recommended that seats should be reserved for OBC students in all scientific, technical and professional institutions run by the Central as well as State Governments. This reservation will fall under Article 15(4) of the Constitution and the quantum of reservation should be the same as in the Government services, i.e., 27 per cent. Those States which have already reserved more than 27 per cent seats for OBC students will remain unaffected by this recommendation. **(13.25)**

Special Coaching Facilities

While implementing the provision for reservation it should also be ensured that the candidates who are admitted against the reserved quota are enabled to derive full benefit of higher studies. It has been generally noticed that these OBC students coming from an impoverished cultural background, are not able to keep abreast with other students. It is, therefore, very essential that special coaching facilities are arranged for all such students in our technical and professional institutions. The concerned authorities should clearly appreciate that their job is not finished once candidates against reserved quota have been admitted to various institutions. In fact the real task starts only after that. Unless adequate follow-up action is taken to give special coaching assistance to these students, not only these young people will feel frustrated and humiliated but the country will also be landed with ill-equipped and sub-standard engineers, doctors and other professionals. **(13.26)**

Institutional Finance and Technical Assistance

Vocational communities following hereditary occupations have suffered heavily as a result of industrialisation. Mechanical production and introduction of synthetic materials has robbed the village potter, oil crusher, black-smith, carpenter, etc. of their traditional means of livelihood and the pauperisation of these classes is a well known phenomenon in the country-side. **(13.27)**

It has, therefore become very necessary that suitable institutional finance and technical assistance is made available to such members of village vocational communities who want to set up small scale industries on their own. Similar assistance should also be provided to those promising OBC candidates who have obtained special vocational training. **(13.28)**

Of course, most State Governments have created various financial and technical agencies for the promotion of small and medium scale industries. But it is well known that only the more influential members of the community are able to derive benefits from these agencies. In view of this, it is very essential that separate financial institutions for providing financial and technical assistance are established for the backward classes. Some State Governments like Karnataka and Andhra Pradesh have already set up separate financial corporations etc. for OBCs. **(13.29)**

Cooperative Societies

Cooperative Societies of occupational groups will also help a lot. But due care should be taken that all the office-bearers and members of such societies belong to the concerned hereditory occupational groups and outsiders are not allowed to exploit them by infiltrating into such cooperatives. **(13.30)**

Business and Industrial Enterprise

The share of OBCs in the industrial and business life of the country is negligible and this partly explains their extremely low income levels. As a part of its overall strategy to uplift the backward classes, it is imperative that all State Governments, are suitably advised and encouraged to create a separate network of financial and technical institutions to foster business and industrial enterprise among OBCs. **(13.31)**

Structural Changes to Tackle the Problem of its Root

Reservations in Government employment and educational institutions, as also all possible financial assistance will remain mere palliatives unless the problem of backwardness is tackled at its root. Bulk of the small land-holders, tenants, agricultural labour, impoverished village artisans, unskilled workers, etc. belong to Scheduled Castes, Scheduled Tribes and Other Backward Classes. "Apart from social traditions, the dominance by the top peasantry is exercised through recourse to informal bondage which arises mainly through money-lending, leasing out of small bits of land and providing house-sites and dwelling space to poor peasants. As most of the functionaries of Government and the top peasantry remain firm. This also tills the socio-political balance in favour of the top peasantry and helps it in having its dominance over others". **(13.32)**

Need for Proper Implementation

The net outcome of the above situation is that notwithstanding their numerical preponderance, backward classes continue to remain in mental and material bondage of the higher castes and rich peasantry. Consequently, despite constituting nearly 3/4th of the country's population, Scheduled Castes, Scheduled Tribes and Other Backward Classes have been able to acquire a very limited political clout, even though adult franchise was introduced more than three decades back.

Through their literal monopoly of means of production of higher castes are able to manipulate and coerce the backward classes into acting against their own interests. In view of this, until the stranglehold of the existing production relations is broken through radical land reforms, the abject dependence of under privileged classes on the dominant higher castes will continue indefinitely. In fact there is already a sizeable volume of legislation on the statute books to abolish zamindari, place ceilings on land holdings and distribute land to the landless. But in actual practice its implementation has been halting, half-hearted and superficial. The States like Karnataka, Kerala and West Bengal which have gone about the job more earnestly have not only succeeded in materially helping the Backward classes, but also reaped rich political dividends into the bargain. **(13.33)**

Radical Transformation of the Existing Relations

It is the Commission's firm conviction that a radical transformation of the existing production relations is the most important single step that can be taken for the welfare and upliftment of all backward classes. Even if this is not possible in the industrial sector for various reasons, in the agricultural sector a change of this nature is both feasible and overdue. **(13.34)**

Enactment of Land Legislation

The Commission, therefore strongly recommends that all the State Governments should be directed to enact and implement progressive land legislation so as to effect basic structural changes in the existing production relations in the countryside. **(13.35)**

At present surplus land is being allotted to SCs and STs. A part of the surplus land becoming available in future as a result of the operation of land ceiling laws etc. should also be allotted to be OBC landless labour. **(13.36)**

Diverse Recommendations

(1) Certain sections, of some occupational communities like Fishermen, Banjaras, Bansforas, Khatwes etc., still suffer from the stigma of untouchability in some parts of the country. They have been listed as O.B.Cs by the Commission, but their inclusion in the lists of Scheduled Castes/Scheduled Tribes may

be considered by the Government.

(2) Backward Classes Development Corporations should be set up both at the Central and State levels to implement various socio-educational and economic measures for their advancement.

(3) A separate Ministry/Department for O.B.Cs. at the Centre and the States should be created to safeguard their interests.

(4) With a view to giving better representation to certain very backward sections of O.B.Cs. like the Gaddis in Himachal Pradesh, Neo-Buddhists in Maharashtra, Fishermen in the Coastal areas, Gujjars in J & K, it is recommended that areas of their concentration may be carved out into separate constituencies at the time of delimitation. **(13.37)**

Assistance from the Central Government

At present no Central Assistance is available to any State Government for implementing any welfare measures for Other Backward Classes. The 18 States and Union Territories which have under taken such measures have to provide funds from their own resources. During the Commission's tours practically every State Government pointed out that unless the Centre is prepared to liberally finance all special schemes for the upliftment of OBCs, it will be beyond the available resources of the States to undertake any worthwhile programme for the benefit of Other Backward Classes. **(13.38)**

The Commission fully shares the views of the State Governments in this matter and strongly recommends that all development programmes specially designed for Other Backward Classes should be financed by the Central Government in the same manner and to the same extent as done in the case of Scheduled Castes and Scheduled Tribes. **(13.39)**

Review after 20 Years

Regarding the period of operation of the Commission's recommendations, the entire scheme should be reviewed after twenty years. We have advisedly suggested this span of one generation, as the raising of social consciousness is a generational progress. Any review at a shorter interval would be rather arbitration and will not give a fair indication of the impact of our recommendations on the prevailing status and life-styles of O.B.Cs. **(13.40)**

8

Mandal Commission in Election Manifestoes, 1989-90

Congress (I) Manifesto

NO MENTION of Mandal Commission as such. The Congress has always enjoyed the full support of backward classes. It is fully committed to their welfare and all round progress. Special programmes will be instituted to support the professional activities and occupations of the backward classes through the provision of better technologies, more generous financial assistance and better marketing. Educational concessions, including scholarships and other schemes of academic improvement, will be extended from the primary to university level to students belonging to the backward classes.

National Front Manifesto

The socially and educationally backward classes will be given special opportunities and substantial reservations in employment, education and public offices will be made.

The recommendations of the Mandal Commission will be implemented expeditiously.

Bharatiya Janata Party Manifesto

In the opinion of the B.J.P, the question of reservation has to be viewed with an open mind free from all prejudices of any kind

For this B.J.P. commends:

1. Reservation should be continued for Scheduled Castes and Scheduled Tribes as before;

2. Reservation should also be made for other backward classes broadly on the basis of the Mandal Commission Report, preference to be given to the poor among these very classes;
3. As poverty is an important contributory factor for backwardness, reservation should also be provided for members of the other castes on the basis of their economic conditions.

Communist Party of India (Marxist) Manifesto

No mention of Mandal Commission

Communist Party of India Manifesto

No mention of Mandal Commission.

9

Government Policy

Statement of the Prime Minister on Mandal Commission

August 7, 1990

THE FOLLOWING is the text of the *suo moto* statement of Prime Minister in the Lok Sabha on decisions on the Mandal Commission Report:-

I am happy today to announce in this august House a momentous decision of social justice that my Government has taken regarding the Socially and Educationally Backward Classes on the basis of the Report of the Mandal Commission.

Hon'ble Members are aware that the Constitution which we gave to ourselves 40 years back envisages that Socially and Educationally Backward Classes (SEBCs) be identified, their difficulties removed and their conditions improved in terms of Article 340(1) read with Article 15(4) as well as Article 16(4). It is a negation of the basic structure of our Constitution that till now this requirement was not fulfilled.

The Second Backward Classes Commission under the Chairmanship of the late Shri B.P. Mandal which was appointed on 1st July, 1979 submitted its report on 31st December 1980. In accordance with our commitment before the people we included this in our Action Plan After examining various aspects of it, I am glad to announce that my Government has taken the following decisions on the Commission's Report:

(i) In order to avail ourselves of the benefit of the long experience of a number of States in preparing lists of Socially and Educationally Backward Classes (SEBCs) and in order to ensure harmonious and quick implementation, we have decided to adopt in the first phase the castes common to both the Mandal list as well as the State Lists.

(ii) The percentage of reservation for the Socially and Educationally Backward Classes (SEBCs) will be 27.

(iii) This reservation will be applicable to services under the Government of India and Public Undertakings.

Hon'ble Members are aware that on 14 April, 1990 at the official function organised to celebrate the birthday of Bharat Ratna Baba Saheb Dr. B.R. Ambedkar at the Ambedkar Stadium, I announced the commencement of the Ambedkar Centenary Year and designated it as the Year of Social Justice. We have taken a number of measures of social justice pertaining to the Scheduled Castes and Scheduled Tribes and other weaker sections like removal of injustice done to Neo-Buddhists vesting of constitutional status and substantial powers to the National Commission for Scheduled Castes and Scheduled Tribes, according due but long delayed honours to Dr. Ambedkar, and so on. The present decisions are in the same line and belong to the tradition of this Government's dedication to the cause of the Scheduled Castes Scheduled Tribes, Socially and Educationally Backward Classes and other weaker sections.

Office Memorandum on Mandal Commission*

Recommendations of the Second Backward Classes Commission (Mandal Report): Reservation for Socially and Educationally Backward Classes in Services under the Government of India

In a multiple undulating society like ours, early achievement of the objective of social justice as enshrined in the Constitution is a must. The Second Backward Classes Commission called the Mandal Commission was established by the then Government with this purpose in view, which submitted its report to the Government of India on

* No. 360/31/90-Estt (SCT), Government of India, Ministry of Personnel, Public Grievances & Pensions, (Department of Personnel & Training), New Delhi, August 13, 1990.

December 31, 1980.

2. Government have carefully considered the report and the recommendations of the Commission in the present context regarding the benefits to be extended to the socially and educationally backward classes as opined by the Commission and are of the clear view that at the outset certain weightage has to be provided to such classes in the services of the Union and their public Undertakings. Accordingly orders are issued as follows:

(i) Twenty-seven per cent of the vacancies in civil posts and services under the Government of India shall be reserved for SEBC.

(ii) The aforesaid reservation shall apply to vacancies to be filled by direct recruitment. Detailed instructions relating to the procedure to be followed for enforcing reservation will be issued separately.

(iii) Candidates belonging to SEBS recruited on the basis of merit in an open competition on the same standards prescribed for the general candidates shall not be adjusted against the reservation quota of twenty-seven per cent.

(iv) The SEBC would comprise in the first phase the castes and communities which are common to both the list in the report of the Mandal Commission and the State Government's lists A.

(v) The aforesaid reservation shall take effect from August 7, 1990. However, this will not apply to vacancies where the recruitment process has already been initiated prior to the issue of these orders.

3. Similar instructions in respect of public sector undertakings and financial institutions including public sector banks will be issued by the Department of Public Enterprises and Ministry of Finance respectively.

(Smt. Krishna Singh)
Joint Secretary to the Govt. of India.

10

Critique of the Policy by Cross Section of Society

Mandal Commission : Dividing to Rule

IT WAS a decision that will live forever in infamy and become the benchmark of the descent of Prime Minister Vishwanath Pratap Singh from leader to demagogue. His announcement on August 7 — two days before Devi Lal's kisan rally in New Delhi — that the Government would implement the recommendations of the Mandal Commission, was initially greeted as a master-stroke calculated to consolidate the backward castes as the new vote bank of the badly mauled Janata Dal.

That Singh was willy-nilly planting the seeds for a new political harvest became even more evident when he used the Red Fort as an electoral platform on Independence Day to reiterate his commitment to implementing the Commission's recommendations, and appealed to the Scheduled Castes and Muslims by repeated references to Ambedkar and declaring Prophet Mohammed's birthday a public holiday.

But as events unfolded during the fortnight it became clear that what Singh was trying to reap was a harvest of shame. He had been reduced, like all power-hungry politicians before him, to a vote-hungry power broker shamelessly using the two elements that have ever bloodied and divided this nation — religion and caste.

(Badhwar, Inderjit, *India Today* September 15, 1990)

Quota for Weaker Sections Must

Referring to the Congress leader's statement that economic status be the criterion for reservation policy. Mr. Bommai reminded Mr. Gandhi that Congress-I Governments in the South have been implementing reservation policy for the backward classes based on caste only.

Mr. Bommai said that implementation of Mandal Commission report was a must to ensure some sort of an opportunity in services for the backward classes. If the oppressed are not given the opportunity there would be bloodshed and revolution in the country.

He said that National Front Government under the leadership of Mr. V. P. Singh had taken its election promise seriously. Achievements in the first ten months was significant, but publicity to the internal differences in the party has swallowed the good work of the Government, he opined.

He further said that there was no difference of opinion among the Janata Dal leaders over the reservation issue, as was being made out by some people.

Asked about the steps his party proposed to take on the issue in the context of the BJP having expressed a different view on it. Mr. Bommai said 'we are holding discussions'.

The percentage of reservation in southern states was more than that recommended by the Mandal Commission, he said, adding, though there was a demand in the south to review it, 'reservation has been introduced only now in the northern parts of the country'. He urged students to call off their on-going agitation over the issue.

The notion that the implementation of the report would affect excellence and merit was incorrect, Mr. Bommai said, "Top ranking and meritorious students may not become good engineers, doctors, administrators, advocates and journalists", he said. How many of you are distinction or rank holders? Are you not doing a good job? he asked the gathered newsmen.

(Bommai, S. R., *Indian Express*, September 9, 1990)

Risking the Mandal Report

The editorials and public protests against the official adoption of the Mandal Commission's 1980 report contrast strangely with the support for it from all the major political parties, including the Congress (I), the Marxists and the BJP. These, of course, are publicly playing the numbers game. Privately, however, they are dismayed that party funding and the control of their organisations may be in jeopardy. However, they are probably happy that the protests represent the first serious public threat to the government.

Though reservations *a la* Mandal makes sense, it would be futile to expect reservations alone to remove social prejudice. That requires social programmes and a strict protection of the rights of the backward classes as equal citizens. As the history of reservation for scheduled castes and tribes indicates, the absence of programmes to better their social status in spite of job and education reservation has left them as vulnerable as they were earlier.

Appropriate though reservations are in the context of India's history of class distinction and neglect of the backward classes, this does not excuse V.P. Singh's manner of working in this case. The hasty adoption of the Mandal Report appears opportunistic in the light of Singh's poor mass base and can be criticised as politically expedient in this new era of consensus politics.

(Business India, September 3-16, 1990)

More Politics than Jobs

Mr. Gandhi, who was addressing the Congress-I Parliamentary Party's valedictory meeting, 'devoted most of his speech to the Government's decision to implement the Mandal Commission recommendations.

"The Prime Minister, Mr. V.P. Singh, had taken the decision in a huff. There was no proper discussion even in the Cabinet and, according to our information, the Mandal Commission was not on the agenda paper even. There were also much quibblings among the Bharatiya Janata Party and the Left parties supporting the Government from outside," Mr. Gandhi pointed out.

Describing the Government's decision to go ahead with 27 per cent job reservation on the basis of the Mandal Commission report, irrespective of consequences, as a "political gimmick", the former Prime Minister said that by backwardness the Constitution makers meant socially and educationally backward classes and not just backward castes. But the Government had arbitrarily changed a concept well-defined in the Constitution. "Yesterday, I was shocked when during the debate on the Mandal Commission in the Lok Sabha, Mr. V.P. Singh did not get up to say that he did not believe in castes," Mr. Gandhi said.

It was shocking that the country had a Prime Minister whose actions encouraged casteism, Mr. Gandhi said reminding his party colleagues that "caste is a cancer in our society".

Spelling out the Congress-I's stand on job reservations issue, Mr. Gandhi said: "We are for helping the weakest and the poorest among backwards. The Congress-I was never against the reservations but it was opposed to the proposal to define caste as the sole factor for determining the economic backwardness. The Mandal Commission had used the economic factor to identify castes but it had not used the economic factor to go beyond caste.

Mr. Gandhi said it was worth noticing that the Constitution had defined backwardness in class terms and not backwardness in caste terms. He called upon his party men to ensure that the caste system was eradicated from society and the country moved towards a casteless society.

The Congress-I men and women should go to people and tell them that the advantage of reservations should not go to the priviledged and vested interests, Mr. Gandhi said adding that "assistance should be given to the truly poor people, to the landless, to people falling in the poorest category."

He particularly asked MPs belonging to Backward Classes to go to the rural areas and tell people "what Mr. V.P. Singh is doing is a total fraud on backward classes and what the other backward classes needed is educational and financial assistance."

(Gandhi, Rajiv, *Hindustan Times*, September 8, 1990)

Time for Second Thoughts

The refusal of the Supreme Court to intervene in the implementation of the Mandal Commission report till it takes up the petitions challenging the Central decision on November 6 should be seen as an attempt to cool down the passions now running riot over the issue. Its impassioned plea to all concerned to refrain from all kinds of agitation as the court is seized of the matter makes this all the more clear. The apex court did not think it necessary to stay the implementation or to enforce *status quo* or to make it mandatory for the Government to seek the court's permission before it took any step in this regard. It went by the Attorney-General's submission that the implementation would take a "reasonable" time and there was no immediate infringement of anybody's rights or privileges. However, the Supreme Court's decision does not prevent anyone who is aggrieved by the impugned government orders from moving the court for redress. In view of the large number of writ petitions filed in various courts against the Government's decision on various grounds, it was in the fitness of things that the court decided to hear them as a composite case.

Since the court can only decide the constitutional validity or otherwise of the Government's decision, the challenge of defusing the explosive situation, which has started taking a heavy toll of lives in States like Bihar, has to be faced by the political leadership. With pro- and anti-reservationists at daggers drawn, a caste conflagration, particularly in the countryside, cannot be ruled out. Although in many places schools and colleges have been closed to keep the students away from the agitation, it has not demonstratively weakened the movement against caste-based reservation as the successive *bandhs* and protest marches even in States where OBCs have already been getting the reservation facility suggest. Only those with a closed mind can underestimate the groundswell of opinion against what is known as the Mandalisation of society. However, the V. P. Singh Government, obsessed as it is in calculating the electoral advantage that it thinks can accrue to it from its decision, is not bothered by what is going on in the north.

Despite the frightening portents visible all around, all that the Government could do was to organise an all-party meeting which was destined to meet with failure as the 27 per cent reservation for OBCs was at the outset declared non-negotiable. The meeting ended up issuing an innocuous appeal to the students to refrain from violence. The Government has been consistently refusing to budge an inch on its stand, perhaps, in the fear that any compromise would antagonise the vote banks it sought to cultivate. Even the fact that apart from parties which prop up the minority Government like the BJP and the Leftists, even a section in the Janata Dal has reservations on the decision does not bother the Government. If it believes in reconciliation and not confrontation, it should immediately start a dialogue with those in the forefront of the agitation with a view to evolving a more equitable system of helping the really deprived sections of society. The agitators should also respond to the Supreme Court's plea for not resorting to violence. The court has provided enough time to all concerned for second thoughts.

(*Hindustan Times*, September 13, 1990)

Weakening the Roots

All over the world, the stress is on talent and merit, because it is by proper harnessing and utilisation of these qualities that the nations go forward and make a mark in the different fields of human endeavour. India has in the past produced great engineers, great doctors, great scientists and technologists. We have also had a distinguished array of civil servants, judges, academicians and defence personnel. Man to man an Indian possesses higher I.Q. and talent compared to the nationals of most other countries. This is proved by the performance of Indian students in foreign universities and institutions. Let us not put a damper on merit by putting a premium on the caste factor under the cover of ameliorating the lot of backward classes. Any attempt to dethrone merit and enthrone in its place mediocrity would spell disaster for the future of the country.

We must not create conditions as would banish and drive away talent from the country and add to the wealth and progress of other countries.

Watchword

The watchword has to be excellence; that has to be the pole star to guide all our strivings. We want all our institutions to be first-rate, for it is thus that we can hold our own in competition with other nations. To have first-rate institutions we must ensure that the human stuff composing those institutions is also first rate. It is a self-deluding fallacy to assume that we can have first-rate institutions with second-rate talent. For instance, you cannot have a first-rate hospital, if its staff consists of sub-standard doctors. It is not merely enough to have hospitals, it is equally important that they should be manned by first-rate doctors.

India's great leaders and social reformers, being conscious of the havoc caused by the caste system and the divisions, discrimination, distortions and demeaning of human dignity it created within some sections of the society, launched a mass educative process highlighting this aspect and the need to eliminate the caste factor. The new move seeks to undo all those labours and to give a perpetual or in any case long lease of life to the caste element.

One of the most sinister aspects of reservation is to enforce this principle not merely at point of initial appointment but also at the time of promotion. Extending the principle of reservation to the stage of promotion would result in startling anomalies. This can best be demonstrated by an illustration: Supposing a candidate from a caste declared backward class with 50 per cent marks is appointed as an Engineer in preference to a candidate with 80 per cent marks. In the very nature of things he would be of sub-standard talent compared to those selected on-merit. After about 7 or 10 years of service when the time comes for promotion to the higher post, the above Engineer with sub-standard talent would be entitled to be promoted just on the basis of caste consideration by bypassing and superseding the other Engineers who were senior to him and possessed better talent. The result would be that despite his deficiency in talent he would become superior to those under whom he worked at one time. One can well imagine the havoc such promotions would wreak on the efficiency of the Department. It would also give rise to disturbing anomalies in the administration of the department, besides causing grave disaffection and frustration.

(Khanna, H.R. *Hindustan Times*, September 13, 1990)

Job Reservations : Pro-side, Con-side and Inside

The privation of millions, other than SCs/STs, would seem to suggest that reservations should be given to backward castes as well as SCs/STs and in that case the addition of a certain percentage say 27 per cent to the existing SC/ST quota of 22.5 per cent may seem to have a justification. While it is undeniable that the backward castes have to be uplifted through social and economic policy, two serious observations are in order. First, after all the effort for four decades to reduce and obliterate caste sentiments, isn't it a tragedy that caste should be consolidated through this backdoor of reservations? Unfortunately, caste remains an important element in the politics of the ballot, but fortunately social policy until this day is geared to the elimination of caste. Here, clearly, there is a head-long collision between long-term social policy and short-term expediency. In other words, reservations by caste — backward or forward — are unacceptable unless by some wooliness of argument or some mixed-up logic we perpetrate the error of diluting our social policy. A consolidation of the caste factor in whatever garb will be preposterous and will have vastly damaging consequences for the country.

Secondly, why should there be a reservation by caste? Because the backward castes are backward and poor, that is to say economically weak. In that case, the real issue is of economic weakness and not its outward expression, the caste. So, why don't we break the outer shell of caste and come to the brass-tacks of economic backwardness and provide suitable reservations in education and jobs for a sensible length of time until the economically weak manage to uplift themselves? Why beat about the bush and talk of caste rather than come to the reality of economic privation? From whatever angle we look at this matter we reach the conclusion that the real issue is the protection of the weak and not of particular castes.

Thus, a sensible system of reservation is one which (a) takes care of the downtrodden and the poor through creation of opportunities at the educational and the first-job stage; (b) identifies the poor by the level of poverty and not by caste; (c) graduates the economically weak as they become stronger; (d) provides additional assistance to the weak through coaching, hostel facilities and scholarships and stipends at the scholastic stage; (e) arranges training programmes for the weak preparatory to admissions to jobs in the public and private sectors and generally promotes self-reliance rather than doles and crutches.

(Khusro, A.M., *Indian Express*, September 13, 1990)

Policy Reservations

Populism is the last refuge of desperate politicians. It would be premature to dump Prime Minister Vishwanath Pratap Singh into that category. But his tunnel-visioned resolve to shove the controversial reservations policy down the country's throat smacks of political expediency.

Whether or not Singh achieves his political objective of cementing the backward castes. Harijans and Scheduled Tribes into a lasting vote bank through implementing the job, educational and promotion quotas recommended by the Mandal Commission in another matter. But the social price that this already deeply and bitterly divided land may have to pay could be horrendous.

Sadly, the religious divide that partitioned this country is being resuscitated by the Ram Janmabhoomi-Babri Masjid battle. And linguistic wars pitch community against community. Add to these tensions a system that formally anoints — indeed, institutionalises — caste as the basis of educational and professional advancement, and you not only highlight but also exacerbate the most fundamental hatreds and prejudices that have lacerated Indian society since time immemorial. The violence that is spreading through Bihar, Gujarat and Rajasthan is a preview of the real horrors that may lie ahead.

The paramount necessity is fairness and the impartial and rigorous implementation of the law. If Dalits are being exploited or massacred in villages in Bihar the law must crack down hard. All cases of discrimination in jobs and education on the basis of caste, sex or religion must be relentlessly prosecuted, even in special tribunals.

The state must function not as a promoter of quotas based on the demography of caste but as a referee guaranteeing equal opportunity at the starting line. It must help pull the disadvantaged into the mainstream by guaranteeing them basic quality education, providing them emergency economic assistance, identifying and helping the brightest of them through aid and scholarships, and paving the way for allowing them to compete in any field they desire.

The Government's larger objective, eradication of poverty, is laudable. But it cannot be achieved by lowering competitive standards. The lasting solution is to expand the economic cake rather than apportion its slices according to some pathetic caste-based formula. This entails a solid commitment to rapid economic growth, and removal of all barriers in the path of production and speedier industrialisation. The answer lies in providing more jobs for more people, not reserved jobs for reserved people.

(*India Today*, September 15, 1990)

Reservations

The resolution of the Congress-I Working Committee adopted on August 30, 1990 is full of ambiguities and contradictions. It will provide a good handle to the opponents of the Congress-I to undermine its position in the States south of the Vindhyas. These States had implemented the provisions of the Constitution relating to the backward classes long ago. It was the Centre which was dragging its feet.

The criticism that the step taken by V. P. Singh "betrays a degree of cynical opportunism, intellectual dishonesty and political malfeasance never before seen at the highest levels of Government" will not wash. It is the Government's action and its impact on the struggle for social justice that needs to be evaluated. The impeachment of V. P. Singh's motive is no substitute for such an evaluation.

I do not wish to dispute the fact that historically the Congress has made a great contribution to the establishment of social justice. It is irrefutable. But the new resolution of the Congress-I will be perceived by the masses as its opposition to measures which have been introduced for their benefit.

The Constitution deliberately did not speak of economically

backward classes; it spoke only of socially and educationally backward classes. Poverty criterion is comprehended by the concept of educational backwardness, which denotes absence of both the tradition of learning as well as poverty. The Constituent Assembly, aware of the historical background, could not therefore be oblivious of the relevance of caste as unit. But the non-use of the expression caste enables the Government to bring in groups of Muslims and Christians who are engaged in lowly occupations, have to live in miserable hovels and are educationally backward.

The discontinuation of caste enumeration in the Census has given rise to unsupported claims by some castes and equally wild refutations of these claims by the privileged minority. It is time this enumeration was resumed during the current Census. Economic criterion can be applied only to those castes, declared by the Mandal Commission to be backward but which after the exhaustive enumeration are found to be more educationally advanced than the national average and the ratio of whose representation in the Central services exceeds their proportion in the total population. But unless the results of the concrete enumeration and statistical data demand revision, the Mandal classification of the socially and educationally backward classes must be accepted.

In my opinion all the *adwija* castes should be included in the backward class reservation. These *adwija* castes should to begin with, be divided into two classes: a) landholding castes; b) non-land holding castes. The first category should be given 12 per cent posts; and the second category 15 per cent.

After the Census enumeration, if it is found that any caste in category (a) above has (i) educational attainments above the national average, and (ii) a share in class I and II of Government services larger than its proportion in the total population, that caste's reservation should be subjected to economic criterion. Similarly, if any caste in category (b) has made enough progress in terms of (i) and (ii) above, that caste, too, should be put in category (a) and be made subject to economic criterion.

In fact this formula should be applied to SCs and STs also and castes which have advanced in terms of (i) and (ii) above should be similarly subjected to economic criterion so that the castes and tribes which lagged behind will secure representation in the nation's administration.

Only by introducing the scientific test of continuing data collection and its analysis can the desired goal of social justice be achieved in terms both of the preamble of the Constitution as well as the firm commitment of the Congress.

(Limaye, Madhu, *Hindustan Times*, September 10, 1990)

Mandal : A Way Out

Lohia View

Dr. Lohia was the first to recognise that in India class cannot be separated from caste. He proposed reservation for Backward Castes. But he was not free from inner doubts. Once he told me regretfully: "They (members of Backward Castes) never fail to demand their share of tickets (for elections). But they never fill their quota for our jail bharo protests!" Perhaps the motivation for caste reservation diluted their revolutionary fervor, I suggested. He fell silent.

Just before the general election of December 1979 Charan Singh had hastily introduced reservation for backward castes in his election manifesto. After the election, during a meeting of the Working Committee, Charan Singh suggested a review of the reservation policy because he feared that it would badly divide society. It was Madhu Limaye, the party's Secretary-General, who advised him not to rush through with a policy reversal so soon after the election as it would badly impair his credibility. Limaye advised him to wait a while before deciding the issue. I hope Limaye will recall that conversation.

The irresponsibility displayed by the champions of the Mandal Commission Report in the Government, V. P. Singh, Ram Vilas Paswan and Sharad Yadav, became evident from a recent episode. The Mandal Report is applicable to employment as well as educational facilities. But after the student protest gained momentum, the Prime Minister stated that the reservation would not be applied to educational institutions. None of his ministers demurred. How can backward castes ever hope to avail the advantages of reservation in any meaningful fashion if they are denied easy access to education which alone will qualify them for reserved jobs? Does this not strengthen the view that the Government announced the reservation policy solely for electoral advantage with no thought to the welfare of those whom it is intended to help?

Instead of reservation, let all the states of the Indian union have representation. Let them have their due share of the Central

Government employment. This is a perfectly just demand because in the all India services each state deserves to be represented in proportion to its size. Once this perfectly reasonable demand is granted, each state, according to the conditions that prevail inside it, should be left free to decide whether it wants any proportion of its Central Government quota of employment reserved for the Backward Castes or not. The will of Uttar Pradesh and Bihar should not be forced on all the other states.

(Puri, Rajender, *Hindustan Times*, September 11, 1990)

Creating New Tensions

The decision of the V.P. Singh Government to extend caste-based reservations by another 27 per cent on the basis of the Mandal Commission Report is motivated primarily by partisan and electoral considerations. It is neither rational nor national. It has created new tensions in society, in addition to the growing discontent caused by rising prices and failure of the Government to tackle the vital issues of Kashmir and Punjab. As a result, Prime Minister V. P. Singh has lost credibility and his minority Government has become shaky.

Reservation of any kind based on birth, caste or religion cuts at the roots of democracy and spirit of Indian Constitution. It creates vested interest in backwardness, casteism and communalism. It, as Dr. B. R. Ambedkar, the best friend of the depressed, himself admitted, is not even in the best interests of its immediate beneficiaries because it destroys their self-confidence. He himself told me that the Scheduled Caste people would not be able to stand on their legs so long as they depended on the crutches of reservation. That is why he advocated total abolition of caste-based reservations in the manifesto of the Republican Party that he founded.

Now that a false step has been taken, Mr. V. P. Singh must show the moral courage to admit his mistake and take steps to minimise its mischief. These steps are:

The backwardness of people must not be mixed up with their caste. There can be rich and poor in a family and every caste. The emphasis should be on the economic rather than the caste factor.

The criterion for economic backwardness must be fixed and those who fulfil them may be given reservation for some time.

Those from the depressed castes, who have improved their lot and have begun rubbing shoulders with the so-called forward people, should be taken out of the purview of the reservation so that the benefits of reservation may reach the really needy and the backward among the Scheduled Castes and Scheduled Tribes. Survey has shown that the benefits of reservation to the Scheduled Castes and Tribes have been cornered by some families in every State.

Because of our faulty economic policies and association of caste with birth, a big chunk of our society has remained backward educationally and economically. Many steps should be taken to ameliorate the lot of society. The most important of them is provision of equal facilities for higher and professional education.

As things are, the higher rungs of public services of India are being monopolised by families which can afford to send their wards to costly English medium public schools. Such schools must either be abolished or provision must be made for at least 50 per cent admission in such schools for children from educationally, economically and socially backward segments of society. The aim should be to pull up the backward and bring them on par with more fortunate elements of society.

The policies being adopted by the V. P. Singh Government will only perpetuate backwardness by creating a vested interest in remaining backward and discourage competition and merit. That will make India a second-rate country, encourage brain drain and further undermine efficiency of administration.

There must be an extensive public debate on the effects of reservation on the basis of past experience and means and methods that should be adopted to pull up the really backward. Any hasty decision taken primarily for electoral gains will prove counter-productive. Even Janata Dal may not get the electoral mileage that it has in mind.

The Mandal Commission Report must be scrutinised in depth by a committee of eminent sociologists, economists and jurists before any steps are taken to implement its recommendations.

(Madhok, Balraj)

Reservations : Double Talk on Castes

Many Problems

There are many problems with the indices used by the Mandal Commission for identifying backward castes. Even if these indices are accepted as valid, the commission overplayed the backward and underplayed the forward elements in identifying most of the backward castes. Basically, it used the cover of the 1931 Census to ignore the upward mobility that has taken place in many castes from 1931 to 1980. It turned a blind eye to this mobility mainly to inflate the number of backward castes and their population. I also suspect it allowed itself to succumb to pressures from the leaders of these castes. During the 10 years after the commission make its recommendations the forward elements in the so-called backward castes have grown, and so has the clout of the leadership in these castes, due to green revolution, land reforms, commercialisation, industrialisation, urbanisation, bureaucratisation, and the growth of local level political institutions. The present government is ignoring not only the changes that have taken place in these castes since 1980 but also the distortions that had crept into the recommendations of the Mandal Commission, again mainly to oblige the leaders of these castes.

The country is still fumbling with the implementation of 22.5 per cent reservations for Scheduled Castes and Scheduled Tribes. The hefty addition of 27 per cent reservations for OBCs is sure to place an enormous strain on the social system. In fact, it is already time to make an objective assessment of the gains of reservations for SCs and STs and draw lessons from it. The main lesson to learn is that in a regime of caste-based reservations the maximum benefit is cornered by the more powerful castes and by the more powerful families within a caste.

To blunt the strong opposition to the Mandal Commission's recommendations several suggestions are now made: (1) reservations for only the economically backward class within every recognised backward caste; (2) a separate quota for all economically backward classes side by side the 27 per cent quota for Other Backward Castes; (3) to add a provision for de-reservation for the children of those who receive benefit of reservation under the present plan; and (4) to exclude educational institutions from the reservation plan and to restrict it to jobs in government and public sector undertakings.

All these suggestions, however, do not alter the basic plan to introduce 27 per cent reservations for the Other Backward Castes. These are stratagems to allow the politicians of these castes to consolidate their position and promote their political interests. What is really required is the realisation of the folly of introducing the cast-based reservations.

Curiously many Leftists and progressives advocate the class-within-caste approach to reservations. Since caste is the first principle in this approach, one wonders how these Leftists and progressives reconcile their declared concern for secularism with the caste principle. Or, do they continue to hang on their long-held illusion that caste is only another form of class?

Knowing the dynamics of caste-based reservations, one can be sure that the OBCs will force the Government to extend reservations to educational institutions in the course of time. These reservations will then have disastrous consequences on these institutions. Human resource development and scientific and technological progress are so crucial for the future of the country, including its defence and security, that we cannot afford to compromise with standards in these institutions. Since caste-based reservations will lead to their deterioration, the very purpose of encouraging children of backward classes to go to these institutions will be defeated. We will be starting a terrible vicious circle from which we will not be able to come out.

Judicious Choices

Public policy requires making judicious choices between alternatives. Surely, we have not yet exhausted all alternatives for bringing about social equality and justice. In fact we have not seriously worked for them. For example, we have not worked seriously for universal primary education — good primary education — as the foundation for good higher education, without which reservations in jobs are meaningless.

By and large the country has worked against the caste badge during the independence movement and for more than 40 years after independence. The caste badge was removed from the Census after 1931. The column on caste was deleted from application forms and other documents. Do we want every Indian to wear that badge again? Do we want the nation to rise to a higher level of caste consciousness?

(Shah, A.M., *Hindustan Times*, September 7, 1990)

Mandal Commission : Where does the Janata Dal Stand?

. . . Where does all this leave V.P. Singh, the man who could have been Mr Clean but chose to be Mr Caste? The Raja was beginning to consider whether — for perhaps the first time in his life — he had made a major miscalculation.

His supporters said that he still clung to his original view that the

Mandal issue would help the Janata Dal to knit together a coalition of backwards that make it electorally unbeatable in U.P. and Bihar. Moreover, they pointed out, he had been vindicated in his belief that no political party could dare oppose reservation.

There were two problems with this view. Firstly, it was true that nobody had openly opposed reservation, but — sensing the mood of the media and the middle class — nearly every party had found the perfect excuse for opposing the Raja's decision to increase reservations. Generally, this was framed in terms of "we are all for the 'backwards' but we oppose the manner in which the Mandal recommendations are being implemented". That this was a politically expedient stand became clear when the all-party meet to discuss Mandal ended in chaos with each participant producing its own reservation formula. Consequently, the Raja stood isolated.

The second problem was that the electoral arithmetic only made sense if there was an election. But *would* V.P. Singh call an election? The MARG poll showed that he would lose and though his supporters pointed out that it was conducted before the decision to back Mandal, it still seemed unlikely that his party had the confidence to face the polls. . . .

(Shukla, Raji, *Sunday*, September 9-15, 1990)

Mandal Mess

Many years ago I was invited to sit on a board to select applicants of the posts of Information Officers. At the time there was only one vacancy which had to be filled in immediately. We interviewed six applicants including a young lady of a Scheduled Caste from South India. She had graduated from an American University; hence it could be assumed that she came from an affluent family. She was, however, blissfully unaware of what was going on in the world as she admitted that she did not read newspapers. To make things simpler for her I asked her if she knew the name of the Chief Minister of Kashmir. She smiled sweetly and shook her head to indicate she did not. To make it even simpler I asked her if the name Sheikh Mohammed Abdullah (he was then CM of Jammu & Kashmir) meant anything to her. Once again she shook her head and replied, "I have not studied Islamic history".

After the interviews were over, the chairman asked us to approve of the name of the lady for the post. "We have no option. A Scheduled Caste candidate has to be recommended and she is the only one we have", he said with an air of finality. He did not explain why we had to go through the exercise of interviewing six candidates when all that was required of us was to affix our thumb impressions on her selection. However, we dutifully did so. What kind of information the lady was able to disseminate to people who came to seek knowledge from her, leaves little room for imagination.

I am still not clear of the exact implications of accepting the recommendations of the Mandal Commission. What is quite clear is that all major political parties have accepted the report and the supporters of the National Front Government cannot be faulted for having accorded them legal sanction. It is also quite clear that besides religion, caste and tribe, consideration will be given to economic status in as much as families earning less than Rs. 10,000 per year (the figure may be revised upwards) will be given similar preferences for being deprived. Motives for doing so are to undo wrongs done to the out-castes and under-privileged over the centuries. What we have to guard against is that in our attempts to do so we do not perpetuate the caste structure and ignore merit of the deserving. I fear that not enough attention was paid to these aspects of the problem and the public response to the steps contemplated. Hence we find ourselves in the midst of a civil strife based on caste differences. Instead of a national consensus on the best means to provide equality of opportunity to those who are unable to compete, we are up against a dogged resistance to any change in the wretched *status quo*

(Singh, Khushwant, *Hindustan Times*, September 8, 1990)

Attack Caste: No Mandal

There is undoubtedly an element of truth in the contention that the National Front Government's decision to reserve 27 per cent of Government and public sector jobs for the socially and educationally backward classes was political move to checkmate Mr. Devi Lal. Not only the timing of the step but the manner in which it has been taken has come in for criticism. Nevertheless, it cannot be denied that the Government's acceptance of the Mandal Commission report has had the effect of setting off a social dynamite on the nation.

It is unfortunate that the agitation by the anti-reservationists and the angry reaction by the pro-reservationists have fed to a confrontation, the like of which the country has not witnessed in recent years. But if the lower castes, particularly the poor among them, could ultimately derive some benefits from the V.P. Singh Government's reservation policy, the nation will find itself on the threshold of a major social transformation.

The caste animosity would not have deepened so much had the decision on the Mandal report come as the result of a national consensus. Mr V.P. Singh and his colleagues certainly erred when they did not seek the support of other political parties, particularly those which have been propping up the National Front Government, on such an important issue like job reservation. The mere mention of reservation in the Janata Dal's poll manifesto alone did not provide sufficient justification to go ahead with the implementation of the Mandal report.

It is worth nothing that of the various suggestions made by the Mandal Commission only the reservation part has been implemented. The right course for the Government would have been to first implement the measures suggested by the commission to improve the socio-educational standards of the backward castes before taking up the question of job quotas.

A time comes when the underdogs gain courage and stand for their gain courage and stand for their rights. In a way, we are passing through such a time and the issues involved in the present social upheaval go far beyond the recommendations of the Mandal Commission. Reservation of jobs on caste lines may be a retrograde step but those who are against reservation should fight the caste system with the same vehemence with which they are opposing reservation. And the Government should bear in mind the need for demolishing caste barriers.

In 1951 Nehru interpreted the Constitution by saying: "After all, the whole purpose of the Constitution as proclaimed in the Directive Principles is to move towards what I may call a casteless and classless society". President Radhakrishnan went to the extent of suggesting that one more clause should be added to the Directive Principles to say that "it shall be the duty of the State to eradicate the caste system for bringing about a casteless society".

As untouchability is banned under the law, the caste system also should be abolished under the Constitution. But abolition of the pernicious system involves associated with it. This is certainly a tall order, but one day or other it has to be accomplished if national unity is to be preserved and social justice is to be ensured.

(Tharyan, P., *Hindustan Times*, September 8, 1990)

Quack Remedies

If the diagnosis is wrong, the prescription will not work. So with the Mandal Commission positive discrimination and affirmative action are valid prescriptions. . . .

Unwise Propositions

Unfortunately all parties are given to populism. The National Front is no exception. It has nailed four propositions to its mast. These are Mandalisation, making the right to work a fundamental right; loan waivers, and workers' participation in management. All are unwise and essentially impracticable. Even a timid watering down of the original promise of loan waivers is hurting co-operative credit which could in turn affect agricultural production and employment. Who suffers? A fundamental right to work, if legislated, will mean guaranteeing about eight million jobs annually (which is the net addition to the labour force), apart from catering to the backlog, or facing potential court action for constitutional default. Why pick up a burden that is simply not going to be carried except by definitional legerdemain. Workers' participation rests on the muddled notion that workers inherently possess a right to management (apart from trade union consultation) as well as such a capability. It has not been proven anywhere. On the contrary.

Similarly, what is all the tomtomming about placing a long list of land reform legislation in the 6th Schedule. This protects these Acts against challenge in any court of law. But has the even longer list of land reform Acts earlier scheduled been implemented? No, Not always, or very inadequately. Whom are we fooling?

Instead of indulging in wasteful and misleading populism, the Government would be better advised to go ahead with the kind of employment-oriented and socially-transforming programmes outlined in its Approach Paper to the Eighth Plan, plus education and health-for-all by 2000. And this to be implemented through decentralised planning and governance or panchayati raj with its promise of wide access and participation. the alternative is to push forward with backwardness and populism towards a Backward Country. The best will go abroad.

(Verghese, B.G., *Indian Express*, September 12, 1990)

Reservations: Lesson from Experience

. . . To go back now to Mandal, the commission's listing of socially and educationally backward classes is a botched job. Such surveys as it conducted were very limited. The data relating to them are not available. Having listed eleven broad criterion for identifying backwardness it had ultimately to fall back on State lists (themselves prepared on no uniform or scientific criterion) and, most amusing of all, "personal knowledge". The result is a hotch potch, with repetitions and mistakes and a lumping together of a number of not-so-disadvantaged groups with genuinely backward, historically disadvantaged ones. There certainly was need, before accepting any of the recommendations of the commission, to have a thorough check of the lists in consultation with the States. The list has a staggering 3,743 Hindu OBCs and one is irresistibly reminded of the Government of India's statement in 1956 on the Kalelkar Commission report of 'the really needy being swamped by the multitude'. Mr V.P. Singh must have the lists carefully examined before finalising eligibility for the concessions he had ordered.

But this will not be enough. The concessions have to be targeted precisely to those that are most in need of them. The introduction of an economic criterion has been suggested for this purpose. There are two principal arguments advanced against this. The first is that, in the circumstances that prevail in India, it is quite possible for a rich family to be socially and educationally backward. This is true, particularly of the rural areas but much less true today than say 40 years ago. Certainly in South India, there are not many well-to-do patriarchs left who sneer at formal education for their progeny. Even social disabilities affect the well to do very little. In any case reservation in appointments to the services is no answer to the backwardness of those who have it in themselves to come out of it. The second argument is that economic status may change and so eligibility should not be based on it. This is a specious argument for what is sought to be done is to determine the eligibility of a person belonging to a backward class for the benefit or reservation on the basis of his (or his parents') economic status at the time he seeks it. At that point of time, the better off BC should not deprive the less well off. Thus, an economic cut-off point for eligibility would be justified and would accelerate elimination of backwardness.

A second step that would ensure specific targeting of the benefit would be to take into account the educational and occupational status of the parents. In other words, if either parent is graduate, and/or has employment satisfying certain present standards, the person concerned should be ineligible for the concession.

Basis for Discrimination

These two offer a clear basis for discrimination among other backward classes. In fact, they should be applied to SCs and STs also to ensure wide distribution of the benefits of reservation among them.

On the percentage of reservations, the Supreme Court would appear to have made *obiter dicta* to the effect that anything more than a total of 50 per cent might not be acceptable but in at least one case that came before it where it was in excess, the reservation was not struck down. In Tamil Nadu and Karnataka the total reservation for SCs, STs and OBCs is already far in excess of 50 per cent. If reservations are an exception to the principal constitutional provision of equality, even 50 per cent might be considered high. In any case, the aim should be to bring it down as more and more classes cease to require special treatment.

There should be a quinquennial review at regular intervals to assess the efficacy of the provisions for reservation and to determine which groups no longer need protection under the terms of Articles 15(4) and 16(4). The idea that reservations are intended to eliminate, and not perpetuate, backwardness must be accepted and acted upon. The Mandal Commission has recommended a duration of 20 years for reservation. Time-limits like this hardly ever work and tend to be routinely extended. Frequent review without a time-limit would work better. But above all, sincere steps have to be taken to remove the root causes of educational backwardness by universalising primary and secondary, and providing generous scholarships and freeships as well as special coaching.

(Ramanathan, K.V. *Indian Express*, September 7, 1990)

Selected Letters to the Editor

Sir, I protest, along with other students of my college, against the implementation of the Mandal Commission recommendations. We are horrified when we think about the future of our country. The Government should not talk about the improvement in quality and standards when it itself spoils them. The Government has no right to ask the researchers to accelerate their space, medical and defence programmes when it fills these research institutions with second-rate staff. This policy will hamper the progress of these programmes, which will prove to be a major setback for India.

We can assure the Government that it cannot suppress the student agitation by *lathi*-charging and tear-gassing the students. Why is the Government scared of an unarmed human chain around Parliament? The closure of schools and the proposed closure of the universities for 30 days clearly expose the government's panic. They also prove the government wrong. The government is making a mockery of democracy by taking a dictatorial stand on the issue and calling for a debate at the same time.

The action of the police, which is a government agency, is deplorable and should be strongly condemned. The police have no right to beat up students who are demonstrating peacefully. It is our constitutional right to protest against something that is wrong. By beating up the Deshbandhu College Principal, the police have further agitated the student community.

The Government should realise its mistake and reconsider its decision.

ASHWINI KUMAR
B.Sc. Physics (Hons) 2nd Year
Shivaji College

Sir, I have a pen-pal in New York named Shelley Baker. She recently asked me what's exactly this so-called reservation system in India. I said it was the cast and not merit which was the criterion of getting a government job here. I felt ashamed when she wrote back:

> "I am looking forward to visiting India next February but I will certainly avoid taking Air India flights as I do no want myself to be crushed due to inefficiency of Indian pilots."

This is how the people of other countries feel about Indian standards. I am dead sure that in no other country in world, there is such suppression of merit. How is India going to progress in science and technology if we select our scientists and technicians on the basis of cast and lack of merit?

JAYSHREE MAHAPATRA
President Students' Union
R.D. College
(*Indian Express*, September 13, 1990)

Sir: Janata Dal spokesmen like Mr. Jaipal Reddy and Mr. Ram Dhan are trying to convince the country that the implementation of the Mandal Report as in their election manifesto and that its implementation had to be done within the first year of the Janata Dal Government. The argument is specious and will not stand close scrutiny.

The Janata Dal has won 142 seats, which is barely 25 per cent of the total Lok Sabha seats. How does this number give it the right to implement such a contentious and divisive measure?

The Janata Dal (National Front) government exists only because of the support of its allies like the BJP and the Communist parties. How can it the totally take for granted or ignore the views of these allies?

Were prior consultations not desirable and called for with these allies before a decision of this nature was taken? Are these allies so attached to their parliamentary seats as to be willing to compromise on such vital issues of national concern? And since when have the communists started recognising castes?

A minority government of 142 Lok Sabha members has no right to inflict its election manifesto on the country. It must not be permitted to, without proper discussion and consultations with its allies and the oppostion where issues of such vital importance to the nation are concerned. The allies and the opposition should not take recourse to opportunism but stand for the good of the country.

No one is against the uplift of the backward classes. However, there must be "method in the madness". This very report can form the basis of discussion by political parties, intellectuals and the representatives of the people affected by the report. A time-bound programme can then be evolved to implement the agreed/modified report without adversely affecting the achievements in various fields of human activity.

Maj.Gen. B.K. MEHTA (Retd.)

Sir, This refers to the news item that Mr Biju Patnaik has sought some changes in the implementation of the Mandal Commission Report (MCR). His suggestions need to be pondered upon, especially by Mr V.P. Singh. Actually, the whole business of reservations needs overhauling. It is basically a political gimmick. Nobody would scrap it even after 100 years because of its political impact. Mr V.P. Singh should also extend these reservations to the armed forced. Why is he afraid to do so?

One news item says that these reservations won't apply to eductional institutions. Then how the hell are they going to have thousands of substandard graduates, doctors and engineers to fill up thousands of reserved jobs for them? The whole system is full of loopholes.

The implementation of the MCR has fully justified Indian students going abroad and settling there. Now more students, including me, will follow suit. But then these very politicians will start crying about "brain drain". They want us to stay here but at the same time won't provide the appropriate atmosphere the whole system is rotting. The three M's — Money, Muscle and Minister — rule this country. We, the students, had envisaged that by bringing in V.P. Singh, we would bring about a change. A change that would root out some problems facing our country, if not all.

The attitude of these politicians can be gauged from the heated argument which took place between Mrs Alva of the Congress (I) and Ms Renuka Chowdhary of the Telugu Desam. When Mrs Alva condemned the lathi-charge on the students outside Parliament. Ms Renuka Chowdhary was on her feet to remind the Congress(I) that they too had ordered a lathi-large and teargassed peaceful women from Andhra Pradesh. The argument between the two MPs shows that they are not concerned about the public but their respective parties. The debates in Parliament have become reduced to allegations and counter-allegations.

The events of the last few days have reminded us or Mr Rajiv Ganddhi's regime — manipulating news and open threats. The whole student community is thankful to your paper for the series of articles it has published against the MCR underlining the repercussions it would have on our country. And also for bringing to light the fact that these reservations will cover 71 per cent of the total jobs in the organised sector rather than one per cent.

We students have a pious duty to get rid of all the dirty politicians of our country. Therefore, what we need is a revolution. We, being students have the necessary power to bring it about so that our country, our society, can progress. And in this struggle, the role of intellectuals and the role of the public are as important as ours.

INDERJEET SINGH
Eco. (Hons), II Year
Shri Ram College of Commerce
(*Indian Express*, September 7, 1990)

Sir, the Central Government going ahead with the reservations of posts for OBCs in utter disregard of the views expressed against it by a large number of eminent jurists, journalists, newspapers, academics, social scientists, politicians, students and others is most unfortunate. The language of reason and logic seems to have lost out to adamancy and arrogance. The tragedy is heightened by the baffling silence maintained by some of the major political parties, although in their heart of hearts they feel that reservations on a caste basis have no justification. Yet for fear of losing votes they dare not speak out. They should rise above petty political considerations and have the courage to call a spade a spade in the larger interest of the nation.

As if to compound the problem, the Government seems to be inclined to consider 5 to 10 per cent reservations (over and above 49.5 per cent for SCs, STs and OBCs) for others also on an economic basis along with additional reservations for religious minorities. But, one should not forget that reservations of any sort reduce the share of merit, which stands the risk of extinction in the reservation process.

A concession once granted becomes a permanent right of the beneficiaries in course of time and no political party in power can subsequently afford to withdraw it for obvious reasons.

It is a well-known fact that a large number of vacancies reserved for SCs and STs remain unfilled due to non-availability of suitable candidiates even by relaxing standards. The same may happen to the posts reserved for OBCs. As such, while it may promote mediocracy at the cost of ment and efficiency, it may serve very little useful purpose. Hence, the futility of reservations in employment.

What is required is to do away with the policy of reservations and instead provide all possible educational/training facilities and financial assistance to economically weaker persons in order to equip them fully for open competitions. — Yours etc.,

R.N. PANDEY

Sir, the system of reservations is bad essentially. That is why the founding fathers of our Constitution did not apply it to the Army, the Navy and the Air Force. Moreover, they applied it only for a short fixed period. It should not have been extended with no end in sight as to time or the lists.

Any system of reservations is wrong. It is against fair play. Reservations on the basis of religion or a branch of it (caste) are against our secular constitution anyway. After all what was the partition of 1947 about, if not for secularism vs religion? — Yours etc.,

SHIAM SUNDER NATH

Sir, the statement of Mr Sharad Yadav that the anti-reservation agitation had been instigated by some politicians with nefarious motives (HT, Sept. 3) is incorrect. The irrational, illogical and blind step taken by the Government is quite obvious to every same person.

We the students of Aligarh Muslim University, mostly belonging to the backward castes, severely condemn the Government's stand on the Mandal Commission's recommendations and agree with the stand taken by the students of DU, JNU and other institutions? — Yours etc.,

MAQSOOD AHMAD AFZAL AHMED and six others

AMU, Aligarh.

(*The Hindustan Times*, September 11, 1990)

11

Education as an Instrument of Social Change with Reference to Backward Classes

THE TERM social change implies changes in attitudes, behaviour, customs, habits, manners, relations and values of people. It also implies change in the styles or ways of living. It may also imply changes in the structure of social institutions.

According to B. Kuppaswami, "when we speak of social change we might assert that there is some change in social behaviour and in the social structure".

Henry Johnson would like to include five kinds of changes under social change : (a) change in social values; (b) institutional changes; (c) change in distribution of possession and rewards; (d) change in personal; and (e) change in abilities or attitudes of personnel.

Social change may be brought about by violent or non-violent means.

Social change may mean addition of new elements or things.

Social change may mean discarding some old elements or old things.

Social change may be sudden or slow.

All aspects or elements may not change at the same rate.

Prof. R.B. Mathur has explained this concept in *The Third Indian Year Book of Education – Educational Research* as "Social change therefore refers to the modification in the organisation and behaviours of the group as expressed in its law, institution, customs, modes and beliefs. The change may be gradual or sudden, evolutionary and revolutionary. When change is supposedly for the better, it becomes 'progress' which is essentially an evolutionary concept".

Nature of Social Change in India

The Indian Constitution with its statements of Fundamental Rights, Directive Principles and the Preamble can be said to represent one broad consensus of the type of society which Indians wish to create.

The salient features of the social change in Indian society as envisaged in the Constitution are:

1. Indian society must be based on the principles of secularism, socialism and democracy.
2. Indian society must be based on justice; social, economic and social.
3. Indian society must provide for liberty of thought, expression, belief, faith and worship.
4. Indian society must be based on equality of status and of opportunity.
5. Indian society must be based on fraternity, assuring the dignity of the individual and the unity of the nation.

The change is inevitable. Society is dynamic. It is in a constant flux. Whether we want a change, whether we like it or not, times are moving fast. Change is inherent in the society.

Among the various factors, mention may be made of these: (i) Westernisation, (ii) Industrialisation, (iii) Urbanisation, (iv) Secularisation, (v) Socialisation, (vi) Educationalisation, and (vii) Modernisation. Laws of the Government also bring about social changes. Social reformers act important instruments of social change.

Education as an Instrument of Social Change

The Education Commission (1964-66) has observed that realization of country's aspiration involves changes in the knowledge, skills, interests and values of the people as a whole. This is basic to every programme of social and economic betterment of which India stands in need.

The Education Commission has pointed out this fact as "If this change on a grand scale is to be achieved without violent revolution (and even then it would still be necessary) there is one instrument, and one instrument only that can be used, *Education*. Other agencies may help, and can indeed sometimes have a more apparent impact. But the national system of education is the only instrument that can reach all the people. It is not, however, a magic wand to wave wishes into existence. It is a difficult instrument whose effective use requires strength of will, 'dedicated' work and sacrifice. But it is a sure and tried instrument, which has served other countries well in their struggle for development. It can, given the will and the skill, do so for India."

Ideas of great leaders have played important role in social change. The influences of great men like Gandhiji of India, Lenin in Russia and Mao Tse-Tung in China are some of the well-known examples of modern history. Ideas like 'Liberty', 'Equality' and 'Fraternity' proved great forces in giving birth to French Revolution which in turn greatly influenced the French Society. Industrial Revolution led to important changes in society.

The well-known American philosopher-educationist John Dewey observes, "Education is the fundamental method of social progress and reform. This it does in two ways; by guiding children towards new values and by assisting the development of intelligence in individual children and increasing society's potential for its own transformation".

Gandhiji wanted to bring about a silent social revolution in India through the Basic system of education. In his words, "The Basic school should be the spearhead of a non-violent social revolution".

All the social reformers have stressed the importance of education as the most important single instrument and medium for bringing about changes in society.

Education can be of great help to people in identifying their limitations and weaknesses or gaps in knowledge. It enables people to gain necessary knowledge and skills necessary for achieving progress.

Education can be very helpful in improving quality of life.

Two Fold Functions of Education in Social Change

The problem of education in relation to social change is two fold:

1. Adjustment to the changing situation.
2. Creation of a new order through change in knowledge, new idea and or in other words education for social progress.

Education is not only concerned with the perpetuation of society but with its improvements also.

Education is both conservative and progressive. Education

transmits the culture of one generation to another. The rising generation has to be conveyed the activities and experiences of the past generation. It has also to be asked to make necessary changes in these activities and experiences to meet the new situations which it will meet. An integration of the old must take place with the new ones. It must be remembered that the communities live in the present on the past and for the future. This means that activities and experiences in the present have to be built on the past and the present will guide the activities of the future. Thus education is continuous, reorganisation and integration of activities and experiences. Education is a constructive agency for improving our society. Brown has stated, "Education brings changes in behaviour, and if its main functions are to remain mere transmission or enrichment of culture, it will fall short of its role in a dynamic society. Education must also provide situations at all age levels but within the maturity and ability of the individual to stimulate a creativeness of mind."

Measures for Bringing About Social Change

Simplifying and ordering the Environment: The activities of the society are complex. So the first duty of the school is to provide simplified environment. It selects the features which are fairly fundamental and capable of being responded by the young. In this way it establishes a progressive order, using the factors first acquired as means of gaining insight into what is more complicated.

Purifying Environment: We cannot import into school life all that exists outside. We shall have to eliminate evil features of the existing environment. By selecting the best for its exclusive uses it strives to reinforce the power of this best.

Wider and Better Balanced Environment: In the school there are children of diverse races, communities, religions etc. They come from different backgrounds. We should train children in tolerance towards other communities, races and religions. The caste, creed and colour should not be a bar to healthy living in the school.

Schools as Miniature Communities: School should be a miniature community. There should be a living traffic with the outside world. We have embarked upon the new experiment of democracy. It is a hard fact that democratic system of government is meaningless till the people learn democratic way of living. So we should also incorporate such activities as School Panchayat.

English Medium Schools and Social Change: The existence of a chain of English-medium schools at all levels of education has been an instrument of creating small privileged groups of English knowing elite. The new and expanding job opportunities are thus monopolised by the members of this group who are getting wealthy in the emerging economic order. This must be stopped.

Medium of Instruction and Social Change: The right to vote, the right to participate intelligently in shaping the policies of the State, demands not merely the right to education, but the right to education in the language of the people. The major failure of the Government of Independent India lies in the fact that it has not fulfilled this major democratic task.

Ensuring Equality of Opportunity: The National Policy on Education, 1986 has observed, "The New Policy will lay special emphasis on the removal of disparities and to equalise educational opportunity by attending to the specific needs of those who have been denied equality so far." Equality of opportunity is very helpful in promoting social change.

12

Equalisation of Educational Opportunity and Social Change

IT IS really very sad that we have not paid adequate heed to the words of wisdom of the Education Commission (1964-66). Non-implementation of its recommendations as outlined in Chapter VI has led to a sorry state of affairs. The Commission, very emphatically observed that "the education of the backward classes in general and the tribal people in particular is a major programme of equalisation and of social and national integration. No expenditure is too great for the purpose."

(6.75)

Education Commission (1964-66)

Relevant observations under 'Towards Equalisation of Educational Opportunity' are:

One of the important social objectives of education is to equalise opportunity, enabling the backward or under-privileged classes and individuals to use education as a lever for the improvement of their condition. Every society that values social justice and is anxious to improve the lot of the common man and cultivate all available talent, must ensure progressive equality of opportunity to all sections of the population. This is the only guarantee for the building up of an egalitarian and human society in which the exploitation of the weak will be minimized. **(6.01)**

Inequalities of educational opportunities arise in various ways. In places where no primary, secondary, or collegiate institutions exist, children do not have the same opportunity as those who have these facilities in the neighbourhood. This handicap should be overcome by the widest dispersal of educational institutions, consistent with economy and efficiency, by instituting an adequate scholarship programme, by providing the needed hostel facilities or by making suitable transport arrangements. It is sometimes not fully appreciated that there are at present glaring imbalances of educational development in different parts of the country: the educational developments in the States show wide differences, and even wider differences are found between the districts. To remove such inequalities, deliberate policies of equalisation of educational opportunities and educational development in the different districts will have to be adopted. **(6.02)**

Another cause of inequality of educational opportunity is the poverty of a large section of the population and the relative affluence of a small minority. Even in the neighbourhood of an educational institution, children from poor families do not have the same chance as those who come from richer ones. To overcome these handicaps, it is desirable to abolish fees progressively, to provide free books, stationery and even school meals and uniforms. In addition, it is necessary to develop a large programme of scholarships. **(6.03)**

Again, differences in the standards of schools and colleges create an extremely intractable form of educational inequality. When admission to an institution such as a university or professional college, is made on the basis of marks obtained at the public examination at the end of the secondary stage, as often happens, the marks do not at all provide a common yardstick for a student from a rural area who attends an ill-equipped school in his village, and a student from an urban area who attends a good city school. To overcome this to some extent at least, it is necessary to evolve more reliable and egalitarian methods of selection, whether for admission to institutions or for award of scholarships. **(6.04)**

Gross inequalities arise from differences in home environments. A child from a rural household or an urban slum having illiterate parents, does not have the same opportunity which a child from an upper class home with highly educated parents has. These inequalities are obviously the most difficult to overcome and here progress essentially depends on the general improvement in the standard of living of the population. But something can be done by arranging that special attention at school is paid to children from the under-privileged groups and by the provision of day-study centres or boarding houses. **(6.05)**

Two other forms of educational inequalities, which are peculiar to the Indian situation, need attention. The first is the wide disparity between the education of boys and girls at all stages and in all sectors of education. The second is the equally wide, or sometimes wider disparity of educational development between the advanced classes and the backward ones — the Scheduled Castes and the Scheduled Tribes. On grounds of social justice as well as for the furtherance of democracy, it is essential to make special efforts to equalise educational opportunities between these groups. **(6.06)**

Like all ideals in life, perfect equality of educational opportunity is probably unattainable. In such matters, however, the essence of the problem is not the attainment of the goal, but an impassioned faith and earnest striving. In a good system of education, there should be a continuous attempt to identify factors which tend to create significant forms of inequality and to adopt measures either to eliminate them altogether or at least to reduce them to the minimum. **(6.06)**

National Policy On Education, 1968

Strenuous efforts should be made to equalise educational opportunity. More intensive efforts are needed to develop education among the backward classes and especially among the tribal people. **(4. C)**

Draft National Policy On Education, 1979

While there has been considerable expansion in all sectors of education in our country, imbalances and inequalities still persist. Girls, Scheduled Castes and Tribes, landless labourers, backward classes and urban slum poor generally continue to lag behind in education. Special effort must be made to identify the problems in these cases and to bring all such people into the fold of education. **(17.1)**

National Policy on Education, 1986

Part III: National System of Education

The concept of a National System of Education implies that, up to a given level, all students, irrespective of castes, creed, location or sex, have access to education of a comparative quality. To achieve this, the Government will initiate appropriately funded programmes. Effective measures will be taken in the direction of the Common School System recommended in the 1968 policy. **(3.2)**

To promote equality, it will be necessary to provide for equal opportunity to all not only in access, but also in the conditions for success. Besides, awareness the inherent equality of all will be created through the core curriculum. The purpose is to remove prejudices and complexes transmitted through the social environment and accident of Birth. **(3.6)**

Part IV: Disparities

The New Policy will lay, emphasis on the removal of disparities and to equalise educational opportunities by attending to the specific needs of those who have been denied equality so far. **(4.1)**

Other Educationally Backward Sections and Areas

Suitable incentive will be provided to all educationally backward sections of society, particularly in the rural areas. Hill and desert districts, remote and inaccessible areas and islands will be provided adequate institutional infrastructure.

Programme of Action, 1986

The following measures have been envisaged:

(i) Measures will be further strengthened to ensure that incentives in the form of scholarships, uniforms, books and stationery, etc. reach the clientale group.

(ii) Priority will be given to the special needs of nomadic, semi-nomadic and denotified communities. **(xiii. 5 j)**

Organisation and Management of Programmes of Education

Detailed guidelines for monitoring will be evolved at the Central and State levels to ensure qualitative implementation of the programmes; standards to achieve optimal efficiency in implementation, will be laid down; consistent with the autonomy of the implementing agencies, norms of accountability shall be defined at all levels. **(xiii. 6)**

A single nodal agency for coordination of all programmes leading to the development of SC/ST and other backward sections may be developed at the Central and State levels. It is suggested that a Standing Committee of the CABE under the Chairmanship of Minister of Human Resource Development (HRD) may be constituted to monitor and review implementation of all educational programmes for SC/ST and Other Educationally Backward Sections at the Central Level. A similar committee under the State Advisory Board of Education may be constituted at the state level. **(xiii. 7)**

In addition to an in-built mechanism for continuous evaluation of programmes, evaluation of important schemes like scholarships, hostels and the proposed incentive scheme may be undertaken by external agencies. **(xiii. 8)**

Education, the Better way for Providing Equality of Opportunity

There is no doubt that no two individuals are alike. They differ in tastes, manners, attitudes and aptitudes, beliefs etc. Any attempt to provide precisely the same educational programmes and opportunities is likely to be met with failure. Equal opportunity implies that the rich and the poor alike should have equal access to the educational system and programmes without any hindrance. All material barriers should be removed. Caste, colour or creed should not put any check on an individual to pursue course of education in accordance with his ability and aptitude.

How does Inequality of Educational Opportunity arise? The Education Commission (1964-66) has mentioned the following causes:

1. *Lack of Educational Facilities* — There are many places and areas in the country where primary, secondary or collegiate institutions do not exist. Children residing therein do not have the same opportunity as those who have these facilities in the neighbourhood.
2. *Poverty of a Large Section of Population* — Children coming from the poor sections of the community do not have the same chance to study in the neighbourhood of an educational institution as those who come from richer ones.
3. *Differences in the Standard of Educational Institutions* — Differences in the standards of schools and colleges lead to educational inequality. Students coming from rural educational institutions do not compare well when admission to professional courses are made on the basics of selection tests.
4. *Differences in Home Environments* — A child from a rural household or an urban slum having illiterate parents does not

have the same opportunity which a child from an upper class home with highly educated parents has.

5. *Disparity in Education of Boys and Girls* — Due to the conservative nature of the Indian society there is a wide disparity between the education of boys and girls.
6. *Disparity due to Advanced Classes and Backward Classes* — Another factor that has led to inequality of opportunity in education is the existence of different types of classes *i.e.* advanced classes and backward ones.
7. *High Private Costs of Education* — The private costs of education required for the textbooks, supplies, co-curricular activities etc., have increased very substantially in recent years in public schools. The parents are required to incur vary heavy expenditure for this purpose.

Promotion of Education among the Backward Classes

1. *Tuition Free Education.* School education is completely free in advanced countries and our country should also gradually work towards a stage when all education should be tuition free.
2. *Reduction in Other Costs.* It is felt that parents are required to incur heavy indirect costs on the education of their children. These indirect costs include costs incurred by parents on textbooks, supplies, uniforms, co-curricular activities, etc.

   (a) *Free text-books at various Stages* — It is, therefore, very essential that a programme of providing free text-books should be given very high priority and introduced immediately at all stages of education.

   (b) *Book-Banks* — A programme of book-banks should be developed in secondary schools and in institutions of higher education.

   (c) *Grants for Purchase of Books* — The top 25 per cent of the students in educational institutions belonging to backward classes should be given grants annually for the purchase of books which need not necessarily be text-books.

3. *Scholarship.* There should be an adequate programme of scholarships so that the best use is made of the available talent.
4. *Transport Facilities.* Adequate transport facilities may be

provided in the rural areas and for the students of backward classes so that students are encouraged to attend educational institutions.

5. *Day-Study Centres and Lodging Houses.* A large number of day-study centres at the secondary and university stage should be provided for students who do not have adequate facilities for study at home. Lodging houses, *i.e.*, places where students can stay throughout the day, and even at night, but go home for food, may also be provided.
6. *'Earn and Learn' Facilities.* As a supplement to the programme of scholarships, facilities for students to earn and play a part of their expenses should be provided on as large a scale as possible.
7. *Special Facilities for Girls.* Special incentives may be provided to the girls.
8. *Admission Policy.* There is a great need to introduce an egalitarian element in admissions to institutions so that students coming from rural areas are not handicapped due to language or some other factors.
9. *Special Assistance to Backward Areas or States.* At the national level, it should be regarded as the responsibility of the Government of India to secure equalisation of educational development in the different states. The necessary programmes for this including special assistance to the less advanced states should be developed.
10. *Compensatory and Remedial Education.* Compensatory education means provision of such special training and incentives as would compensate for the initial disadvantages experienced by the children of the culturally, economically and socially deprived groups. The compensatory measures include free school uniform, text-books, meals etc. It also includes remedial classes. In the ordinary classes, where instruction is traditionally geared to the need of the average child, the slow learner children have to work under a great hardship. They need individual attention, special remedial help and probably also a modified curriculum to suit their rate of learning. In some educationally advanced countries special schools have been established for this category of children. Such a feasibility may be explored in our country in big cities. Special classes in ordinary schools can also be held very profitably. Such a

treatment is likely to be very useful for their emotional and social development also. Guidance and counselling services have an important role to play in the education of such children.

11. *Common School System.* A common school system of public education should be evolved in place of present system. It should be maintained at an adequate level of quality and efficiency so that no parent would ordinarily feel any need to send his child to the institutions outside the system such as independent or public schools. Such a step will be very helpful towards eliminating the segregation that now takes place between the schools for the poor and the under-priviledged classes and those for the rich and the priviledged ones. The existing 'caste' system in the educational system should be gradually abolished.

Role of the Teachers

The teachers can play an important role in developing a favourable school climate conducive to the educational progress of Backward Classes and Castes. Some suggestions in this regard are given here:

(i) The teacher's own example in his behaviour towards students belonging to these castes is the most effective and powerful way to build up a congenial climate.
(ii) The school staff should ensure non-discrimination between the children of different communities.
(iii) The school staff should avoid the use of the caste names or derogatory words while calling roll or naming children.
(iv) Teachers should provide equal opportunities to all the children to participate in the curricular and co-curricular activities of the school, including games.
(v) Frequent meetings between the staff, school teachers and parents should be arranged. The details of the schemes for promoting education amongst them should be explained to the parents at these meetings. It should be impressed upon them that they must continue the education of their children.
(vi) Special attention should be paid to motivating parents for the education of girls.
(vii) Teachers should suggest to illiterate parents the advantages gained by attending functional literacy classes in the centre.

Education, the Better Way

Observations made by Shri H.R. Khanna in *the Hindustan Times* dated the September 14, 1990, invite careful attention:

> "Let us give the best of education to those in backward classes, apart from the general education to the children born in those classes. Let us give them abundant financial aid to pursue their studies and encourage them by giving large number of scholarships and other encouragements. It would be proud day in the history of the country if we can produce a number of Ambedkars in different fields on the strength of their own talent and merit. That would be the best way to uplift the members of the backward classes. The backwardness of these classes is a great stigma on our national polity.
>
> The best way to expiate for the wrong done to these sections of the society is to give to the children of the backward classes proper education from the very start and afford them all facilities for higher education, apart from improving the living standards of those classes and not by undermining the efficiency in different departments of the State."

13

Towards an Enlightened and Humane Society*

THE FOLLOWING extract of the Resolution constituting the Committee for Review of National Policy on Education (NPE), 1986, spells out the specific concerns of the National Front Government about the new education policy for establishing an enlightened and human society.

> "Despite effort at social and economic development science attainment of independence, a majority of our people continue to remain deprived of education, which is one of the basic needs for human development. It is also a matter of great concern that our people comprise 50 per cent of the world's illiterate, and large sections of children have to go without acceptable level of primary education. Government accords the highest priority to education both as a human right and the means for bringing about a transformation towards a more humane and enlightened society. There is need to make education an effective instrument for securing a status of equality for women, and persons belonging to the backward classes and minorities. Moreover, it is essential to give a work and employment orientation to education and to exclude from it the elitist aberrations which have become the glaring characteristic of the educational scene. Educational institutions are increasingly being influenced by casteism, communalism and obscurantism and it is necessary to lay special emphasis on struggle against this phenomenon and to move towards a genuinely egalitarian and secular social order. The National Policy on Education, 1986 (NPE), needs to be reviewed to evolve a

---

* A Perspective Paper on Education, Committee for Review of National Policy on Education (NPE) 1986, New Delhi, September 1990.

framework which would enable the country to move towards this perspective of education." **(1.1)**

The paper published by the Review Committee highlights the urgency of educational development in the country and especially of the Backward classes and sections.

The struggle for survival is more urgent for many people of India than educational needs. Therefore, education and its planning must be organically linked with the larger socio-cultural, economic and political context. Specifically it must be linked with live issues of development. Then it will be possible for education to play a catalytic and interventionist role. Only then. **(1.2)**

Almost half of the children in the age group of 6 to 14 either do not enter the school at all or drop out at an early stage. Of these, according to a recent National Sample Survey, about one-third to one-half find school either boring, irrelevant or threatening (i.e. failure in examinations). Almost another 40 to 45 per cent of them have to stay away from school due to strong economic compulsions and the demands of home and family life. Only about 5 per cent of the children manage to reach the higher secondary stage and a smaller percentage go on to higher education. A negligible number from the disadvantaged sections are able to get admission to the excellent professional institutions, due to poor quality school education apart from their socio-economic backgrounds. The calibre of these making it to excellent institutions might have perhaps been better had they been drawn from a larger social base of children. Efforts to link education with life have not met with any appreciable degree of success and our goal of attracting all children to the schools and increasing their retention has remained largely unfulfilled. **(1.3)**

While we have many achievements to recount at the higher levels of learning the constitutional mandate of providing elementary education to all till the age of 14 has remained a testing illusion. And this, in spite of such huge quantitative expansion of primary schools, so as to make available a primary school within one kilometre from the residence for every child. The educational pyramid has no solid and strong base to stand on even today, not to speak of the poor quality of education itself. In fact, the pyramid is precariously balanced upside down. The decreasing proportion of allocations to elementary education over the last seven plans has aggravated this structural imbalance. (The share of Plan and Non-Plan allocations for

Elementary Education in the States/UTs has remained stagnant in recent years. As a percentage of GNP, share of this sector of education has come down since 1985-86). Nor have the attempts to provide a complementary structure, through non-formal education and adult literacy helped in the rectification of this imbalance, though these programmes do involve substantial financial outlays. **(1.8)**

The real challenge is to provide and ensure that an education of comparable quality is made available to all through the evolution of a Common School System. The challenge is also one of identification and removal of elitist aberrations that have crept into the educational system over the years: and of remedying the erosion of community involvement in making the educational system work. Are we committed to stop "tinkering with the existing situation, and moving forward with faltering steps and lack of faith", and to act on the conviction that "Indian education needs a drastic reconstruction, almost a revolution"? (Quotes from Dr. D.S. Kothari's Foreword to the *Education Commission Report*, 1964-66). **(1.9)**

The principle of equitable opportunity for all as a path of educational development in the Indian context is to be preferred to segregated nurturing of talent amongst a few in separate schools. This will ensure an egalitarian social order, as well as scope for achieving the nation's full potential for 'excellence' by broadening the social and ethnic base of education. Indeed, in the ordinary course, the teacher does identify and respond to talented children. Therefore, the appropriate course would be to specially train the teachers to enable talented children to learn at a faster pace without segregating them from other children and involve them in group or peer learning processes that encourage non-competitive environment. In this view, in any case, further encouragement of Navodaya Vidyalayas may not be justified. **(II.vi)**

In order to promote 'social cohesion and national integration', a Common School System is to be built up over a ten-year time-frame, both through persuasion and essential legislation. As a first step, the quality of government, local body and aided schools is to be improved, so as to transform them into genuine 'Neighbourhood Schools'. The question whether and how the Common School System should gradually reach out to include private schools as well should be examined. **(II.vii)**

Education for women's equality is to be redesigned with a view to:

(a) create essential conditions for all girls to successfully participate in school education and reduce drop-out rate amongst them by linking an effective programme of Early Childhood Care and Education with every primary school of India, at the same time providing in the community a complex of support services for making available drinking water, fuel, fodder and health care; and

(b) remove gender bias and eliminate sex-stereotyping from the structure, content and process of education by taking into account the broader social framework which has so far denied empowerment of women. **(II.viii)**

The phenomenon of regional disparities is to be tackled with a view to allocating additional intellectual and financial resources to educationally and socially backward areas to compensate for the past deprivations of the people, mostly belonging to scheduled castes and tribes. Other backward communities and minorities (particularly women among them) living in these areas and to decentralize planning and implementation through area specific and disaggregated perceptions of what and how it needs to be done. **(II.ix)**

Common School System

The Common School system was recommended by the Kothari Commission. It was accepted in the National Policies of 1968 and 1986. The Policy of 1968 states:

> "To promote social cohesion and national integration the Common School System as recommended by the Education Commission should be adopted. Efforts should be made to improve the standard of education in general schools. All special schools like Public Schools should be required to admit students on the basis of merit and also to provide prescribed proportion of free studentships to prevent segregation of social classes. This will not, however, affect the rights of minorities under Article 30 of the Constitution."

The concept has not, however, been translated into action so far. This is one of the reasons for development of exclusiveness in the school system, in the sense that provision of education of a comparable quality to the poorer sections has not been feasible and the affluent sections have had access to education in expensive privately managed institutions. In order to bring the Common School System into practice, the following actions would be required:

— Provision of significantly increased outlay for elementary (particularly primary) education. This would help in the building up of the required levels of infrastructure and quality of education thereby transforming Government, local-body and aided schools into genuine Neighbourhood Schools.

— Provision of special allocations for improvement of school system in backward areas, urban slums, tribal areas, hilly tracts, desert and marshy areas, drought and flood-prone zones, coastal belts and islands.

— *Ensuring* instruction for all in the medium of mother-tongue at the primary level, particularly for linguistic minorities: active encouragement of teaching in the regional languages at the secondary level: and discontinuance of State aid to the schools imparting education otherwise than in the medium of mother-tongue/regional language.

— Phased and time bound implementation of the Common School System within a ten-year time frame; and essential minimum legislation, particularly to dispense with early selection process, tuition fee, capitation fee etc.

— Exploring ways of including the expensive private schools into the Common School System through a combination of incentives, disincentives and legislation. **(III.2)**

Removal of Regional Disparities

The country being very large, marked by striking diversities in terms of language, culture and resource endowments, blanket policy options, strategies, investment patterns and targets do not help in tackling the problem of regional and sub-regional disparities. No doubt, efforts have been made in the past to deal with the problem of inter-state disparities by special planning and allocation of funds for educationally backward States/UTs. This, however, is not adequate. There are, indeed, backward areas within States that could be construed as educationally not backward in terms of certain parameters. 'Approach to the Eighth Five Year Plan' lays much store by decentralisation in planning. Therefore, there is need for identification of backward areas at the district and sub-district levels. District, block and village level profiles have to be prepared in meaningful planning for educational development.

It follows that target setting for educational development also has to be disaggregated and area specific (even gender specific), whether it be for Universal Elementary Education, Adult Education or Vocational Education. Full scope would have to be given for diversified content planning, plural learning strategies and variable ways of non-formalising the school, according to the socio-cultural milieu of different regions. Special efforts are needed to develop learning resources in regional languages to reduce inequities. It is only in this way that backward classes could be provided education of comparable standards without which reservations for job opportunities cannot be meaningfully availed of by them. **(III.7)**

Resources

Considering the Constitutional directives the need for State intervention in education for reasons of equity and social justice, and the gigantic magnitude of the clientele to be provided education, public expenditure, indeed, has to be very significant. Over the years, no doubt, the percentage of GNP spent on education has been increasing. In 1950-51, it was 1.2 per cent. In 1986-87, it was 3.9 per cent. But the actual requirements are far in excess of the present level of expenditure. It is also much below the level of 6 per cent of the GNP envisaged in NPE, 1986. As stated elsewhere, India ranks 115th in the world in terms of investment in education as a percentage of GNP. Amongst countries with a population of 10 crores and above, India is at the very bottom barring Bangladesh. Share of educational plan expenditure came down to 3.55 per cent in the Seventh Plan from 7.86 per cent in the First Plan.

Within Education, intra-sectorally, there have been serious distortions in outlays. The share of Elementary Education decreased to 29 per cent in the Seventh Plan, from 56 per cent in the First Plan. Over the same period, share of University and general education increased from 18 per cent to 44 per cent. These retrogressions are serious. Considering that the rate of return on elementary education, is considerably higher than in tertiary education. This could be perceived as much more glaring, viewed from the angle that certain University Scholarships, reportedly, have been higher than the fees charged. The tertiary level student fees, not having meaningfully increased over the years, there is a strong case for their upward revision. (The student fees also are far lesser than per student cost.)

Government share in the overall expenditure on education increased from 57.1 per cent in 1950-51 to 77.9 per cent in 1979-80. The share of local bodies and internal resource generation and of private agencies has significantly come down. (Data for years later than 1979-80 are not available.)

Strategies for augmenting resources for education and distribution of the same would need to be : a significant increase in public expenditure – at least 6 per cent of the GNP; substantially larger allocations in the Central as well as State budgets: mobilisation of resources from the community and through local bodies; increased ratio of allocation for Elementary Education: non-divertible allocation within Elementary Education for special sections such as women, SC/ST/OBC communities etc.; equitable formula for enhancing the fee structure for higher education, simultaneously with offer of scholarships for the weaker sections and student loan facilities: and alternative measures like graduate taxes on the users of the services of graduates. **(III.9)**

14

List of Other Backward Classes Recommended by the First Backward Classes Commission (Kalelkar)

Alphabatical list to facilitate users to identify the backward class in respective States.

ABBREVIATIONS USED FOR THE STATES

AJMER	AJ
ANDHRA STATE	AP
ASSAM	AS
BHOPAL	BH
BIHAR	BI
BOMBAY	BO
COORG	CO
DELHI	DE
HIMACHAL PRADESH	HP
HYDERABAD STATE	HY
KUTCH	KU
MADHYA BHARAT	MB
MADHYA PRADESH	MP
MADRAS	MD
MANIPUR	MA
MYSORE STATE	MY
ORISSA	OR
PATIALA & PUNJAB STATES UNION	PP
PUNJAB	PU
RAJASTHAN	RA
SAURASHTRA	SA
TRAVANCORE-COCHIN	TC
TRIPURA	TR
UTTAR PRADESH	UP
VINDHYA PRADESH	VP
WEST BENGAL	WB

Abbasi, Bhishti, Sakka (DE)
Abdal (BI)
Acharaj (RA)
Acharaj, Dakaut, Gujru (HP)
Acharaj, Panchal Brahman, Changar (PU)
Acharja (PP)
Acharji, Agariya (WB)
Acharya, Acharji (WB)
Ad-Bhopa (RA)
Adhori (VP)
Adi-Saiva (MD)
Adi-Telaga (AP)
Adodia (SA)
Agamudaiyan (Excluding, Vellala) (MD)
Agaria, Aghria, Aghria (OR)
Agasa (BO)
Agasa (HY)
Agasa (MD)
Agasa (MY)
Aghore (WB)
Aghori (BI)
Agnikula Kashatriya, Pallekapu, Pallereddi, Palli, Vannireddi, Vanni Kapu, Vannikula Kshatriya (AP)
Agnikula Kshatriya, Palli, Vanniyakula Kshatriya (MD)
Agradana, Agradani, Agradani (WB)
Agrahari (UP)
Agrahari Vaishya (BI)
Agri (BO)
Agri Kharwal (DE)
Ahar (UP)
Aheri, Aheria, Heri, Naik, Thori, Tori, Aheria (PP)
Aheria, Aheri Heri, Naik, Thori, Turi, Aheri (PU)
Ahibasi (UP)
Ahir (AJ)
Ahir (BH)
Ahir (KU)
Ahir (MA)
Ahir (MB)
Ahir (PU)
Ahir (RA)
Ahir (SA)
Ahir, Ahir Sonar, Ahir Sonar (BO)
Ahir, Bargahi Brijbasi, Jadav (VP)
Ahir, Bargahi, Bhurtiya (UP)
Ahir, Ghosh, Goala, Jadav, Yadav (WB)
Ahir, Ghosi (DE)
Ahir, Gola, Golla, MekalaGolla, Punnu Golla, and Yadava (OR)
Ahir, Gola, Yadav, Gaura, Goala Bagal, Ghosi, Gaddi (BI)
Ahir, Jadav (MP)
Ahom (AS)
Airavar, Ayiravaisya (MD)
Aiyarakulu (AP)
Akkasalig Sonar (BO)
Akkasaliga (HY)
Alia (OR)
Alitkar (BO)
Alkari (BO)
Alwar (TC)
Amaguntamala (AP)
Amanatiya (OR)
Amant, Amat, Amath, Amat, Amath (WB)
Amat (BI)
Ambalakaran (MD)
Ambigaru (BO)
Ambika (MD)
Amma Kodaga (CO)
Anarpay Mala (AP)
Andhiya Domb, Chonel, Domb, Christian Domb, Dombo, Mirgani Domb, Ponaka Domb, Telaga, Ummia, Audiniya Domba (AP)
Andhiyadiya Domb, Audiniya, Domb, Chonel, Domb, Christian Domb, Domb, Mirgani Domb, Ponaka Domb, Telaga, Ummia (MD)
Andi Pandaram (MD)
Anglo-Indians (Eurasians) (TC)
Annadan (MD)
Anne Boyina Palli (AP)
Annupagoundar (Ramnad, Coimbatore, Madura, Tinnevelly) (MD)
Ansar, Julaha, Momin (UP)
Arab (SA)
Arain Rayee, Kunjra (DE)
Arain, Kunjra, Rayee, Bhandi Waddar, Dandhi Dasa, Dhunia, Ghatti Waddar, (BO)

Arakalu (AP)
Arakh (UP)
Arakh (VP)
Archukatlavandu (AP)
Are Maharati (AP)
Are Maharati (S. Kanara) (MD)
Arekatika (HY)
Arer (BO)
Arya (S. Kanara) (MD)
Arya Kshatriya (AP)
Arya Sarollu, Daruwala, Sharigaru (HY)
Arya Vaishya (CO)
Asara (MB)
Asthana Golla (Coimbatore and Malabar Distts.) (MD)
Atagara, Devanga, Audiniya Domb (AP)
Atagora, Devanga, Audiniya Domb, Ayira vaisya (MD)
Atari (BO)
Atashbaz, Tirgar (UP)
Atishbaz (HP)
Atit (UP)
Atith, Gosain (BI)
Atte Vikkal (BO)
Audhia (MP)
Audhias (Oudhias) (UP)
Audhie, Avadhi, Avadhi (VP)
Ausula (HY)
Ayer (KU)Bagal (WB)
Ayodha Kapu (AP)
Ayodhareddi, Kambalathar, Kendi, Kottai Reddi, Rajakambala Naicker, Reddi Ganiga (MD)
Ayri (CO)

Babar, Nai, Ved, Hajam (RA)
Babria (BO)
Badahi, Barhi, Barhai, Viswakarma, Bagal (BI)
Badaka (MP)
Badani (BO)
Badasuda (OR)
Badera (RA)
Badgi (BO)
Badgujar (BO)
Badhai (BO)
Badhair, Barhai, Bindhani, Sutradhar and Badhira, Badhira (OR)
Badhi, Barhai Dhiman, Brahman (PU)
Badi (Nepali) (AS)
Badi (Nepali) (MA)
Badi (Nepali) (WB)
Badiga (HY)
Badigar (VP)
Badwa Goswami (UP)
Badyakar, Dhuli, Nagarchi, Sabdakar (TR)
Bagadi (BO)
Bagaria, Barhai (PU)
Bagaria, Beldia (RA)
Bagdi (BI)
Baghia, Baree, Bawar, Payak, Singhiwala, Vaidyanai (MB)
Baghwan, Mali (UP)
Bagri (VP)
Bagri, Gujarat Baori, Marwar Baori, Marwar Waghri, Salat Waghri (BO)
Bagria (PP)
Bahari (PU)
Bahurupi (BO)
Bahurupi (MP)
Bairagi (BH)
Bairagi (BI)
Bairagi (DE)
Bairagi (MY)
Bairagi (VP)
Bairagi, Baragi, Baragi (PP)
Bairagi, Bava, Gosavi, Gosai (BO)
Bairagi, Bawa (KU)
Bairagi, Jogi (RA)
Bairagi, Nath, Gossain (HP)
Bairwa (Berwa, Jatiya, Bola, Meghwanshi) (AJ)
Bairwa (DE)
Baishnab (TR)
Baishya Kapali, Kapali (WB)
Bajadar, Bajania, Bedey, Bediya (excluding, Bediya in S.C.), Bajania (WB)
Bajania, Kannatia (MB)
Bajenia (BO)
Bajir (BO)
Balasanthosh (HY)
Balasanthu (HY)
Balasi (OR)
Baldhia Bhat (RA)
Balegar (HY)
Balija, Oda Balija, Togara, Kita Balia

(OR)
Baloch (if settled in Saurashtra) (SA)
Balolika (MD)
Balsantoshi (BO)
Banajiga (MY)
Bandekar, Komti, Kudale, Maratha Vani, Pednekar, Sangameshwari, Narwekar, Patne (BO)
Bandhara (BO)
Bandhara Khati (SA)
Bandi (BO)
Banerwala (DE)
Banjara (BH)
Banjara, Baldia (RA)
Banjara, Berwa, Bola (AJ)
Banjara, Kuta (UP)
Banjara, Labana (MB)
Banjara, Lamana, Baragahi (VP)
Banjara/Vanjari, Labhan/, Lamane, Mathura, Nayak/, Nayakda, Thuria (MP)
Banka (OR)
Banna (CO)
Banoudhiya Rajputs (PU)
Banua, Buna, Bunna, Buno (WB)
Baori (RA)
Bara (SA)
Baragi, Bairagi, Bairagi (PU)
Barai, Bargahi (UP)
Barai, Tamboli (BH)
Barai, Tamboli (DE)
Barai, Tamboli (PU)
Barai, Tamboli, Tamoli, Chaurasia, Barhai, Barhi (BI)
Baraik (TR)
Baraji, Barui, Barhai (OR)
Barcha (BO)
Barchain, Chai, Chain (WB)
Barhai (UP)
Barhai, Carpenters, Baree (MB)
Barhai, Khati, Tarkhan (DE)
Barhai, Kundera, Sutar (VP)
Barhai, Tarkhan (PP)
Barhunda (BH)
Bari (BI)
Bari (BO)
Bari (DE)
Bari (MP)
Bari (RA)
Bari (UP)
Bari, Baria, Baria (VP)
Bari, Tamboli (MP)
Baria (AS)
Baria, Koli Baria (BO)
Barika, Bhandhari, Beja, Napit and Nai, Barui (OR)
Barker (BO)
Barmera, Bava (BO)
Barna Brahman, Patit, Brahman (WB)
Barnwal Bania (BI)
Baroi Chauraia, Kumavat, Panwari, Purabia, Tamboli, Bawar (MB)
Baroi, Barui, Barujibi, Barui, Barujibi (AS)
Barot, Bawa (KU)
Barra (PU)
Baruasankar, Beja (OR)
Barui (TR)
Barui, Barujibi, Barujibi, Bedey, Bediya (WB)
Barwar (PU)
Basdewa/Vasdeo/Vasudewa (MP)
Baseda (RA)
Basudev, Harbola, Jaga, Kaparia Kapdi (VP)
Batham (BI)
Bathi (PP)
Bathi (PU)
Battada (AP)
Battada (MD)
Battal (BO)
Batterha (PU)
Batwal (PU)
Bauri (TR)
Baver (MB)
Bawa, barber (SA)
Bawaji (MY)
Bawaria (UP)
Bazigar (BO)
Bazigar, Nat, Qalandar, (Excluding those in, S.C.) (DE)
Beda (MY)
Bedar, Berad, Naikmakkalu, Naikwadi, Nayakaru, Talvar, Valmiki (BO)
Bedia (TR)
Bedia/Beria/Biria, Dukar-Kolhati, Kolhati (MP)
Bediya, Sapera (BI)

Bega (HP)
Behna (VP)
Behna, Dhunia, Pinjara (MB)
Behna, Pinjara (BH)
Beldar (BI)
Beldar, Berad (BO)
Beldar, Kharol (MB)
Beldar, Telegu-Munnarkapu (MP)
Benata Oriya, Benati, Benati (OR)
Bentkar, Bentkars, Bentkars (OR)
Beparla (SA)
Beragi (UP)
Beria (UP)
Beria, Bedia, Bedia (RA)
Beria, Chhara, Dasa, Gujarathi Kolhati, Kanjar Bhat, Kanjari, Kanjar, Sansia (BO)
Beria, Kasera (PU)
Berua (WB)
Besta, Gangaputra (HY)
Bestar (BO)
Bestha (AP)
Bestha (MD)
Beta, Hensi, Hesi (PU)
Betera, Betra, Betra, Bhandari (OR)
Betru (HP)
Bhaat, Bhat, Bhat (HY)
Bhabhulia (DE)
Bhadbhuja (BO)
Bhadbhunja (by caste) (MP)
Bhadhuja (MB)
Bhadi-Waddar, Matti-Wadder, Waddar (MP)
Bhadre (MP)
Bhagat (RA)
Bhagat (UP)
Bhagia (BO)
Bhaitia (BO)
Bhakta (TR)
Bhal (BO)
Bhalya (BO)
Bhampta, Bhampta (Rajput), Dong-Dasar, Ghantichor, Uchlia, Bhampta (Rajput) (BO)
Bhamta, Bhamti, Bhamti (MB)
Bhand (BO)
Bhand (DE)
Bhand (PP)
Bhand (PU)
Bhand (UP)
Bhand, Bhavaya (SA)
Bhandari (AP)
Bhandari (MD)
Bhandari, Bhandara (in, Gujarat), Bhandara (in Gujarat) (BO)
Bhangi (WB)
Bhangi, Dom (UP)
Bhangi, Halalkhor, Lalbegi and Mehtar (Excluding those in S.C.) (BI)
Bhangi, Hela (MB)
Bhania (OR)
Bhanja Purana (OR)
Bhanjara Dhai (PU)
Bhanmati, Bhanta/Bhamta, Bhanta/Bhamta (MP)
Bhansali (KU)
Bhant (WB)
Bhantu (MB)
Bhar (BI)
Bhar (MP)
Bhar (TR)
Bhar (WB)
Bhar, Rajbhar (UP)
Bharadi (BO)
Bharari (MB)
Bharawa (RA)
Bharbhooja (DE)
Bharbhuja (MB)
Bharbhuja (PP)
Bharbhuja (VP)
Bharbhuja, Bhurji, Kandu (UP)
Bharbhunja (BH)
Bharbhunja (PU)
Bharbhunja (RA)
Bharewa (VP)
Bharia-Bharihar (MP)
Bharwad (KU)
Bharwad (outside Nesses, area in the forests of, Alech, Gir & Barada), Bhopa Rabari (SA)
Bharwad, Rabari (BO)
Bhaskar (BI)
Bhat (BH)
Bhat (BI)
Bhat (BO)
Bhat (DE)
Bhat (KU)
Bhat (WB)

Bhat, Bhatra, Darpi, Ramaiya, Bhatra (PU)
Bhat, Charan (RA)
Bhat, Charan, Maru, Sotiya, Salvi (MB)
Bhat, Deti (HP)
Bhat, Jasondhi (VP)
Bhat, Sanghadia (SA)
Bhat, Taga Bhat (UP)
Bhat/Brahmabhat, Charan (MP)
Bhatarajulu (OR)
Bhathiara (BI)
Bhathiara, Razzaqi (WB)
Bhati Rajput, Karadia, Nardoda, Bhoyan, Bhoyah, Bhoy (SA)
Bhati, Chang, Ghirath (PU)
Bhatiara (RA)
Bhatiara, Bhisti (DE)
Bhatiya (WB)
Bhatiyara (MB)
Bhatiyara (UP)
Bhatraja (HY)
Bhatraju (AP)
Bhatraju (MD)
Bhatraju (MY)
Bhatua (OR)
Bhavaiya, Targala (BO)
Bhavasar (RA)
Bhavasar Kshatriya (AP)
Bhavin (BO)
Bhavsar (BO)
Bhavsar (KU)
Bhavsar, Chippa, Nilgar, Nirali, Rangari (MP)
Bhawasar, Rangari, Rangrez (HY)
Bherihar, Gareri, Gadaria (BI)
Bhil (SA)
Bhilaya (SA)
Bhima (VP)
Bhinhar (TR)
Bhinjia (TR)
Bhiro (RA)
Bhishti (BH)
Bhishti (MB)
Bhishti (UP)
Bhishti (VP)
Bhishti, Sakka (RA)
Bhisti, Bhurji, Bhurtiya (UP)
Bhisti, Pakhali (BO)
Bhisty (MP)
Bhogam, Ganika, Kalavanthula (HY)
Bhogam, Sani, Kalavantulu, Devdasi (OR)
Bhoi (BO)
Bhoi (HY)
Bhoi (KU)
Bhoi, Bhoyan, Bhoyah, Bhoy (SA)
Bhoi, Dhiwar, Kahar, Mallah, Navda (MB)
Bhoi, Ezingabhui, Kahar, Turha (MP)
Bhoi, Kahar, Kewat, Mallah, Dhimar (BH)
Bhoi, Sagarvanshi Mali, Mali, Saini (RA)
Bhojak, Sevak (RA)
Bhojki (PU)
Bhokta (OR)
Bhopa, Manbhao (MB)
Bhoyar (MP)
Bhuhalia, Lohar (PU)
Bhuiya (TR)
Bhujan (OR)
Bhujru, Chang, Changar (PU)
Bhujwa (VP)
Bhuk (BO)
Bhuliya, Bindhani (OR)
Bhunji (BI)
Bhunvaya, Bhavaiya, Bhawari, Bhavaiya, Bhawari (RA)
Bhupar (BO)
Bhura Brahman (PU)
Bhurtiya (VP)
Bhute (BO)
Bhutia, Brijbasi (VP)
Bidia (MB)
Bikak (BO)
Bilas Naik (BO)
Bilimagga (CO)
Billava (CO)
Billava Maliah Billava (MD)
Biloch (PU)
Bin (TR)
Bind (BI)
Bind (TR)
Bind (UP)
Binjara, Vanjari, Vanjara (BO)
Binjhia, Binjhwar, Birjia, Brijia, Binjhwar (WB)
Birhor, Birjia, Brijia, Buna, Bunna, Buno (WB)

Birjhia (OR)
Bisati (UP)
Bissoy (AP)
Bogada (OR)
Bogari (BO)
Boldari (RA)
Bolodhia (OR)
Bondil (AP)
Bondil (MD)
Bondili (HY)
Bondili (OR)
Boreka, Gopal, Carpenters, Charan, Chaurasia (MB)
Boriabaf, Rassiban (HY)
Botakusuda (OR)
Botehra (PU)
Bowariya (MP)
Boya (AP)
Boya (CO)
Boya (HY)
Boya (MD)
Brahman (in Kangra, District) (PU)
Britia, Kahar (VP)
Budabukkala (AP)
Budbudkala (HY)
Budbudki (BO)
Budubudike (MY)
Bugri (BO)
Bujhri (Brahman) (HP)
Bukka (HY)
Bukkitgar (BO)
Bumij (TR)
Bundabestha (MY)
Burud (HY)
Burud, Medar (BO)

Chack, Chai, Chain (WB)
Chai, Kewat, Mallah, Sorahiya (UP)
Chain (BI)
Chak (DE)
Chakala (AP)
Chakala (HY)
Chakar, Daroga, Hazuri, Lambuat, Charan (RA)
Chakkala (TC)
Chamadia (BO)
Chamadia Khatki (SA)
Chamta (RA)
Chamtha (BO)
Chamtha (SA)
Chanara (KU)
Chandal, Namasudra (BI)
Chandlagara (BO)
Chandor (RA)
Changar (PP)
Chaniatia, Daya Maha-Brahman, Gujargaod, Brahman (RA)
Chapota, Chaurasia (BI)
Chapparband (BO)
Chaptogara (S. Kanara) (MD)
Charan (KU)
Charan, Gadhavi (BO)
Charan, Maldhari (outside, Nesses area in the forests, of Alech, Gir and Barada) (SA)
Charg (PU)
Charodi, Chhara (BO)
Chasadhoba Haladhar, Halari, Satchasi (WB)
Chatada, Chattada, Srivaishnava, Chattada, Srivaishnava, , Chonel Domb, Christian Domb (MD)
Chatadi, Chattada, Sri Vaishnava, Chattadasri Vaishnava, Chonel Domb, Christian Domb (AP)
Chauhan, Chippa (MP)
Chaukalshi (BO)
Chaurasia, Tamboli (VP)
Chaurth (BO)
Chavalakkaran (TC)
Cheeta (RA)
Chhadipti (UP)
Chhimba, Chhipi, Chhipa (PU)
Chhimba, Chimpa, Darzi, Tank, Chimpa (PP)
Chhimba, Darzi, Dakaut, Darzi, Deti (HP)
Chhipa (AJ)
Chhipa (MB)
Chhipa (RA)
Chhipi (UP)
Chhipi, Tank (DE)
Chhippa (UP)
Chigari Betegar (BO)
Chik (BI)
Chik (OR)
Chik, Chikwa, Kasai, Kassab, Chikwa (WB)
Chikwa, Qussab (UP)

Chikwa, Qussab (VP)
Chipa (VP)
Chipar (BH)
Chipi, Darzi (VP)
Chippa (in Gujarat) (BO)
Chippa, Kuntulu (HY)
Chippar, Rangrez (BH)
Chippollu, Mera (HY)
Chirimar (DE)
Chirimar (PU)
Chirimar (WB)
Chirimar, Darzi (PP)
Chirmar, Mirshikar (BI)
Chita (AJ)
Chitari (MP)
Chitari, Naqqashi (HY)
Chitra (OR)
Chitrakar (OR)
Chitrakathi (BO)
Chittrakar (WB)
Choodi Farosh, Daruwala (HY)
Choongar (BH)
Choudang (AS)
Chunari, Lonari (BO)
Chunera (SA)
Chunkar, Sunkar (MP)
Chunvalia Koli, Chunvaidia, Chunvadia (SA)
Churia (OR)
Churigar, Lakhera (RA)
Churihar, Manihar (UP)
Churihara (BI)
Churihara, Lahera (WB)
Chutiya (AS)

Dabagar (BO)
Dabgar (SA)
Dafali (BI)
Dafali (DE)
Dafali (UP)
Dafali (WB)
Dafali, Dholi (BH)
Daffer (SA)
Dahalias (OR)
Dahej (VP)
Daibagya, Daivagna, Ganak (AS)
Daiya, Darpi (PU)
Daiya, Dhaiya (DE)
Dakaut (AJ)
Dakaut (PU)
Dakaut, Prade, Daiya (DE)
Dakot, Garo, Gakudia (RA)
Dalera (UP)
Damai (Nepali) (MA)
Damai (Nepali), Daivagna (AS)
Damami (Dholi, Nagarchi), Dholi (AJ)
Damami, Daroga (RA)
Dana (VP)
Dandrolu, Dyandrawar (AP)
Dangi (BH)
Dangi (BI)
Dangi (UP)
Dangi, Darzi (VP)
Dangi, Daya Maha Brahman (RA)
Dangua (OR)
Danwar (of Gorakhpur) (UP)
Darji (OR)
Darji, Meru (MP)
Darji, Shimpi, Dasa (BO)
Daroga (AJ)
Darzi (BH)
Darzi (DE)
Darzi (MB)
Darzi (MY)
Darzi (RA)
Darzi (SA)
Darzi (UP)
Darzi, Idrisi (BI)
Darzi, Idrisi (WB)
Dasari (AP)
Dasari (HY)
Dasari (MD)
Dasari (MY)
Dasari (OR)
Davari, Davari Gosavi, Nath Panthi, Davari Gosavi (BO)
Debhar (BI)
Deevanga (HY)
Deha, Dhaya, Dhea, Dhaya, Dhea (PP)
Dehuri (OR)
Deons, Devadasi (OR)
Depala (BO)
Depala Dhobi (KU)
Depala, Dhobi, Dhobi (SA)
Desali, Dhuli (TR)
Deshwali, Mina (MB)
Devadasi Caste, Natuva (HY)
Devadika (S.Kanara), Devanga, Domb

(MD)
Devakuditalayari, Devanga (AP)
Devali (BO)
Devalkar (AP)
Devanga (CO)
Devanga (MY)
Devangi, Dora (OR)
Devdig (BO)
Dewang, Jandra, Koskati, Lingayat, Dukar-Kolhati (MP)
Dey, Sudra Das (AS)
Dhakad (BH)
Dhakad, Keer, Kirar (MB)
Dhakar (AJ)
Dhamin (BI)
Dhanak, Dhai (PU)
Dhanak, Dhanka, Dhanuk, Gokhi, Dhanka, Dhanuk (RA)
Dhandi, Dhadhi, Dhadhi (RA)
Dhaner (OR)
Dhangar (BH)
Dhangar (HY)
Dhangar, Dhiwar (MB)
Dhangar, Gadri/Gadaria, Hatgar/Hatkar, Kurmar, Mirdha (MP)
Dhangar, Kurbar (BO)
Dhanka (MP)
Dhanuk (BI)
Dharala, Patanwadia (BO)
Dharhi, Pawaria, Singharia Tanwar (UP)
Dhasa (WB)
Dhavad (BO)
Dhebra, Dhimar, Dhivar, Gabit, Harkantra, Mangeli, Mangela, Page, Sankuri, Dhimar, Dhivar (BO)
Dheh (PU)
Dhekaru (BI)
Dhekaru (WB)
Dhenuar (WB)
Dhimar (BI)
Dhimar, Dhinwar, Jhinwar, Kahar, Mallah, Dhiman Brahman, Dhinwar (PU)
Dhimar, Dhiver, Dhiver (UP)
Dhimar, Kewat (MP)
Dhinwar, Jheer, Jhinwar, Kahar (HP)
Dhinwar, Jhinwar, Kahar, Mallah (PP)
Dhinwar, Jhinwar, Kahar, Nishar (DE)
Dhobi (DE)
Dhobi (excluding those in S.C.), Dhimar (BH)
Dhobi (excluding those, in S.C.) (OR)
Dhobi (HY)
Dhobi (MP)
Dhobi (PP)
Dhobi (PU)
Dhobi (RA)
Dhobi (UP)
Dhobi (VP)
Dhobi, Hawari, (Excluding those in S.C.) (BI)
Dhobi, Parit (BO)
Dhogri (PU)
Dhoki (BO)
Dholi (BO)
Dholi (MP)
Dholi, Nagarchi (RA)
Dhosali (PU)
Dhukkar (BO)
Dhulia, Kosti/Kushta/, Kosthi, Lingayat Hatgar, Charan (MP)
Dhunia, Dhunkar, Dhunkar, Dora (OR)
Dhunia, Dhunkar, Ezingabhui (MP)
Dhunia, Mansoori, Naddaf, Gadaria, Gaddi (BI)
Dhunia, Masoori (WB)
Dhunia, Naddaf (BH)
Dhunia, Naddaf, Dom (UP)
Dhunia, Pinjara, Kadhera, Dhunnewala, Dhunnewala (DE)
Dhunkar, Kadore, Dhunia (MB)
Doga (MY)
Dombara (HY)
Dombara (MY)
Dombari (HY)
Dombari, Dong-Dasar (BO)
Dombo, Dombo (AP)
Dommara (AP)
Dommara (HY)
Dommara (MD)
Donga Dasari (AP)
Donga Yata (AP)
Doodekula (HY)
Dosad (TR)
Dosali (PP)
Drazi, Sai (KU)
Dudekula (MD)
Dudekula, Dyandrawar (AP)

Dudekulu (OR)
Dumal (OR)
Durgamurogeru (BO)

Eediga (HY)
Eeliga (HY)
Elmar (BO)
Eravallar (MD)
Erragoala (OR)
Eshava, Thiya (TC)
Ex-Tea-garden labourers (AS)
Ex-tea-garden labourers (TR)
Ezhavathy, Vathi (TC)
Ezhuthasan (TC)
Ezhuvan, Illuvan (Malabar) (MD)

Fakir (BH)
Fakir (DE)
Fakir (KU)
Fakir (OR)
Fakir (RA)
Fakir, Sain (VP)
Fakir, Sain (WB)
Fakir-Bandarwala, Gadri/Gadaria (MP)
Faqeer (HY)
Faqir (PU)
Faqir (UP)
Faquir (MB)
Futgudi, Gabit, Gadhavi (BO)

Gach, Mandewala (DE)
Gachaki (MP)
Gadaria (DE)
Gadaria (PP)
Gadaria (PU)
Gadaria (RA)
Gadaria, Gadri, Gari, Gadri, Gari (BH)
Gadariya (VP)
Gadariya, Gauriya (UP)
Gadariya, Ghosi (MB)
Gaddi, Garri (DE)
Gaddi, Ghosi (UP)
Gaddi, Ghosi (WB)
Gadhai (SA)
Gadheri (BI)
Gadheri, Garri (DE)
Gadic Lohar, Gadolia, Lohar, Lohar, Garo (RA)
Gadlia (SA)
Gadole, Gaddoli, Longoliha, Lohpita, Gaddoli (MB)
Gadolia (Gadodia), Gadodia (AJ)
Gahamandi (MP)
Gahelra (BO)
Gain (WB)
Gainey (Nepali) (MA)
Gainey (Nepali), Ganak (AS)
Gajula (HY)
Gajulu (OR)
Galada Konkani (MD)
Galkata (SA)
Gam Vakkal (BO)
Gamalla, Gowda, Kalali (AP)
Gamalla, Gowda, Kalali (MD)
Gamantiya (OR)
Ganda (WB)
Gandharap (BO)
Gandharb (BI)
Gandharp (UP)
Gandhi (UP)
Gandhila (UP)
Gandhiya, Gauriya (UP)
Gandla (AP)
Gandla (MD)
Gandla, Gangaputra (HY)
Gangai, Ganesh (BI)
Gangakula (MY)
Gangauta, Gangota, Gangota (BI)
Gangavar (AP)
Gangavar (Coimbatore, Distt.) (MD)
Gangelddulavar (HY)
Gangi Reddula (AP)
Gangin (TR)
Gangwar, Ganesh, Gareri, Ghosi, Gaura, Goala, Gola (BI)
Ganiga (CO)
Ganiga (MY)
Ganiga, Ganika (HY)
Ganiga, Ghanchi, Teli (BO)
Ganiga, Nagavamsam (AP)
Ganika Nagavamsam (MD)
Ganika, Kaniyan (TC)
Ganjam Reddi (Ramned, Madura, Tinnevelly, Distts) (MD)
Ganju (TR)
Ganju, Gunju (OR)
Gaoli, Gwal (BH)
Gaoli, Lingayat-Gaoli (MP)

Garadiga (MY)
Garai, Kalu (WB)
Garasia (in Gujarat) (BO)
Gareri (TR)
Garhwal (MP)
Garpagari, Nath (MP)
Garudi (KU)
Garudi (SA)
Garudi, Modikar (BO)
Garwadi/Garaddi (MP)
Gatti (S. Kanara) (MD)
Gauria, Gwar, Gwaria (PU)
Gavada, Gavdi, Gavdi (BO)
Gavandhi (BO)
Gavandi (HY)
Gavara (AP)
Gavli (BO)
Gavli (SA)
Gawaria (AJ)
Gawaria, Gadolia Lohar, Garudia (RA)
Gayari (MB)
Gayari (RA)
Gazula Balija (AP)
Gend (BO)
Gengettinavaru (HY)
Ghadi (BO)
Ghadshi, Ghanchi (BO)
Ghai (HP)
Ghai (PU)
Ghami (MB)
Ghancha (KU)
Ghanchani, Rangaswami (RA)
Ghanchi, Ghancha, Ghanacha, Ghancha, Ghanacha (RA)
Ghanchi, Ghancha, Ghancha (SA)
Ghandaria, Ghantichor (BO)
Ghantia (SA)
Ghariya (VP)
Gharuk (BO)
Gharuk, Kahar, Kamkar, Ghosi (UP)
Gharwali (BO)
Ghasiara (PP)
Ghasiara (RA)
Ghasiara, Ghirath (PU)
Ghasiara, Ghosi (DE)
Ghatti Ghare, Ghosi, Gopal (MB)
Ghatwal, Ghosh, Ghosi, Goala (WB)
Ghisadi (BO)
Ghosh, Gop, Gowala, Gop (AS)
Ghosi (MP)
Ghosi (PP)
Ghosi (PU)
Ghosi (VP)
Ghosi, Gnosi, Gnosi (BH)
Ghosi, Gokhi, Gujar Goad Brahman, Hajam (RA)
Ghur (MY)
Gingra (OR)
Gir (BO)
Giri (UP)
Girigiria, Gola, Golla (OR)
Girni-Waddar (BO)
Goala (TR)
Goala, Gopala, and, Gowdo, Gopala, Gowdo (OR)
Godaba (AP)
Golarana (BO)
Golla (CO)
Golla (MY)
Golla, Gol, Gol (BO)
Golla, Iddayar Konar, Yadav, Gowda (MD)
Golla, Iddayar, Konar, Yadav (AP)
Golla, Yadav (HY)
Gond (WB)
Gonda (WB)
Gondaliga (MY)
Gonde, Gowda (AP)
Gondhali (BO)
Gondhali (HY)
Gondhali (MP)
Gondhaliga (HY)
Gongadikar (BO)
Goniga (MY)
Gontia (VP)
Goondla (HY)
Gopal, Gosavi, Gosai (BO)
Gopal, Pangala Gopal (MP)
Gorhi, Gosain (BI)
Gorkha (UP)
Gorkha, Gosain, Gujru (HP)
Gorkhodu, Gowala (AS)
Gosain (BH)
Gosain (VP)
Gosangiwar (MP)
Gosayi (MY)
Gossain (UP)
Goundla, Gowda, Gowda (HY)

Gowala (PP)
Gowda (CO)
Gowli (HY)
Gowliga (CO)
Gowliga (HY)
Grahabipra Brahman, Jyotish, Sakaldarpee, Brahman (OR)
Gramani, Shanan (MD)
Gudheri (WB)
Gudia, Gurja, Gunja, Gujra (OR)
Gudigar, Gujarat-Baori (BO)
Gudigara, Iddayar (MD)
Guhar, Jatiya (AJ)
Gujar (AJ)
Gujar (DE)
Gujar (MB)
Gujar (MY)
Gujar (UP)
Gujar Kadia, Kadia (in, Gujarat), Gujarati Kolhati (BO)
Gujar, Gwal (BH)
Gujar, Harbola (VP)
Gulgulia (BI)
Gunagi (BO)
Gundi (TR)
Gurav (BO)
Gurav (MP)
Guri (TR)
Gurira (BO)
Gurkha (MY)
Gurou (HY)
Gwala (DE)
Gwala, Gwar, Gwaria (PU)

Habbu (BO)
Habra (OR)
Habura (MP)
Hadi (PU)
Hajam (KU)
Hajam, Ibrahimi, Haladhar, Halari (WB)
Hajam, Kalseru Navaliga, Kelashi, Nabhik, Nai, Nhavi (BO)

Hajam, Nhavi, Nai, Barber (SA)
Hajjam (HY)
Hajjam (MB)
Hajjam (MP)
Hajjam (OR)
Hajjam (UP)
Hajjam, Ibrahimi, Halalkhor (BI)
Hajjam, Nai (DE)
Hajjam, Nai (PU)
Hajjam, Nai, Heri (PP)
Hajuri Daroga, Hela (MB)
Halalkhor (excluding, those in S.C. list) (WB)
Halalkhor (UP)
Halalkhor, Hazuri (RA)
Halepaik (BO)
Hali Kaibartta (AS)
Hali, Heri, Hensi, Hesi (PU)
Hallikar (MY)
Halvakki Vakkal (BO)
Halwai (MA)
Halwai (UP)
Halwai (WB)
Halwai, Kandu, Kanu, Hawari, Ibrahimi, Idrisi (BI)
Hammal (MB)
Hanbar (BO)
Hansi (OR)
Haranshikari (BO)
Hari (PP)
Haridas (in East, Khandesh) (BO)
Harikalyan, Harkantra (BO)
Harjala (UP)
Harni, Hatgar/Hatkar (MP)
Hassimi (UP)
Hati (BO)
Hati (SA)
Hatkar (HY)
Hawari (WB)
Hegde, Kuruba (AP)
Heggade (CO)
Hela (RA)
Hela (VP)
Hela, Ibrahimi, Idrisi, Jadav (WB)
Helav (BO)
Herbi (DE)
Higer (BO)
Hijra (DE)
Hijra (UP)
Hill Tribes of Himalaya and Chittagong, hill tracts (WB)
Hingora (KU)
Hiragar, Sargara (BO)
Holar, Valhar (BO)
Hollar, Jadav, Jandra (MP)

Hoogar (HY)
Huga Lohar, Lohar, Lohpeta, Jadav, Jaga (VP)

Idiga (MY)
Idiga, Setti Balija (AP)
Idiga, Setti-Balija (MD)
Ilgar (BO)
Illathar, Pannikkar, Pillamar, Sarayakara, Sirkudipillai, Illuvan (MD)
Irulan (MD)
Isaivellalar, Melakarar, (Tanjore Distt.) (MD)

Jachak Mir Dhadhi (SA)
Jachak Mir Dhadi (KU)
Jada, Nekar (HY)
Jadupatia (BI)
Jaga (BO)
Jagaria (BO)
Jagiasi (from Sind) (BO)
Jagyasi (AJ)
Jagyasi Bhagat, Jogi (RA)
Jain (MY)
Jajak (from Sind) (BO)
Jajri (BO)
Jakhria Jakreja (BO)
Jakkula (Guntur Dist.) (AP)
Jalari (AP)
Jallad (DE)
Jambovanodai (AP)
Jambuvanodai (MD)
Janappa Chetty (AP)
Jandara (AP)
Jandara (MD)
Jandra (HY)
Jangalu (OR)
Jangam (AP)
Jangam (MD)
Jangam (MP)
Jangra, Lodhi, Jasondhi (VP)
Jarugamalli (AP)
Jat (BH)
Jat (BI)
Jat (BO)
Jat (HP)
Jat (KU)
Jat (MB)
Jat (SA)
Jatia (BO)
Jatigar (BO)
Jaunpuri Bania (BI)
Javeri, Johari (BO)
Jeoni (WB)
Jethi Mal (KU)
Jetty (AP)
Jetty (MD)
Jetty (MY)
Jhandi, Sonar (MP)
Jhangra Brahman, Khati (PU)
Jhara (TR)
Jhatkia Sikh, Jhinwar (DE)
Jhatkia, Kasab, Jhinwar (PP)
Jhodia (OR)
Jhoja (UP)
Jilaya (SA)
Jingar (BO)
Jingar (HY)
Jingar (MB)
Jogde (MB)
Jogi (AP)
Jogi (BH)
Jogi (BO)
Jogi (DE)
Jogi (HY)
Jogi (MD)
Jogi (MY)
Jogi (VP)
Jogi Nath, Jhinwar (PU)
Jogi Vadi (SA)
Jogi, Jugi, Jugi (BI)
Jogi, Jullaha (UP)
Jogi, Nath, Yogi (TR)
Jogi, Yogi (OR)
Jogin (BO)
Joginath (MB)
Jogivadi (KU)
Jogtin, Johari (BO)
Jolaha, Momin (AS)
Jolaha, Momin, Jyotish, Kalavantulu (OR)
Jonakan (TC)
Joshi (BO)
Joshi (MB)
Joshi (VP)
Julaha (AJ)
Julaha (excluding those, in Scheduled Castes), Kahar (PU)

Julaha (if not Harijans), Jhinwar, Jheer, Kahar (HP)
Julaha (RA)
Julaha, Kahar (PP)
Julaha, Momin (BH)
Julaha, Momin (HY)
Julaha, Momin (MB)
Julaha, Momin (VP)
Julaha, Momin, (Excluding, those in S. C.), Kahar (DE)
Julaha, Momin, Kassab, Kasai, Kunjra, Kharwi, Laddaf, Lad Vanjari, Mann Waddar, Matti Waddar, Maratha Kolhati, Mitha, Momin, Naddaf, Pardeshi Bhoi, Raj Bhoi, Rajput Lamani, Rajput Vanjari, Rayee, Shilavat (BO)
Jyotshi Brahman (UP)

Kaasaar, Kasar (HY)
Kabad, Kabadia, Kamad, Kamadia, Kabadia, Kamad, Kamadia (RA)
Kabar, Kaleari, Kabari (VP)
Kabariya (UP)
Kabbaliga Kabberu, Kabberu (HY)
Kabbaligar (BO)
Kabbera (S. Kanara) (MD)
Kabirpanthi, Ramdasiya, Ravidasia (MB)
Kacchi (UP)
Kachagandhivaru (HY)
Kachari (BO)
Kachchi, Kahar (BH)
Kachera, Lakhera (MP)
Kachhi (MP)
Kachhi (RA)
Kachhi (VP)
Kachhi Koeri, Murai, Murao (DE)
Kachhi, Kushwaha Kshatriya, Kadore, Kahar (MB)
Kachhia, Kachi, Kachi, Kadia (in Gujarat) (BO)
Kachi (HY)
Kadar (BI)
Kadera (VP)
Kadera, Kahar (MP)
Kadera, Kahar (VP)
Kadhere, Kahar (UP)
Kadia (SA)
Kaduppatan (Malabar, Distt.) (MD)
Kaghzi (BI)
Kagzi (WB)
Kahar (AJ)
Kahar (BO)
Kahar (MY)
Kahar (RA)
Kahar, Kalu (WB)
Kahar, Rawani (BI)
Kaibertta (BI)
Kaikadi, Kalavanthulu (HY)
Kaikadi, Pamlor (BO)
Kaikolan, Songunthur, Kalali (MD)
Kaikollan (TC)
Kaikollan, Kalali (AP)
Kaiserwani, Kasera, Thathera (BI)
Kakal, Kakar, Kakar (KU)
Kalal (BO)
Kalal (HP)
Kalal (RA)
Kalal, Kalar, Kalar (BH)
Kalal, Kalar, Kalar (MB)
Kalal, Kalwar, Kalwar, Kadhera (DE)
Kalandar (BI)
Kalar, Kapdi, Kaparia (VP)
Kalar, Khatri-Maratha (MP)
Kalari Kurup Kalari, Panickar, Kalaripanicker (TC)
Kalavant (BO)
Kalavanthula (AP)
Kalavanthula (MD)
Kalawati (HY)
Kalbelia (BH)
Kalbi, Kulbi, Kangshia (RA)
Kalingi (AP)
Kalingi, Kintala-Kalingi (OR)
Kalkutika (HY)
Kall-waddar, Kalseru Navaliga, (BO)
Kallan, Kaniyan (TC)
Kallan, Parimalai Kallan, Kambalathar (MD)
Kallunder, Kannatia (MB)
Kalota (BH)
Kalwar (AS)
Kalwar (UP)
Kalwar Bania (BI)
Kamalapuri Vaishya, Teli (UP)
Kamar (OR)
Kamar, Karmakar (AS)
Kamar, Karmakar (WB)

Kamar, Karmakar, Karmakar (TR)
Kamar, Lohar, Karamkar (BI)
Kamati (BO)
Kambar (HY)
Kamboh, Kamkar, Kandu (UP)
Kamboj, Kamboh, Kamboh (PU)
Kami (Nepali) (AS)
Kami (Nepali) (MA)
Kamlapuri Vaish Teli, Kandu, Kanu, Karamkar, Kasera (BI)
Kamli (BO)
Kammalan, (Kamsala, Viswa Brahman, Viswa), Kamsala (AP)
Kammalan, Kamsala, Viswabrahmin, Viswakarma, Kamsala (MD)
Kammar (BO)
Kammari (HY)
Kammari (OR)
Kammi (BO)
Kan (WB)
Kanada (BO)
Kanbi, (except Lova Kanbi otherwise styled as Patidar of, the Kaira Distt. and the, North and South Daskroi talukas of the Ahmedabad, Distt.) (BO)
Kanbi, Karadia Nardoda (SA)
Kanchagar, Kanjari, Kanjar, Kanjar Bhat (BO)
Kanchan, Kanjar (PP)
Kanchari (AP)
Kanchari (HY)
Kanchari (OR)
Kanchugar (HY)
Kandarpa (OR)
Kandera (BH)
Kandh (WB)
Kandu (WB)
Kandu, Kamakar (AS)
Kandu, Kanu, Kanu (MA)
Kanera, Khangar (UP)
Kanet Rajput (HP)
Kangar (DE)
Kangar Batwalo (MP)
Kangashia (SA)
Kangehra (PU)
Kangerha, Kanjar, Kasab (PP)
Kangh (TR)
Kangi, Kangshia (RA)
Kanisu, Kaniyar Pannikkar, Kanitha Pulaver, Kanitha Pulaver, Kaniyar Pannikkar (MD)
Kaniyar (MY)
Kanjar (MP)
Kanjar, Kanchan, Rachband, Kanchan (PU)
Kanjar, Sansia (VP)
Kannadiyar (MD)
Kannaeli (DE)
Kansara (BO)
Kansari (OR)
Kansari, Kangsakar, Kangsakar, Kapali (WB)
Kanuh (BO)
Kanvi (RA)
Kaora (BI)
Kapali (TR)
Kapdi (BO)
Kapu (Srikakulam &, Vizag Distt.) (AP)
Kapu, Koppulakapu (OR)
Kapudia (OR)
Kapuria (WB)
Karad (RA)
Karani (WB)
Karar, Kirar (VP)
Karaun (BI)
Kare Vakkal (BO)
Karha, Karmaker (WB)
Karhara (OR)
Karia (BO)
Karikala Bhaktulu, Kami, Bhaktula, Pattusali, Padmasali, Sale, Sali, Saliyan, Senapathulu, Thogata. (MD)
Karnatak-Vishwa Brahman, Panchal (BO)
Kartias (OR)
Karush (UP)
Karvi (BO)
Karwal Nut (BI)
Karwal Nut, Nat, Kasai (WB)
Kasaar, Kasar (HY)
Kasab (Qasab) (AP)
Kasab, Kasai, Quraishi, Kasai (OR)
Kasab, Kasai, Qureshi, Kasai (BI)
Kasai (AJ)
Kasai (KU)
Kasai (MY)
Kasai (SA)
Kasai Maji, Kassab (WB)
Kasai, Kassab, Quraishi, Kassab (AS)

Kasai, Qussab, Quraishi (DE)
Kasar (BO)
Kasar, Kasera, Otari, Tamera/Tambatkar, Thathera (MP)
Kasarwani (UP)
Kasaundhan (UP)
Kasbi, Kasera, Kewat (MP)
Kasera, Keer (MB)
Kasera, Kewat (BH)
Kasera, Tamera (VP)
Kasera, Tamera, Thathera (PP)
Kasera, Thathera (RA)
Kasera, Thathera (UP)
Kasgar (UP)
Kashikapdi, Tirmali (BO)
Kasia (BO)
Kasodan Bania (BI)
Kassab (BH)
Kassab (HP)
Kassab, Kasai, Quraishi, Khatik (MP)
Kassab, Khati (PU)
Kassab, Qassab, Kasai, Kasai (RA)
Katabu, Killiket (BO)
Katari (BO)
Kathgara (MY)
Kathi, Kelashi (BO)
Kathodia, Kherwa (RA)
Kathputli Nachanewala (DE)
Katipapala (HY)
Kauri, Kori (VP)
Kavathi, Kerala-Muthali, Sakravar, Kerala Muthali (TC)
Kavuthiyan, Kendi (MD)
Kechai (TR)
Keer (AJ)
Keer, Kirar, Kewat (UP)
Keot, Keuta, Keute, Keuata, Keuta, Keuata, Keute (OR)
Kepmari (AP)
Kesera, Temara, Thathera, Thathiar (DE)
Keut, Kewat, Kewat (BI)
Kewat, Kundera (VP)
Khagi, Khangar, Kirar (UP)
Khajirin (OR)
Khalasi (KU)
Khalasi (SA)
Khamgara, Khatri-Maratha (MP)
Khandual (OR)
Khangar (BH)
Khangar (BI)
Khangar, Mirdha, Kirar (VP)
Khangar, Mirdhan, Kharol, Kirar (MB)
Khant (SA)
Khant, Khorwa (RA)
Kharadi (BO)
Kharak (BO)
Kharak (SA)
Kharga (WB)
Kharia (WB)
Kharol (AJ)
Kharol (RA)
Kharur, Kharwa, Kharwa (BO)
Kharvi (S. Kanara) (MD)
Kharwa (KU)
Kharwa (SA)
Kharwar, Kherwar, Khewar (WB)
Khasia (SA)
Khatgune, Khati (DE)
Khathi (HY)
Khati (AJ)
Khati (from Sind) (BO)
Khati (OR)
Khatia (MP)
Khatik (Only Suryavanshi) (PP)
Khatik (only Suryavanshi), Koeri (DE)
Khatri (AP)
Khatri (MD)
Khattri (BO)
Khatua (OR)
Khatwe (BI)
Khavas (BO)
Khawas (KU)
Khawas (SA)
Khelkari, Kolhati (BO)
Kheltas (BI)
Khetauri (BI)
Khetri, Killiket (BO)
Khodra, Kintala Kalingi, Kita Balija (OR)
Khondal (OR)
Khumbhakar (TR)
Khurdalta (RA)
Khyara (WB)
Kichha (KU)
Kintala Kalinga, Konar (AP)
Kirad, Kolhati (BO)
Kirar (BH)
Kirar/Kirad, Kolhati (MP)
Kisan (UP)

Koch (BI)
Koch, Rajbanshi (AS)
Koda (OR)
Kodaga of Yedavanar and, Suriabinads (CO)
Kodar, Kori (VP)
Koeri (BI)
Koeri (UP)
Kohli (PP)
Kohli (PU)
Koiri (WB)
Kolari, Muniyani (South Kanara) (MD)
Kolasi (S. Kanara) (MD)
Kolhati, Kolhatni (HY)
Koli (SA)
Koli (Son) (BO)
Koli Malhar (BO)
Koli Suryavanshi (BO)
Koli, Koli Bariya (BO)
Koli, Koskati, Kosti/Kushta/Kashti (MP)
Koli, Kuli (OR)
Koliy, Urali Nair (MD)
Kollar, Kuli, Koppula Kapu (OR)
Komarpaik (BO)
Komarpantha, Komti (BO)
Konar (TC)
Konchi Korava (HY)
Kongadi (BO)
Kongu Chettiar (Coimbatore Distt.), Konar (S (MD)
Koppala Velama (AP)
Koracha (AP)
Koracha (MD)
Koranga (BI)
Korava (HY)
Korcha (BO)
Kori (from Sind) (BO)
Korku (BI)
Korva (BO)
Korvanji (BO)
Koshi (BO)
Koshti (HY)
Koshti (MB)
Kot (BO)
Koteyar, Sheragara, Kshatriya (S. Karana), Kettai Reddi (MD)
Kotil (MP)
Kotwal Kotwalia, Kotwalia (BO)
Kotwal, Kutwar (BH)
Kuccharia (from Sind), Kudale (BO)
Kuchband (PU)
Kuchbandha (MP)
Kuchbandhia (BI)
Kuchbandiya (MB)
Kuda (OR)
Kudal Desahasti Gowd (MD)
Kudamatia (OR)
Kudavakkal (BO)
Kuduma (OR)
Kudumbi (TC)
Kulait (PU)
Kulal, Kumbhar, Kumbar (OR)
Kulala (MD)
Kulala, Kummari, Kummari, Kuruba (AP)
Kulama (BO)
Kulbandhiya, Kumavat (MB)
Kulta, Kumbhar, Kumhar (OR)
Kuluva (TC)
Kumahar (BH)
Kumar (BH)
Kumar, Khumbhakar, Kumhar, Kumbhakar, Kumhar (WB)
Kumar, Rudra Paul of, Cachar (AS)
Kumara Kshatriya (MD)
Kumbara (CO)
Kumbara (HY)
Kumbara (MY)
Kumbaran (TC)
Kumbhakar, Kumhar, Prajapati, Kumhar (BI)
Kumbhar (BO)
Kumbhar (HY)
Kumbhar, Kulbi (RA)
Kumbhar, Prajapati (SA)
Kumhar (AJ)
Kumhar (HP)
Kumhar (KU)
Kumhar (MB)
Kumhar (PP)
Kumhar (UP)
Kumhar, Prajapati (PU)
Kumhar, Prajapati, Kunjra (DE)
Kumhar/Kumbhar (MP)
Kummara (HY)
Kunbi (BH)
Kunbi (Maratha) (MB)
Kunbi Tillori (in the Ratnagiri and

Kolaba Distts.) (BO)
Kunbi, Kurmar (MP)
Kunchavakkal (BO)
Kunchi Korava (BO)
Kunchita Kapu (AP)
Kunchitiga (MY)
Kundigar (UP)
Kunjra (RA)
Kunjra (VP)
Kunjra, Kashwaha Kshatriya (MB)
Kunjra, Rain (UP)
Kunjra, Rayeen (BI)
Kunjra, Rayeen (WB)
Kunnuvar Mannadi (MD)
Kupadhar Kushiari Rarh, Kushiari (AS)
Kurba (HY)
Kurma (HY)
Kurmi (DE)
Kurmi (MA)
Kurmi (MP)
Kurmi (OR)
Kurmi (PP)
Kurmi (PU)
Kurmi (TR)
Kurmi (VP)
Kurmi, Kurbar (BO)
Kurmi, Kurmi Mahto, Kurmi Mahto (BI)
Kurmi, Kuta (UP)
Kurmi, Kutwar (BH)
Kurmi, Labana (MB)
Kurmi, Lahera (WB)
Kuruba (BO)
Kuruba (MY)
Kuruba, Kurumba (MD)
Kuruhini Chetty, Kurumba (MD)
Kusavan (TC)
Kuvinchetty (HY)

Labana (AJ)
Labana (DE)
Labana (HP)
Labana, Lakhera, Lambuat, Lohar (RA)
Labana, Vanzara (PU)
Labbai (MD)
Labbai (MY)
Labbai (TC)
Lad, Lad Sonar, Lad Sonar (BO)
Ladar (MY)
Laddaf (HY)
Ladia/Ladhia/Laria, Lakhera, Lingayat, Lingayat-Gaoli, Lingyat Hatgar (MP)
Lahakar, Laheri, Laheri, Lalbegi (BI)
Lahera (UP)
Lakhera (AJ)
Lakhera (BH)
Lakhera, Lamana (VP)
Lakhera, Langoliha (MB)
Lakhera, Manihar (DE)
Lakhera, Manihar (PP)
Lakhera, Manihar, Lohar (PU)
Lakheri (BO)
Lakhra (OR)
Lakshmir (BO)
Lalbegi (PP)
Lamani, Lambada, Lambada (BO)
Langha (KU)
Langha (SA)
Larai (BO)
Larhia, Lodhi, Lohar, Lohpeta (VP)
Laskar (TR)
Liari, Radhi, Niari (OR)
Lingayat (CO)
Lingayod (only of, rural areas) (MY)
Lobana (UP)
Lodh (UP)
Lodha (AJ)
Lodha (BO)
Lodha (HY)
Lodha (RA)
Lodha (SA)
Lodha (TR)
Lodha, Lodhi, Lodhi (BH)
Lodha, Lodhi, Lodhi, Lohpita (MB)
Lodha, Lohar (BI)
Lodhi (MP)
Lodhi, Lodh, Lodha, Maha Lodh, Lodh, Lodha (DE)
Lohar (AJ)
Lohar (BO)
Lohar (HY)
Lohar (if not Harijan) (HP)
Lohar (MA)
Lohar (MP)
Lohar (PP)
Lohar (TR)
Lohar, Luhura, Luhura (OR)
Lohar, Vishwakarma (UP)
Loi (MA)

Lok, Lonari (BO)
Lome (VP)
Lonari (HY)
Lonia, Lunia, Ode, Odiya, Lunia (MB)
Lubana (BO)
Lubana (PP)
Luhar (BH)
Luhar (DE)
Luhar (In Gujarat) (BO)
Luharia, Luvaria, Lunvaria, Luhar, Luvaria, Lunvaria, Luhar (SA)
Lund (BO)
Lunia, Murha, Nunia (VP)
Lunia, Nonia (MP)
Lunia, Nunia (BH)
Lunia, Nunia, Mali, Mallah, Manihar (UP)
Luvaria, Luharia, Lohar, Luharia, Lohar (KU)

Machhi, Machhera, Machhera (DE)
Machhi, Mali, Mali, Mallah, Manbhao (MB)
Machhi, Tandel (BO)
Machhua (OR)
Machhua (WB)
Machula (BO)
Madambi (MD)
Madari (BI)
Madari (KU)
Madari (PP)
Madari (PU)
Madari (SA)
Madhvia (SA)
Madivala (AP)
Madivala (CO)
Madivala (MD)
Madugar, Medavar, Mahendra, Medara, Mahendra (MD)
Magadha, Magadhi-Goral, Magadhi Goral (OR)
Magar, Mangar, Mangar, Mansoori (BI)
Maghi, Maghia, Maghia (OR)
Magura (OR)
Maha Brahman, Mali (RA)
Mahadarda (WB)
Mahajir (BO)
Mahali (HY)
Mahata (WB)
Mahatam, Rai Sikh (PU)
Mahatam, Rai, Mallah, Manihar (PP)
Mahato (WB)
Mahawat (RA)
Mahendra, Medara (AP)
Mahendra, Medari (HY)
Mahesya (OR)
Mahia (BO)
Mahind (BO)
Mahisya, Mahisya Das, Mahisya Das (AS)
Mahratta (MY)
Mahratta (non-Brahmin) (AP)
Mahratta (Non-brahmin) (MD)
Mahunta (OR)
Mahuriya (BI)
Mairal (BO)
Maiya, Mahiya, Mahiya (SA)
Majhwar (BI)
Makarani (KU)
Makhar (BO)
Makrani (SA)
Mala (MP)
Malakar Mali (BI)
Malakar, Mali, Mali (WB)
Malal, Malhor, Malhor (BI)
Malayali (MY)
Malayaman, Moopanar, Nainar, Nathaman, Parakavakulam, Surithiman, Maliah Billava (MD)
Malayan (Malabar) (MD)
Male (AP)
Male (S.Karana) (MD)
Maleya (CO)
Malhar (BI)
Mali (AJ)
Mali (BO)
Mali (HY)
Mali (KU)
Mali (OR)
Mali (SA)
Mali (VP)
Mali, Mali Korchia, Paddamali, Paikomali, Mali Korchia (AP)
Mali, Mali Korchia, Paiko mali, Peddamali, Mali Korchia (MD)
Mali, Mallah (BH)
Mali, Marar (MP)
Mali, Phool Mali, Saini, Mallah, Manihar

(PU)
Mali, Saini, Pholl Mali (HP)
Mali, Saini, Sauthia, Sagarwanshi Mali, Nayak, Maha Lodh, Mandewala, Manihar (DE)
Mallah (Except those in the list of S. C.), Mali (BI)
Mallah, Mansoori (WB)
Managali (OR)
Manbhav, Mangela, Mangel, Maratha Vani (BO)
Manbhav/Mahanubhav, Purohit (MP)
Mandatan Chetty (MD)
Mandulavaru (HY)
Mangala (HY)
Mangala (MD)
Mangala, Medara (AP)
Mangaria (BO)
Manghli (QR)
Manigar (HY)
Manihar (VP)
Manihar, Maratha (Kunbi), Maru Sotiya (MB)
Manipuri (AS)
Manipuri, Nagarchi (TR)
Manjar, Marar, Mathura, Matti-Waddar, Meru (MP)
Manjhi (UP)
Manka Kanbi (KU)
Mapilla (CO)
Mappila (TC)
Mappilla (MD)
Marasi (UP)
Maratha (HY)
Marati (CO)
Maravan (MY)
Maravan (TC)
Maravar (MD)
Mari (SA)
Marich, Marwar Baori, Marwar Waghri, 17) (BO)
Markanda (BI)
Maruthuvar, Medara, Medavar, Melakarar, Mirgani Domb (MD)
Marwada (KU)
Marwada, Maldhari (SA)
Masan Jogi, Medari (HY)
Masania Jogi (DE)
Matak Moran (AS)
Mathuiar (BI)
Matial (WB)
Matva (SA)
Maulik (BI)
Mauriari (BI)
Mavi (MB)
Me (KU)
Me, Medar (BO)
Meda (MY)
Medara, Mehtar (BI)
Medara, Mekala Golla (OR)
Meengar (fishermen in, Karnataka) (HY)
Mehara (RA)
Mehrat, Meghwanshi (AJ)
Mehtar (Muslim), Mera, Momin (HY)
Mehtar, Mirdha, Momin (VP)
Memar, Raj (DE)
Mena (Outside Alwar, Bundi, Bharatpur, Dholpur and Udaipur division, excluding Jahajpur Tehsil, Miras (RA)
Meo, Mewati, Mewati (DE)
Mer (BO)
Mer (KU)
Mer (SA)
Merani (KU)
Merasi, Miras (RA)
Merasi, Mirasi, Mirasi (DE)
Merat (RA)
Merh Rajput (PU)
Meru Kshatriya, Mirgani Domb (AP)
Met (RA)
Metapathi Pandaram-Veerasaiva, Vairagi, Vairavi, Veerasaiva, Yogeswar (TC)
Mettan (TC)
Mewati (BH)
Mewati, Mina (MB)
Mewati, Momin, Murai, Naddaf, Nai, Naik, Naqqal, Nandbai, Nat, Niyaria, Nunia (UP)
Mewati, Rachband (PU)
Mhali, Nai/Nhavi (MP)
Mina (BH)
Mina (BO)
Mina (PP)
Mina (PU)
Mina, Mirdha (MP)
Mina, Nagarchi (AJ)
Minka, Momin (OR)
Mirasi (PP)

Mirasi (PU)
Mirasi, Mirdhan, Momin (MB)
Mirdha, Momin, Naddaf (BH)
Miriasin, Mirshikar (BI)
Mirshikar (WB)
Miyana (KU)
Miyana, Sanghadi (SA)
Mochi (Excluding those, in S. C.), Momin, Murai, Murao, Nat (Excluding those in S. C.), Nai (DE)
Mochi (in Gujarat), Modikar (BO)
Mochi (KU)
Mochi (PU)
Mochi (SA)
Mochi, Naik, Nai (PP)
Modak, Momin, Moran (AS)
Modakmera, Modi, Nichundia Modi, Modi (BI)
Modi Banda (MD)
Modi Randa (AP)
Mogaveera (S. Kanara) (MD)
Moger (BO)
Mogia, Nagarchi, Nai (RA)
Mohani (BI)
Moili (S. Kanara) (MD)
Momin (BI)
Momin (WB)
Momin, Julaha, Nai/Nhavi (MP)
Mond-Golla (MD)
Mondi-vogola (AP)
Mondiwaru (HY)
Moniagar (Tinnevelly, Madura Distts.), Moopanar (MD)
Moothakammala Musuka, Balija (MD)
Moranjhiria (BO)
Morao, Murai (UP)
Morapora Brahmin (WB)
Moria (AS)
Muchhia (MB)
Mudiraj, Mutharasi (HY)
Muduva (MD)
Mug (WB)
Mukhari (MD)
Mukhi (AS)
Muli, Muliya, Muliya, Muniyani (MD)
Multani (HY)
Multani (MY)
Multani (RA)
Mund Patta (AP)
Munda (SA)
Mundama, Naddaf (BI)
Munnoorwar, Munnoorkapu, Munnoorkapu (BO)
Munnur, Munnurkapu, Munnurkapu, Mutharasi (HY)
Murli Vaghya (BO)
Murraha, Murha (VP)
Mussavar (PU)
Musukunta Nadu Vellala, (Tanjore Distt.) (MD)
Mutracha (MD)
Mutracha, Nagavamsam (AP)
Muttakkampatti (MD)
Muttiriyan (MD)
Myadara (HY)

Nabha (BO)
Nadar Hindu (TC)
Nador (BO)
Nagaram (AP)
Nagaram, Nagavamsam (MD)
Nagartha (MY)
Naghori, Nai, Naikmakkalu, Naikwadi (BO)
Nahar, Nai, Napit, Niari (OR)
Nai (AJ)
Nai (BH)
Nai (MB)
Nai, Nath (HP)
Nai, Nunia (VP)
Naicken (TC)
Naik (MB)
Naik (RA)
Naiko (TR)
Naita, Nayata (MB)
Naiya, Namasudra (BI)
Najjar, Naqqashi, Natuva (HY)
Nakkale (AP)
Nalband (BI)
Nalband (PU)
Nalband (WB)
Nalband, Nayak (DE)
Namdev Maharatta (North, Arcot Distt.), Nainar (MD)
Namdev Mahratta (AP)
Namdhari, Namdhari Paik, Numdhari Paik (BO)
Nandiwale (BO)

Nanga (BO)
Nangar (BO)
Nangraj, Narwekar (BO)
Napit (AS)
Napit (TR)
Napit, Nai, Nai (MA)
Napit, Nat (WB)
Napita (CO)
Naqqal, Nishad (DE)
Nar, Naï, Naik (PU)
Narikoravan, Nathanman (MD)
Nat (BH)
Nat (BO)
Nat and Nattadas, Nath (TR)
Nat, Nath (MP)
Nat, Navda, Nayata (MB)
Nat, Nichundia Modi (BI)
Nat-Bajania Bajigar (SA)
Nat-Bajania-Bzigar (KU)
Nath, Nath Panthi, Nayakaru (BO)
Nath, Nunia (BH)
Nath, Yogi (AS)
Nath, Yogi (WB)
Nathbawa (KU)
Nathbawa, Nhavi (SA)
Natuva (MY)
Navudian (MD)
Nayak (AJ)
Nayak (TR)
Nayak/Nayakda (MP)
Nayar (MY)
Nayer, Nhavi (BO)
Nayidaru (HY)
Nayinda (MY)
Neeli (HY)
Neelkanti, Nekar (HY)
Neria, Ode, Odiya (MB)
Neygi (MY)
Neyyalu (AP)
Nhavi (HY)
Niaria (RA)
Nilara (BO)
Nilgar (BO)
Nilgar, Rangrez (RA)
Nirshikari (AP)
Nirshikari (BO)
Nishad (Mallah Tyar, Bind, Khulvat Goria, Vankar, Bathua, Kewat, Manjhi), Quraish, Rajbanshi, Rarh, Rudra Paul of Cachar only (AS)
Noila (OR)
Nokkar (MD)
Noniya (BI)
Noongar, Panchal Brahman, Phool Mali (PU)
Nuhura, Nuhuraj, Nuhuraj, Oda Balifa (OR)
Nunia (TR)
Nut, Pinjara (BH)

Od (AJ)
Od (BO)
Od (KU)
Od (SA)
Odan (TC)
Oddar, Odde, Vadde, Veddai, Vodde, Oddc (MD)
Odde, Odder, Vadde, Veddai, Vodde (AP)
Odiya, Paddamali (AP)
Ojha (VP)
Omeyita (OR)
Oshthama (BO)
Otari (BO)
Otta Nicken, Pandaram Veerasaiva (TC)

Padamsali, Sali (BO)
Padaria, Pamaria, Pandara, Pandara, Pamaria (OR)
Padayachi (Villayan, Kuppan) (South Arcot, and Salem Distts.), Padmasali, Paiko Mali, Panikkar, Palli (MD)
Padhar, Padhiar (outside, Jhalawad District), Padhiar (SA)
Padharia (BO)
Padiar (BO)
Padka (MP)
Padmasali, Sali, Saliyan, Swakulasali (MY)
Padmasali, Sali/Sutsali, Salewer (MP)
Padmashali, Sale (HY)
Padti, Page (BO)
Pagi (In Karwar), Thakarda, Pakhali, Pamlor, Panchal (BO)
Pahar, Panwari, Payak, Pinjara, Purabia (MB)
Paidee, Paikomali (AP)
Paik (TR)

Paiko (OR)
Paisari Bania (BI)
Pakhali Bhisti (KU)
Pakhali-Bhisti (SA)
Pal (OR)
Pala Ekari (AP)
Palavyakula Kshatriya, Palle Kapu, Pallc Reddi (AP)
Palhari (MP)
Palli (OR)
Pamaria (BI)
Pamaria (UP)
Pamula (AP)
Pan (TR)
Panchkalashi (BO)
Pancholi (BO)
Panda (of Uttarakhand, only) (UP)
Pandaram (MY)
Pandaran (TC)
Pandither (TC)
Pando (BI)
Pangadikara (AP)
Pangania (BI)
Panguas (OR)
Pangul (BO)
Pangul (HY)
Panjira (OR)
Panka (MP)
Panka (VP)
Panki (TR)
Pannayar, Panniyar, Panniyar, Parakavakulam (MD)
Panthi, Patit Brahmin (WB)
Panura (BO)
Parasher (MP)
Paravathara Jakulam, Pattanavan, Sambadavar. (MD)
Pardeshi Bhampta (BO)
Pardeshi Thakur, Parit (BO)
Pardhi (HY)
Pareet (HY)
Parel Madivala, Parimalaikallan (MD)
Pargha (BI)
Parivar (MY)
Parivarbunt (MD)
Parkha, Patanwadia (BO)
Parthi (MP)
Parumban (TC)
Pasi (TR)
Patara, Patra (OR)
Pategar (BO)
Pathara (UP)
Patharphora, Sangtarash, Prajapati, Prade, Panjara, Qalandar, Qussab, Quraishi (DE)
Patharvat (BO)
Patharwat (HY)
Pathrut, Patne (BO)
Pathuria, Patra (OR)
Patka/Patki, Patwa, Patwa (MP)
Patkar (HY)
Patnulkaran, Pattanavan (MD)
Patradavaru (BO)
Pattaria, Saliya (TC)
Pattariyar (Tinnevelly and, Madura Distts.), Pattusali, Paddamali (MD)
Pattasali, pattusali, Pattusali (OR)
Pattunulkaran (AP)
Patua (WB)
Paturia (UP)
Patvckar (BO)
Patwa (DE)
Patwa Bania (BI)
Patwa, Pawaria, Qassab (UP)
Patwa, Phadal (RA)
Patwa, Qussab (VP)
Pavaiya, Pednekar (BO)
Payak (RA)
Pedditti Golla (AP)
Pceris (TC)
Pendhari (BO)
Penja, Pinja, Pinja, Rai (PP)
Perika (HY)
Perike (AP)
Perike Balija (AP)
Perki (MP)
Peruvannan (MD)
Phasechari (BO)
Phool Mali (HY)
Phudgi (BO)
Phulari (HY)
Picchigunta, Ponaka Domb (AP)
Pichakuntla (HY)
Pico higunta, Pillamar, Ponaka Domb (MD)
Pindara (MP)
Pinja, Prajapati, Ramaiya, Rai Sikh (PU)
Pinjara (HY)

Pinjara, Pinjari, Pinjari (BO)
Pinjara, Prajapati (SA)
Pinjara, Qassab, Rangaswami, Rangrez (RA)
Pinjari (HY)
Pinjari (MY)
Pinje, Phool Mali, Saini (HP)
Piraj Pota (BO)
Pirali (WB)
Pita, Punnu Golla, Quraishi, Radhi (OR)
Polia, Rajbansi, Resiya, Prajapati, Qureshi, Rajbanshi (BI)
Poosala (HY)
Poraya (Coimbatore Distt.) (MD)
Powar (MP)
Pradhan, Rangrez (BH)
Pulluvan (Malabar Distt.) (MD)
Punnan Vettuva Gowndar, Rajakambala Naicker (MD)
Puragiri Kshatriya (AP)
Pusala, Pusalavadu, Pusalavadu (AP)
Putligar (MP)

Qasa, Qassab, Quarashi, Qassab, Quraishi, Rangari, Rangrez, Rassiban (HY)
Qassab, Ramdasiya (MB)
Quraish, Rabari (BO)

Rabari (KU)
Rabari, Bhopa Rabari, (outside the Nesses area, in the forests of Alech, Gir and Barada) (SA)
Rachawar (MY)
Rachevar (BO)
Raddi (BO)
Radha (UP)
Raghvi, Raghvanshi (MP)
Rahwani, Rain, Rajbhar (UP)
Rai, Rehbari (RA)
Raighatwal (TR)
Raikari (BO)
Raj Pardhi (BO)
Rajaka (AP)
Rajamuria, Rangari (MP)
Rajapur (S. Karana), Reddi Ganiga (MD)
Rajgir (VP)
Rajput (CO)
Rajput (only in Kangra, District) (PU)

Ramaiya (UP)
Rami Mali (BO)
Ramoshi (BO)
Rangaraju (in Kurnool, Dist.) (AP)
Rangari (BO)
Rangraz (UP)
Rangraz, Raj, Rayee, Saini, Sagarwanshi Mali (DE)
Rangredh, Rangraz, Rangrez, Sain, Sansia (VP)
Rangres, Rayeens, Razzaqi (WB)
Rangrez (BI)
Rangrez (MP)
Rangrez (UP)
Rangrez, Ravidasiya (MB)
Ranguni (OR)
Rao (BH)
Raot/Rawt, Raoti (MP)
Rar (UP)
Raul, Ravalia, Rawal, Rawalyogi, Ravalia, Rawal, Rawalyogi (BO)
Rauniyar (UP)
Rautara, Sonar (UP)
Rautia, Rawani, Rayeen, Resiya (BI)
Raval (KU)
Raval (SA)
Rawa (UP)
Rawat (AJ)
Rawat (BO)
Rawat (MY)
Rawat (RA)
Rebari (AJ)
Reddi (Ganjam) (AP)
Reddi of Reddika origin (AP)
Reddi, Reddika, Reddika (OR)
Rehar, Rehara, Rer, Rehara, Rer, Saini (PU)
Rengi Reju (OR)
Rohangia, Roshangia, Roshangia (WB)
Rohar (MP)
Rona (AP)
Rona (MD)
Rona (OR)
Routia (OR)
Ruchbandhia (MP)
Runiar Bania (BI)
Rupai, Sabdakar (TR)

Sad, Santia, Santia (RA)

Sadar, Sali, Saliyan (MY)
Sadh, Singharia (UP)
Sadhu (AJ)
Sadhu Chetty, 24 Manai, Teluga Chetty, Teluga, Chetty (AP)
Sadhu Chetty, Teluga, Chetty, 24 Manai Telugu, Chetty, 24 Manai Telugu Chetty, (MD)
Sagar (BO)
Sagar (SA)
Sagar, Uppara (HY)
Sagara, Uppara (AP)
Sagara, Uppara, Sarayakara, Sale, Sali, Saliyan, Sambadavar (MD)
Sagarpesha, Sakaldarpee Brahman, (OR)
Saha, Sahu, Suri, Sahu (AS)
Saha, Sain (WB)
Sahadev Joshi (BO)
Sain (BI)
Saini (BO)
Sais/Sayees, Shis, Salewar, Sali/Sutsali (MP)
Saisutar, Zalawadi (BO)
Saiz, Sakka, Sangtarash, Santhia (DE)
Sakka (HP)
Sakka, Sagarvanshi Mali, Saini (RA)
Sakravar, Saliya (TC)
Sakulashali, Sale (HY)
Salat (excluding Sompur, Salat) (SA)
Salat (Excluding Sompura, Salat) (KU)
Salat, Salat Waghri, Sali, Sangameshwari (BO)
Sali, Salia, Salia, Sani (OR)
Sali, Salvi (MB)
Saliyan (Padamsali, Pattusali, Senapathulu, Kauni Bhaktulu, Sale, Thogata, Sali, Kerikal, Bhaktulu) (AP)
Saloi (AS)
Sandhi (SA)
Sangar (BO)
Sanghar, Sai (KU)
Sangtrash (HY)
Saniyar (MY)
Sanjogi, Sankuri, Sansia (BO)
Sankhakar, Sankheru, Sankheru, Satchasi (WB)
Sankhari (OR)
Sanoria (BH)
Sansi (OR)
Sanyasi, Sapera (BI)
Sapera (AJ)
Sarania (BO)
Sarania (SA)
Saranjia (MP)
Sarbaria (BI)
Sarekari, Sargara (BO)
Sarki (Nepali) (AS)
Sarki (Nepali) (MA)
Saroda (BO)
Sarvade (BO)
Sarwan (BO)
Satani, Sharigaru (HY)
Satani, Swakulsali (MY)
Satarkar (BO)
Sathwara (KU)
Sathwara (SA)
Satiaya, Sindhi (RA)
Saunta, Sauta, Saita (BI)
Sauntis (OR)
Savar, Sayar, Sayar (WB)
Scheduled Castes converted to Christianitv (AP)
Scheduled Castes converted to Christanity (MY)
Scheduled Castes converted to Christianity (TC)
Scheduled Castes converted to Christianity (VP)
Scheduled Castes converted, to Christianity (HY)
Scheduled Castes, converted to Christianity (MD)
Scheduled Tribes in three areas when they leave, their habitat and settle, in others' parts of Assam (AS)
Sedar (MD)
Seerithigoudu, Senapathulu (MD)
Segidi (OR)
Sehar, Sonsi, Sevak, Sindhi (RA)
Senaikudyan, Senaithalaivar, Senaithalaivar (MD)
Senia, Setti Balija, Shanan, Sheragara Kshatriya of, S.Kanara, Sirkudi Pillai (MD)
Setti Ralija (of Vizag, East and West Godavari, Krishna Distts.), Setti Balija (AP)
Shedia (KU)

Sheikhras (BI)
Sherogar (BO)
Shikari (BO)
Shikkaligar, Shimpi (BO)
Shimpi (HY)
Shimpi (KU)
Shimpiga (HY)
Shorgir (PP)
Shorgir (PU)
Siddi (BO)
Siddi (Outside Nesses, area in the forests of, Alech, Gir and Barada) (SA)
Sidi (KU)
Sikh (AJ)
Sikh (KU)
Sikh (TC)
Sikh Harijan (AP)
Sikh Harijan (AS)
Sikh Harijan (MA)
Sikh Harijans (BH)
Sikh Harijans (BI)
Sikh Harijans (CO)
Sikh Harijans (HY)
Sikh Harijans (MY)
Sikh Harijans (OR)
Sikh Scheduled Castes (MD)
Sikhs (BO)
Sikhs (DE)
Sikhs (PP)
Sikhs (PU)
Sikhs (RA)
Sikhs (SA)
Sikhs (TR)
Sikhs (VP)
Sikhs (WB)
Sikligar (AJ)
Sikligar (PU)
Sikligar (RA)
Sikligar (VP)
Sikligar, Singhiwala (MB)
Singhikaut, Singhiwals, Singhiwals, Tamera, Tank, Tarkhan (PP)
Singhiwala, Singhikaut, Singhikaut (PU)
Singiwala, Sonar, Sunkar (MP)
Sinkos (OR)
Sirkiwala, Sonsi (RA)
Sithula (OR)
Sitria (OR)
Situlia (OR)
Siviar (Coimbatore, Distt.) (MD)
Siyal (BO)
Siyane (MB)
Soeri, Sonar, Sorahiya (UP)
Soi, Tamboli (PU)
Solangi (BO)
Somakshatriya (HY)
Sonar (DE)
Sonar (HY)
Sonar (MB)
Sonar, Sunar, Sunar (MA)
Sonar, Sutar, Tamboli, Tamera (VP)
Sonar, Swarnakar (WB)
Sonar, Swarnakar, Swarnakar (BI)
Sondhia, Tamboli (MB)
Soni (KU)
Sonowal, Sudra Das, Suri (AS)
Sourashtra (TC)
Sourashtra, Surithimar, Telaga, Teluga Chetty (MD)
Sourastera (AP)
Sozhia Chetty (MD)
Srisayana (AP)
Suda (OR)
Sudgadsidda (BO)
Sudugadusiddha (HY)
Sukiar (BI)
Sukuli, Tanti (OR)
Suleru (BO)
Sulia (OR)
Sumra (KU)
Sumra (SA)
Sunagar (BO)
Sunar, Tamboli (BH)
Sundi (BI)
Sundi, Sutradhar (OR)
Sunkar (MP)
Sunkar, Taga Bhat (UP)
Suppalig (BO)
Surabhi Janga (HY)
Surhi Bania, Tamboli, Tamoli, Thathera (BI)
Sut (AS)
Sutar (RA)
Sutar, Suthar, Suthar (BO)
Sutar, Tamboli, Tamera/Tambatkar, Telugu Mannarkapu (MP)
Sutar, Wadhai (HY)
Suthar (SA)

Suthria (from Sind) (BO)
Sutradhar (TR)
Sutradhar, Swarnakar (WB)
Suwar (BO)
Swakula Sali (AP)

Taga, Tagah, Tagah, Tank, Tarkhan, Tamboli (DE)
Taga, Vanzara (PU)
Tak Bodar, Telaga (AP)
Takankar, Talvar including Kanade, Talvar (BO)
Takari (BO)
Tamadia Purana (OR)
Tambat (BO)
Tamboli (RA)
Tamboli, Tamuli, Tamuli (MA)
Tamboli, Tandel, Targala (BO)
Tambuli, Tamli, Tamli (WB)
Tamil (OR)
Tammali (HY)
Tamoli (UP)
Tana, Tanti (OR)
Tank (AJ)
Tanti, Tantri, Tantripal, Tantri, Tantripal (AS)
Tanti, Tantubaya, Tantubaya (WB)
Tantuvai, Tatwan, Tanwar, Tatwan, Teli, Thathera, Tirgar (UP)
Tapodhan Brahmin (BO)
Targala Bhavaya (KU)
Targala, Bhavaya (SA)
Tariatai (KU)
Tariatai (SA)
Tarkada (SA)
Tarkhan (if not Harijan) (HP)
Tarkhan (PU)
Taru (BO)
Tatapu (AP)
Tati, Tanti, Tanti (TR)
Tatiyajan (AS)
Tavate (BO)
Tawaif (MB)
Tea-garden labourers (AS)
Tea-garden labourers (TR)
Telaga (CO)
Telaga (OR)
Telaga of Telagu (HY)
Telaga Pamula (AP)
Telegu Banjig (BO)
Telegu Madiraj (BO)
Telegu Munnoorwar, Teli (BO)
Telenga Pamola (OR)
Teli (AJ)
Teli (BH)
Teli (BI)
Teli (HY)
Teli (if not Harijan) (HP)
Teli (MA)
Teli (MB)
Teli (Nepali) (AS)
Teli (Nepali) (MA)
Teli (Nepali) (WB)
Teli (OR)
Teli (PU)
Teli (VP)
Teli (WB)
Teli, Temara, Thathera, Thathiar (DE)
Teli, Thathera (MP)
Teli, Thathera, Thori, Tori (PP)
Teli, Thathera, Ved (RA)
Teli, Yogi (AS)
Telikula, Teluga Chetty (AP)
Telunga Patty Chetty (MD)
Tenugollu (HY)
Thakar, Thakarda (BO)
Thakarda (KU)
Thakarda (SA)
Thakurhar (BO)
Thambat (HY)
Thambatgar (HY)
Thami (HP)
Thami, Vaidyanai (MB)
Thandal Vannan, Thiya (TC)
Thanwar, Wasdeo (VP)
Thanwin (HP)
Thanwin (PU)
Thatari (OR)
Thathera, Kasera, Thori, Turi (PU)
Theba (KU)
Thegotaveerkshatriya (AP)
Thetwar (MP)
Thiyya (Malabar Distt.), Thogata (MD)
Thogti (HY)
Tholuva-Naicker, Vettala, Karanaicker (MD)
Thondaiman (TC)
Thori (BO)

Thoroya (CO)
Thoti Burud, Thuria (MP)
Thottai Naickan (MD)
Thottiyar (TC)
Thuria (OR)
Thurpu Kapu (AP)
Thurpukapu (MD)
Tiar (BI)
Tigala (BO)
Tigala (Tigla), Tigla, Ummia, Uppara (AP)
Tigala, Tigla, Tigla (MD)
Tigala, Vanniya Kulu, Kshatriya (MY)
Tikulhara, Vishwakarma, Yadav (BI)
Tili (WB)
Timaliya (BO)
Tippera (WB)
Tirgar (BO)
Tirguli, Tirmali (BO)
Tirmale (MP)
Tirwalli, Turha, Waddar (MP)
Tiyar (UP)
Tiyaro, Togara (OR)
Tondaman, Ummia, Uppara (MD)
Traditional Buddhists (WB)
Tudug-Waddar, Uchlia (BO)
Tulleru, Uppara (HY)
Tulukkan (TC)
Turha (BI)
Turha, Yadav, Yogi (WB)
Turi, Yogi (TR)

Udasi (BO)
Ulra (BO)
Umar Bania, Vishwakarma (UP)
Uppar (BO)
Uppara, Vanniyakula Kshatriya (MY)
Ural Goundan, Urali Nair, Vadde (MD)

Vada Baliza of Ganjam, and Vizag Distts., Veddai, Vadde (AP)
Vaddar (BO)
Vadhala (KU)
Vadhala (SA)
Vadi (BO)
Vadugan Vaduvan, Vaduvan (MD)
Vadugan, Vaduvan, Vaduvan (AP)
Vadukan, Vairagi, Vairavi (TC)
Vagher (BO)
Vagher (KU)
Vagher (SA)
Vaghra (KU)
Vaghri (BO)
Vaghri (SA)
Vaidu (BO)
Vaishya Thakur (BO)
Vaiti (BO)
Vakkal (in Kanara Distt.), Valhar, Valmiki, Vanjara, Vanjari (BO)
Vakkaliga (MD)
Valaian (MD)
Valan (N. Malabar) (MD)
Valand (KU)
Valand (SA)
Valimiki of Rayalaseema, Vanne Reddi (AP)
Valla Nagam, Veddai (MD)
Vaniar (MD)
Vaniyan, Vathi (TC)
Vanjara (SA)
Vankar Khatri (BO)
Vannan, Vanniyakula Kshatriya, (MD)
Vanniar, Vanni Kapu, Vanni Kulakshatriya, Viswa Brahman, Vishwakarma, Vodde (AP)
Vanza (BO)
Vanza (KU)
Vanza (SA)
Vanzara (KU)
Varala (HY)
Vasudeo (HY)
Vasudev (BO)
Vathi (MD)
Vavad (SA)
Vedva Gaghri (SA)
Velaan, Veera Saiva (TC)
Velakatalavan (MD)
Velama (OR)
Veluthadan (Malabar) (MD)
Veluthdan, Veluthedathu, Nair (TC)
Verna Golla (OR)
Vettikaran, Vettalakara Naickers, (MD)
Vettuva Gownder (MD)
Vidur (BO)
Vijantri (BO)
Vilakkathala Nair (TC)
Vilakkathalavan (TC)
Vilkurup (MD)

Vilkurup (TC)
Vina Tulavina, Yadava, Yogi (OR)
Vir (BO)
Virakodi Vellalar, Viswa Brahmin, Viswakarma, Vodde, Yadava (MD)
Viramushti (HY)
Viswakarma (MY)
Viswakarmala (TC)
Vokkaliga (CO)
Vokkaliga (only from, rural areas) (MY)
Vokkaliga, Wodayar, Yadava (AP)
Vyasokta (WB)

Wadar (HY)
Wadari (BO)
Waddar (HY)
Waddara, Wadhai (HY)
Wadla (HY)
Waghri Pardhi (BO)
Wanha (MP)
Wanham (BO)
Wansfoda (BO)
Warthi, Yadav (HY)

Yadava (MY)
Yadava, Yogoeswarar (TC)
Yaklar, Zalawadi (BO)
Yerkilwar, Yerkula (MP)
Yoggeeswara (MD)

Zharekari (BO)

15

The List of Other Backward Classes Enumerated in the Second Backward Classes Commission (Mandal)

Alphabatical list to facilitate users to identify the backward class in respective States.

ABBREVIATIONS USED FOR THE STATES

ANDAMAN & NICOBAR ISLANDS	AN
ANDHRA PRADESH	AP
ARUNACHAL PRADESH	AR
ASSAM	AS
BIHAR	BI
CHANDIGARH	CH
DADRA AND NAGAR HAVELI	DN
DELHI	DE
GOA, DAMAN & DIU	GD
GUJARAT	GU
HARYANA	HR
HIMACHAL PRADESH	HP
JAMMU & KASHMIR	JK
KARNATAKA	KA
KERALA	KE
MADHYA PRADESH	MP
MAHARASHTRA	MR
MANIPUR	MA
MEGHALAYA	ME
MIZORAM	MI
ORISSA	OR
PONDICHERRY	PO
PUNJAB	PU
RAJASTHAN	RA
SIKKIM	SI
TAMIL NADU	TN
TRIPURA	TR
UTTAR PRADESH	UP
WEST BENGAL	WB

Abbasi, Bhishti, Sakka (DE)
Abdal (BI)
Acharaj, Panchal-Brahman, Changar (CH)
Achari, Viswakarma, Kammalar, Thattan, Thatchan, Porkollar, Assari, Chary (TN)
Acharya, Acharji (WB)
Achukatlavandhu (AP)
Achukatlavandlu (PO)
Adhiri (BI)
Adhori (MP)
Adi Karnataka (AP)
Adi-Dravida (OR)
Adi-Karnataka (OR)
Adidharmi (MP)
Adikari (WB)
Adikarnataka (MP)
Adiya (excluding Coorg District) (KA)
Adodia (GU)
Agamudayar of Southern Tamil Distts. belonging to Mukkulathers, Agamudayar of Northern Tamil Distts., Thozhu or Thuluva Vellala (TN)
Agamudiyas (including Thuluva Vellalas) (PO)
Agamundi (AP)
Agaria, Agariya (TR)
Agaria, Agariya (WB)
Agariya (BI)
Agaru (AP)
Agaru, Jurakula (PO)
Agasa (KE)
Agasa (PO)
Agasa, Madivala, Sakala, Sakalavadu, Shakala, Tsakala, Vannan, Dhobi, Parit, Rajaka (KA)
Ager (RA)
Aghamudayar, Vellari, Madali, Agahamudaya, Aghambadiar, Barichatty, Kondaliyar, Palegaru (AP)
Agharia, Agaria, Aghria (OR)
Aghore (WB)
Aghori, Karkarmunda (KA)
Agnani (KA)
Agnikula Kshatriya (Pallekapu, Palloreddi, Vannekapu, Vannereddi) (PO)
Agradana, Agradani (WB)
Agri (DN)
Agri (GU)
Agri (UP)
Agri Kharwal (DE)
Agri, Agale or Kolan (MR)
Aguri — Vaishya, Sudi, Halwai, Roniyar, Pansari, Modi, Kasera, Kesarwani, Kathera, Siduriya-Bania, Mahuro-Vaishya-Awadh-Bania, Kaith-Bania (BI)
Aheri (MP)
Aheria, Aheri, Heri, Naik, Thori, Turi (HP)
Aheria, Aheri, Heri, Naik, Thori. Turi (PU)
Aheria, Aheri, Naik, Heri (CH)
Aheria, Aheriya (UP)
Aheria, Ahiria, Heri, Aheri, Naik, Thori, Turi (HR)
Ahir (Yadav, Gope) (RA)
Ahir, Ayar-Boricha, Yadav (GU)
Ahir, Bharvad, Yadav (DN)
Ahir, Gavala, Goala, Gwal, Kansa, Thakur, Jadav, Yadav (MP)
Ahir, Gawala, Gowala, Rao, Yadav (HR)
Ahir, Ghosi, Gwala, Yaduvanshi/Yadav (UP)
Ahir, Goala, Gope, Sadgope, Yadav, Gola, Gawar (WB)
Ahir, Yadav, Gowli (MR)
Ahir, Yadav, Gwala (CH)
Ahir, Yadav, Gwala (DE)
Ahir, Yadav, Gwala (MA)
Ahom (AS)
Ahom (ME)
Aiyanavar (TN)
Ajila (AP)
Ajila (OR)
Alavan (KE)
Alavan, Alavar, Alwar and Azhavar (TN)
Alitkar (MR)
Alwar (PO)
Amaat (BI)
Amant, Amat, Amath (WB)
Ambalagars (TN)

Ambalakaran (PO)
Ambalakaran, Ambalakarar, Vallamber (TN)
Ambalakarma, Ambalakaran (KA)
Ambalakkaran (KE)
Ambika (PO)
Amblar, Ambathan, Ambithan, Ezhavatery, Kalrnikurup, Maruthuvar, Naiken, Pandithar Villakkithalanavi (KE)
Ampattan (KE)
Ampattan (TN)
Anandan (PO)
Andh (KA)
Andipandaram (TN)
Andipandaran (PO)
Anduram (KA)
Anglo Indian (PO)
Anglo-Indian (KE)
Ansari (Muslim) (WB)
Ansari (UP)
Ansari, Julai (Muslims) (KA)
Apatani (MI)
Arain (PU)
Arain, Rayee, Kunjra (DE)
Arakh (UP)
Aranadan (KA)
Aranedan (OR)
Aravala (AP)
Arayan (Nulayan), Araya (PO)
Arayan, Arayar (Nulayar) (TN)
Arayas (KE)
Arayavathi (TN)
Arayavathis (KE)
Archak Brahmins (AP)
Archakari Vellala (TN)
Archakatalavandu (PO)
Ard-Pop (HP)
Are Mahrati (PO)
Are-Marathi (AP)
Arekatika, Katika (AP)
Aremaharti (KE)
Arundatilu (H) (AN)
Arunthuthiyar (OR)
Arya (KE)
Arya (PO)
Arya Mala (AS)
Arya, Dingra (HP)
Aryakshatriya, Chittari, Chitrakara, Giniyar, Nakahs (AP)
Aryan (KE)
Aryavathi Nairuseri) (PO)
Asada (RA)
Asara (MP)
Asur (AS)
Asur (OR)
Asur (TR)
Atagara (AP)
Atagara, Atagora (PO).
Atar (AP)
Atar (KA)
Atar (MR)
Atazri (KA)
Athiya (MP)
Audhie, Avadhi (MP)
Audhiya (MP)
Audhiya (MR)
Auji (UP)
Ayyanavar (where they are not Scheduled Castes) (TN)

Baagawan Tamboli (Muslims) (KA)
Badaga (AP)
Badaga (KA)
Badaga (KE)
Badaga (OR)
Badaga (PO)
Badaga (TN)
Badagar (TN)
Badak (MP)
Badak (MR)
Badak (UP)
Badaka (MP)
Badasuda (OR)
Badera (RA)
Badhai, Ade-Gaur, Chaurasia, Pansari, Sutar, Suthar, Tudolia, Viswakarma (MP)
Badhai, Badai, Barahi, Dhiman, Jhangra-Brahman, Khati, Kondal, Ramgarhia, Tarkhan, Taryal, Vishwakarma (HP)
Badhai, Barhai, Bindhania, Sutradhar, Badhira and Badhria (OR)
Badhai, Barhai, Khati, Tarkhan, Jangra-Brahmin, Viswakarma (DE)
Badhi, Barhai, Dhiman-Brahman (CH)
Badi (DE)

Badi (MP)
Badi (Nepali) (MA)
Badi (Nepali) (WB)
Badi, Chinaora, Melori, Odmata, Uranamara (HP)
Badia (MR)
Badia, Beaja, Biria, Dukar, Kolthati, Kolhati (MP)
Badigar (MP)
Badwa (RA)
Badyakar, Dhuli, Nagarchi, Sabdakar (TR)
Bafan (Muslims) (GU)
Baffand (JK)
Bag (WB)
Bagal (WB)
Bagal, Batalian, Bhut, Dangi, Dhame, Hir, Harbansia, Jalaria, Kaushal, Manadia, Marbansia, Manem, Masaun, Mehton, Mule, Nagia, Parmar, Sangutva, Sial, Thunalia (PU)
Bagalu (AP)
Bagalu (KA)
Bagalu (MR)
Bagaria (CH)
Bagaria (HR)
Bagata (KA)
Bagata (KE)
Bagata (TN)
Bagdi (Marwar Baori, Marwar, Waghri, Salat Waghri) (MR)
Bagdiya (RA)
Bagdo (BI)
Baghia, Baree, Bawar, Payak, Vaidyanai (MP)
Bagria (HP)
Bagria, Bagaria (PU)
Bahari (CH)
Bahelia (TR)
Bahti (HP)
Bahurupi (MP)
Bahurupi (MR)
Baiga (AS)
Baijara (AS)
Bailapatar, Bailaptar, Bikapatar (KA)
Baipari (OR)
Baira (KA)
Baira (OR)
Bairagi (DE)
Bairagi (MP)
Bairagi (OR)
Bairagi (UP)
Bairagi, Baregi (PU)
Bairagi, Bava, Bavaji, Byragi, Bavani (KA)
Bairagi. Gosai, Udasi (MR)
Bairi (UP)
Bairwa, Berwa (DE)
Baishnab (TR)
Baishya Kapali (WB)
Baiti (TR)
Bajadar, Bajania, Bedey (WB)
Bajania (MR)
Bajania, Bajenia (KA)
Bajania, Kannatia (MP)
Bajel (SI)
Bajgar (MP)
Bajigar (MR)
Bajigar (UP)
Bakad, Bant (RA)
Bakadra (KA)
Bakerwal, Bakkarwal (JK)
Bakharia (UP)
Bakuda (AP)
Bakuda (OR)
Balasanthanam (AP)
Balasanthanam (KA)
Balasanthanam (MR)
Balasanthoshi (KA)
Balasanthu, Bahurupi (AP)
Balasaria, Bhagat, Bhara, Gagan, Kanwan, Kawandal, Kawdeya, Khiri, Kunkani, Loda, Lodha, Lodia, Mandi, Niwan, Ramka, Thira (HR)
Balija (AN)
Balija, Bajajiga, Naidu, Bogam Telaga, Telaga, Balaja, Setty Balija, Kasban, Munnur, Mutrasi, Matracha, Janapan, Balegara (KA)
Balolika (PO)
Banchada (RA)
Bandara (AP)
Bandari (KE)
Bandi (AP)
Bandi (MR)
Bandi (OR)
Bandi (UP)
Banerwala (DE)

Banjara (AS)
Banjara (WB)
Banjara, Banjara Nats, Lobana, Vanjara, Kanjar, Kanchan (HR)
Banjara, Banjare, Nal, Naik, Nayak, Kangi, Sirkiband, Labana, Dhan-kute Banjara, Banjara Sikh, Brijwasi (UP)
Banjara, Banjari, Vanjara, Mathura Banjara (A), Goar Banjara, Lambada/Lambara, Lambhani, Charan Banjara, Labhan, Mathura Labhani, Kuchikiwale Banjaras, Laman Banjara, Laman/Lamani, Laban, Dhali/Dhalia, Dhadi/Dhari, Singaris, Navi Banjaras, Jogi Banjaras, Banjari, Shingde, Banjara, Lambade, Phanade Banjara, Sunar Banjara, Dhalya-Banjara, Shingadya Banjara (MR)
Banjara, Gamalia, Baladia, Sirkiwala, Labana or Labhana, Manu Banjara, Bamania Banjara, Bagora, Digora (RA)
Banjara, Goar Banjara, Lambana/Lambara, Lambhani, Charan Banjara, Labham, Mathura Labhan, Kachitiwala Banjara, Laman Banjara, Laman/Lambani, Laban, Dhali/Dhalia, Dhadi/Dhari, Singari, Navi Banjara, Jogi Banjara, Banjari, Mathura Banjari, Bamania Banjara (MP)
Banjara, Gour (TR)
Banjara, Gour, Badi, Labana (JK)
Banjara, Lambadi, Lamani, Sugali (GD)
Banjogi (TR)
Banjogi (WB)
Banka (OR)
Banna, Bannagar (KA)
Banoudhiya-Rajput (CH)
Banpar (BI)
Bansphor (MA)
Bant (excluding Belgaum, Bijapur, Dharwar and North Kanara District) (KA)
Bantu (AP)
Bantu (KA)
Bantu (MR)
Banua, Buna, Bunna, Buno (WB)
Baoria (MP)
Baoria (MR)
Baragahi, Labana, Labhan, Lamame, Mathura, Nayakda, Thuria (MP)
Baragi, Bairagi (CH)
Baragi, Bairagi (HP)
Baragi, Bairagi (HR)
Baragiri (WB)
Barahar, Basod (RA)
Barai (BI)
Barai Jambali (MP)
Barai, Atwasa, Badhai, Baiwal, Dagesar, Dingar, Jungid-Brahman, Jhangra-Brahman, Kavigar, Khati, Kliokar, Mayal, Suthar, Tarkhan, Vishwakarma (RA)
Barai, Tamboli (CH)
Barai, Tamboli (DE)
Barai, Tamboli (HR)
Barai, Tarboli, Tamboli (PU)
Baraik (TR)
Barar (MP)
Barar (RA)
Barar (Umati) (AN)
Barari (MP)
Barchain, Chai, Chain (WB)
Barda (KA)
Barda (RA)
Bargi (MP)
Bargunda (RA)
Barhai (AS)
Barhai, Badhai, Barai, Chauvasia, Jangid-Brahman, Khati, Kolash, Lote, Panchal, Tarkhan, Vishwakarma (UP)
Barhai, Kundera, Barhai Sutar (MP)
Barhi, Badhai, Bishwakarma, Khati, Sutradhar (WB)
Barhi, Bimrao, Dadoi, Dhawal, Dhiman, Jangiar, Jangid-Brahman, Jangra-Brahmin, Khati, Kashyap, Manithiya, Rajotia, Ramgarhia, Suthar, Tarkhan, Viswakarma (HR)
Barhunda (MP)
Bari (BI)
Bari (DE)
Bari (UP)
Bari or Barai (MR)
Bari, Baree (MP)
Baria (AP)
Baria (AS)
Baria (MP)
Baria, Koli Baria (MR)

Bariji or Barui (OR)
Barika, Bhandari, Beja, Napit and Nai (OR)
Bariki (KA)
Bariki (KE)
Bariki (TN)
Barjubi (AS)
Barjubi (ME)
Barlur (KA)
Barma (HR)
Barna-Brahmin, Patit-Brahmin (WB)
Baro (WB)
Baroi (AS)
Baroi (MP)
Baroi, Barui (ME)
Barot, Vahivancha (GU)
Barra (CH)
Barra (HR)
Barui (AS)
Barui (TR)
Barui, Barujibi (WB)
Barwar (CH)
Barwar (HR)
Barwar (PU)
Basdewa, Vasdev, Vasudewa (MP)
Basor (AS)
Basor (RA)
Baspher (TR)
Basphor (AS)
Basphor (BI)
Basudev, Harbola, Jaga, Kaparia, Kapdi (MP)
Batera (PU)
Bathal, Battal, Batler, Battar (KA)
Bathi (CH)
Bathini (AP)
Bathini (KA)
Bathini (MR)
Bathudi (WB)
Battada (AP)
Battada (KA)
Battada (KE)
Battada (OR)
Battada (TN)
Battera (HR)
Batterha (CH)
Batterha (HP)
Baura (UP)
Bauri (AS)
Bauri (TR)
Bauria (DE)
Bauriah (UP)
Bavacha, Bamcha (RA)
Bavcha (MR)
Baver (MP)
Bavocha (GU)
Bavri or Baori (GU)
Bavuri (KA)
Bavuri (KE)
Bavuri (TN)
Bawa, Atit Bawa, Bharathari, Bharti, Deshnami Bawa, Dhashnam, Gangajalia, Giri, Gosai, Goswami, Ramanandi, Kapdi, Margi, Nath Bawa, Puri, Vairagi Bawa (GU)
Bawari (RA)
Bawaria (MP)
Bawtar (KA)
Bayar (UP)
Bazgar, Bazigar (UP)
Bazigar (JK)
Bazigar (KA)
Bazigar, Nat, Kalandar (excluding those in S.C.) (DE)
Beda (Drum-beaters/Pipers) (JK)
Beda (HP)
Beda, Bedaru, Valimiki, Barki Bedar, Privara, Bendar, Boya, Bedar, Nayaka, Bedar Nayak, Naikomakkalu, Naikwadi, Palegar, Romoshi, Talwar, Valmiki, Valmikimakkalu, Vedan (KA)
Beddi (AS)
Bedia (AS)
Bedia (UP)
Bedia, Bediya (TR)
Begari (AP)
Begari (KA)
Begari, Bedar, Berad, Naikawadi, Talwar, Walmiki (MR)
Behana (UP)
Behha, Pinjara, Dhunia (MP)
Behurupi (KA)
Bekhada (BI)
Beldar (AS)
Beldar (TR)
Beldar, Bachgotra (BI)
Beldiya (BI)
Bellara (AP)

Bellara (KA)
Bellara (OR)
Bemariha (MP)
Bengali (MP)
Bentkar (BI)
Bentkar (OR)
Bentkar (WB)
Berad (Bedar) (KA)
Beri (Muslims) (KA)
Beria (CH)
Beria (HR)
Beria (KA)
Beria (MP)
Beria (PU)
Beriah (UP)
Berrer (PU)
Berua (TR)
Berua (WB)
Besdewa (MR)
Beshtar, Bunde-Bestar (KA)
Bestar, Sachaluwaddar (MR)
Bestha, Beztha (Jalarula Nagavadaity) (PO)
Bestha, Siviar (TN)
Bestha-Anikali, Jelare, Ratna Balaji, Uppila, Vade Balaji (AP)
Beta, Hensi, Hesi (CH)
Beta, Hensi, Hesi (HP)
Beta, Hensi, Hesi (PU)
Beta, Hersi or Hesi (HR)
Betare or Betra (OR)
Bhaat (MR)
Bhadbhunja (MR)
Bhadi-Waddar, Matti-Waddar, Waddar (MP)
Bhadre (MP)
Bhaduja (MP)
Bhaduria (MP)
Bhakta (TR)
Bhalia (GU)
Bhampta or Ghantichore or Pardesi, Pong, Dasar, Uchila, Rajput-Bhamta, Bhamta, Bhamti, Kumati, Pathrut, Takari, Uchale (MR)
Bhampta, Ghantichor, Pardesi-Bhampta (RA)
Bhamta (AP)
Bhamta, Bhamti, Bhanmate, Bhanta, Bhanmate (MP)
Bhamta, Bhompta, Pradeshi, Bhampta, Bhomtra, Takari, Uchillian, Rajput Bhamta (KA)
Bhamta, Pardeshi Bhamta (GU)
Bhand (CH)
Bhand (DE)
Bhand (JK)
Bhand (MP)
Bhand (MR)
Bhandari (GD)
Bhandari (MR)
Bhandura, Billawar (MR)
Bhangi (excluding those in Scheduled Caste) (WB)
Bhangi, Khakrob (Sweepers) (JK)
Bhania (OR)
Bhant (WB)
Bhanta (MR)
Bhantu (MP)
Bhanumati (RA)
Bhaot, Bhatraju, Bhatraj, Bohrot (KA)
Bhar (BI)
Bhar (TR)
Bhar (UP)
Bhar (WB)
Bharadi, Balasantoshi, Kinggriwale, Nathbava, Nath Jogi, Nath Panthi, Davari Gosavi (MR)
Bharai Tarkhan (JK)
Bharaik (AS)
Bharari (MP)
Bharatar (where they are not Scheduled Castes) (TN)
Bharbhooja (DE)
Bharbhuja (BI)
Bharbhuja (MP)
Bharbhuja, Bharbhunja, Kalenera (HR)
Bharbhuja, Bhujawala (WB)
Bharbhunja (CH)
Bharbhunja, Bharbhuja (HP)
Bharbhunja, Bharbhuja (PU)
Bhardi, Bharagi (KA)
Bharewa (MP)
Bhari, Rode (PU)
Bharia, Bharihar (MP)
Bharud (MP)
Bharud (RA)
Bharunja (JK)
Bharwad, Mota Bhai Bharwad, Nana

Bhai Bharwad, Kabari, Baria Mota Bhai, Chosla, Janapada (where they are not Scheduled Tribes) (GU)
Bhaskar (BI)
Bhat (DE)
Bhat (JK)
Bhat (WB)
Bhat, Bhatra, Charan, Darpi, Ramiya (HR)
Bhat, Bhatra, Darpi (HP)
Bhat, Bhatra, Darpi, Ramiya (CH)
Bhat, Charan (RA)
Bhat, Charan, Brahmbhat, Jasondhi, Mary, Maru, Sotiya, Salui, Salvi (MP)
Bhat/Bhatt (BI)
Bhathiara (Muslims) (BI)
Bhathiara (UP)
Bhathiara, Razzaqi (WB)
Bhati, Chang, Ghirath (CH)
Bhatiara (DE)
Bhatiya (TR)
Bhatiya (WB)
Bhatiyara (MP)
Bhatra, Bhat, Darpi, Digpal, Ramiya, Rana, Rathore, Rau, Swali (PU)
Bhatraju (AP)
Bhatraju (other than Kshatriya Raju) (TN)
Bhatraju (PO)
Bhatta (AS)
Bhatu Turka (AP)
Bhatua (OR)
Bhauh (Sagavanshi-Mali) (RA)
Bhavaiya or Targala (MR)
Bhavassar Kshatriya, Banagarajulu. Rongare, Darji, Simpi (PO)
Bhavin (KA)
Bhavin (MR)
Bhavsar, Chippa, Nilgar, Nirali, Rangrez, Rangari (MP)
Bhil (AS)
Bhil (UP)
Bhillala (MR)
Bhillava (KE)
Bhima (MP)
Bhina Koya (MR)
Bhinhar (TR)
Bhinjia (TR)
Bhir (TR)
Bhishti, Bhisty (MP)
Bhisti or Pakhali (MR)
Bhogta (OR)
Bhoi (MP)
Bhoi, Bhoiraj, Dhimar, Zinga-Bhoi, Kevat-Bhoi, Bhanara Bhoi, Kirat Bhoi, Machhindra Bhoi, Palewar Bhoi, Kahar Bhoi, Pardeshi Bhoi, Shrimali Bhoi (GU)
Bhoi, Kharvi, Dhiwar Bhoi, Zinga Bhoi, Pardeshi Bhoi, Raj Bhoi, Kahar, Gadia Kahar, Kirat, Machwa, Manzi, Jatia, Kewat, Dhiwar, Dheewar, Dhimar, Palewr, Machhendra, Navadi, Malhar, Malhav, Gadhav-Bhoi, Khadi Bhoi, Khare Bhoi, Dhevra Dhuria Kahar (MR)
Bhojki (CH)
Bhokta (AS)
Bhokta (OR)
Bhot (MP)
Bhotia (WB)
Bhottadas, Boto Bhottada, Muria Bhottad, Sano Bhottada (KA)
Bhottadas-Bodo Bhottada, Muria Bhottada and Sano Bhottada (TN)
Bhottadas-Bodo Bhottada, Muriabhattada and Sano Bhottada (AP)
Bhottadas-Bodo-Bhottada, Muria-Bhottada, and Sano Bhottada (KE)
Bhottodas-Bodo Bottadu, Muria Bhottada and Sano Bhottada (PO)
Bhoyar (MP)
Bhoyar (Pawra) (MR)
Bhrhmi (DN)
Bhubalia-Lohar (CH)
Bhubalia-Lohar, Garhi-Lohar (HR)
Bhubhalia (DE)
Bhugal (WB)
Bhuhalia (HP)
Bhuhalia (PU)
Bhuihar, Bhuiyar (BI)
Bhuiya (TR)
Bhujan (OR)
Bhuji, Bharbhuja (RA)
Bhujru (CH)
Bhujwa (MP)
Bhul (UP)
Bhuliya (OR)

Bhumias, Bado Bhumias and Bhuri Bhumia (PO)
Bhumias-Bhumia and Bodo Bhumia (KE)
Bhumias-Bhuri Bhumia and Bodo Bhumia (TN)
Bhumias-Bhuri Bhumia and Bodo Bhumia (AP)
Bhumias-Bhuri-Bhumia and Bodo Bhumia (KA)
Bhumij (AS)
Bhumij (MA)
Bhumij (ME)
Bhumij, Bumij (TR)
Bhundari (PO)
Bhura-Brahman (CH)
Bhura-Brahman (HR)
Bhura-Brahman (PU)
Bhurji, Bharbhuja, Bharbhunja, Bhunj, Bhunjia, Kandu, Kashodhay (UP)
Bhurtiya (MP)
Bhute, Bhope (MR)
Bhutia (MP)
Bhuyan (AS)
Bidakia (MP)
Bidia (MP)
Bijoria (MP)
Billava (PO)
Billava (TN)
Biloch (CH)
Bin (TR)
Bin (WB)
Binapatta (KA)
Bind (BI)
Bind (TR)
Bind (UP)
Bindli (AP)
Bindli (KA)
Bindli (MR)
Binedhanies (OR)
Bingi (KA)
Binjhawar (WB)
Binjhia (TR)
Binjhia (WB)
Binjia (AS)
Binjina (BI)
Binjina (WB)
Birarea (RA)
Birhor (AS)
Birhor (TR)
Birjhia (OR)
Birjia (AS)
Bissoy (PO)
Bissoy, Barangi Jodia, Bennagi, Dadua, Frangi, Hollar, Jhoriya, Kollai, Konde, Paranga, Penga Jodia, Sodo and Takora (KA)
Bissoy-Barangi Jodia, Bannangi, Daduva, Frangi, Hollar, Jhoriya, Kollai, Konde, Paranga, Penga-Jodia, Sodo Jodia and Takora (TN)
Bissoy-Barangi Jodia, Bannangi, Daduva, Godo Jodia, Hollar, Jheriya, Kollai Konde, Paranga, Pergajodia, Prangi, Takora (AP)
Bissoy-Barangi Jodia, Bennangi, Bollar, Daduva, Frangi, Jhoriya Kollai, Konde Pranga, Penga Jodia, Sodo Jodia and Takora (KE)
Bissoy-Barangi Jodia, Bennangi, Daduva, Frangi, Hollar, Jhoriya, Kollai, Konde, Paranga, Pengajodia, Sodo Jodia and Takoara (OR)
Bogad-Bogadi, Bagodi, Bagadi, Bagdi, Bogodi (KA)
Bogada (OR)
Bolodhia (OR)
Bondil (TN)
Bondili (PO)
Bondo (AS)
Bonya (PO)
Boreka, Gopal (MP)
Boro, Boro Kachari (MA)
Boro-Kachari (ME)
Botehra (CH)
Bowri (AS)
Bowria (JK)
Boya, Balmiki (AP)
Boyan (PO)
Boyar, Oddar (TN)
Boyas (TN)
Brijbasi (MP)
Brijia (TR)
Brijia (WB)
Budabukhalas (TN)
Budabukkalas (AP)
Budbukk (AP)
Budbukk, Budbudki, Budbukala, Devari, Joshi, Burbook (KA)

Bukka (AP)
Burbook (AP)
Burbook (MR)
Burganakaliga (AP)
Buruashankar/Barna Shankar, Beja (OR)
Burud (GU)
Burud, Medar (MR)
Butakusuda (OR)
Buttal (MR)
Byagari (KA)
Byagari (KE)
Byagari (OR)
Byagari (PO)
Byagari (TN)

C.S.I. (Formerly S.I.U.C.) (TN)
Caulota, Kolota (MP)
Chaak (WB)
Chachati (KA)
Chachati (KE)
Chackaravar (KE)
Chackaravar (TN)
Chadar (MR)
Chagar (HR)
Chahang (PU)
Chain, Chayeen (BI)
Chak (DE)
Chakala, Chawla, Dhobi, Rajaka, Chakali, Vannar (AP)
Chakkala (KE)
Chakkala (PO)
Chakkiliyan (AP)
Chakkiliyan (OR)
Chakrawadya Dasar (GU)
Chakrawadya Dasar (KA)
Chakrawadya-Dasar (MR)
Chakrawadya-Dasar (RA)
Chalavadi (KE)
Chalavadi, Chalvadi (OR)
Chalvadi, Chamnayya (RA)
Cham Bukutti (KA)
Chamana (RA)
Chamar (AS)
Chamboti (KA)
Chamling (WB)
Chamtha (MR)
Chanal (UP)
Chanchati (TN)
Chandal (KA)
Chandal (MR)
Chandalagade (MR)
Chandra Vedia (MP)
Chandrabhanshi (Kahar) (BI)
Chang (HR)
Chang, Chahang (HP)
Changar (HP)
Channan, Chaliya (KE)
Chanou (BI)
Chantia (GU)
Chapota (BI)
Chapparband, Chapparbandsa (Muslims) (KA)
Chaptegar, Chaptegara (KA)
Chaptegra (KE)
Chaptogra (PO)
Chara, Chhar, Chhara (KA)
Charan Banjaras (AP)
Charan or Gadhavi (MR)
Charan, Charan Gadhavi (where they are not Scheduled Tribes) (GU)
Charan, Gadvi (DE)
Charg (CH)
Charodi, Chhara (MR)
Charodi, Mestha (KA)
Chasadadhoba, Haladhar, Halari, Satchasi (WB)
Chasi-Kaibartta (TR)
Chasi-Kaibartta (WB)
Chatadi (Chattada or Srivaishnava) (PO)
Chatiyar, Chakkale Chattiyar, Telegu, Vanikavaisya, Vanniar (KE)
Chatri-Agnikulaksatryya, Bombili (AP)
Chatti (KE)
Chatwal (BI)
Chaudhari (where they are not Scheduled Tribes) (GU)
Chaupal (OR)
Chavalakaranas (PO)
Chavalakkaran (KE)
Chavalakkaran, Chavalakkarar (TN)
Chayakkaran (KE)
Chayakkaran (TN)
Cheeta (RA)
Chekkalas whose normal occupation is oil crushing like Cap Vaniyans (PO)
Chelapa (HP)
Chena-Dasaru, Chenna-Dasar, Holaya-Dasar (RA)

Chenchu (KE)
Chenchu (TN)
Chenchu or Chanchwar (MR)
Chenchulu (AP)
Chere (AS)
Chero (OR)
Cheruman (AP)
Cheruman (OR)
Chettadara (PO)
Chetties (Kottar Chetties, Parakka Chetties, Elur Chetties, Attingal Chetties, Pudrakkada Chetties, Iraniel Chedtties, Sri Pandara Chetties, Telugu Chetties, Udayamkulangara Chetties, Wynadan Chetties and Palavara Chetties) (KE)
Chettu or Chetty (including Kottar Chetty, Elur Chetty, Pathira Chetty, Pudukkadai Chetty, Valayal Chetty) (TN)
Chetty/Balija (AN)
Chhapparband (MR)
Chhara, Adodia, Sansi (GU)
Chhara, Kanjar, Nat (MR)
Chhimba, Chhipi (CH)
Chhimba, Chimba, Darzi, Soi (HR)
Chhipa, Apurba, Bhati, Bhagarwal, Chauhan, Chippa, Dayer, Jasod, Nama, Namdeo, Padihar, Pamsar, Solanki, Surage (RA)
Chhipi, Bhata, Mochela Pandla, Rohita, Untal (HR)
Chhipi, Tank (DE)
Chick Banik (AS)
Chidar (RA)
Chik (Muslims) (BI)
Chik (OR)
Chik (UP)
Chik, Chikwa, Kasai, Kassab (WB)
Chikbaraik (OR)
Chikwa (Kassab) (UP)
Chimbe, Battu, Brah, Chhimbe, Chhipi, Chimba, Chimpa, Darzi, Dhami, Jassal, Kareer, Kainth, Madahar, Purba, Rekhroy, Sappal, Sarao, Siria, Srao, Tank (PU)
Chimbe, Chipi, Chimpa, Darzi, Soi (HP)
Chimur (MR)
Chintala (AP)
Chintala (KA)
Chintala (MR)
Chipar (MP)
Chipi, Darzi, Meru (MP)
Chippa (MR)
Chirath (including Chabang and Bahri) (PU)
Chirimar (CH)
Chirimar (DE)
Chirimar (HP)
Chirimar (HR)
Chirimar (PU)
Chirimar (WB)
Chitari (MP)
Chitra, Chitrakar (OR)
Chitra, Chitrkar (KA)
Chitrakar (WB)
Chitrakathi (MR)
Chitrakathi-Joshi (KA)
Chodhara (RA)
Chodhra (MR)
Choongar, Chunkar (MP)
Chopan (JK)
Chopemari (AP)
Choudang (AS)
Choudang (ME)
Chouhan (TR)
Chowdhari (AS)
Christian Chamar (GD)
Christian Mahar (GD)
Christians converted from Scheduled Castes (MR)
Chuhar or Chuhra (KA)
Chunal (UP)
Chunara (GU)
Chunchar (KA)
Chunera (UP)
Chuppolu (Mera) (AP)
Churia (OR)
Churihara, Lakhera, Lahera (WB)
Churihara, Manihar (BI)
Chutia, Chutiya (AS)
Chutiya (ME)
Chuvalia Koli (GU)
Converted Christians from Scheduled Caste (PU)
Converts to Christianity from Scheduled Castes irrespective of the generation of conversion (TN)

Converts to Christianity from Scheduled Castes (PO)

Dabgar (GU)
Dabgar (MP)
Dabgar (MR)
Dafalange (Muslim) (BI)
Dafale (Muslim) (BI)
Dafali (DE)
Dafali (WB)
Dafali, Dholi (MP)
Dafer (Hindus & Muslims) (GU)
Dafla (MA)
Dafoli (UP)
Dahalia (OR)
Dahez (MP)
Daiya (CH)
Daiya (HP)
Daiya (PU)
Daiya Dhaiya (DE)
Dakalaru (RA)
Dakaleru (GU)
Dakaleru (MR)
Dakaut (CH)
Dakaut (RA)
Dakaut, Bhargava, Dakot, Jyotshi, Ransahab (HR)
Dakaut, Dahkaut (PU)
Dakaut, Prade (DE)
Dalera (UP)
Dalu (TR)
Dalu (WB)
Damai (Nepali) (MA)
Damai (TR)
Damal (OR)
Damala (AP)
Damali-Faqir (JK)
Damami (RA)
Dana (MP)
Dandari (AS)
Dandasa, Dandasi (KE)
Dandasi (AS)
Dandasi (KA)
Dandasi (TN)
Dang-Dasar (KA)
Dangi (BI)
Dangi (MP)
Dangua (OR)
Daoli, Daola (HR)
Daoli, Daola (PU)
Daoli, Doala (CH)
Darji (OR)
Darji, Bhavasara, Hindumera, Maratha, Merti, Rangari, Rangrez (AP)
Daroga (RA)
Darvesa (KA)
Darzi (DE)
Darzi (Hindu and Muslims), Bhavasar, Kshatriya, Chippi, Chippiga, Simpi, Shimpi, Shiv Shimpi, Sai, Mirai, Rangari, Rangrez, Nilari, Namdev, Rangare, Neelagar (KA)
Darzi (MR)
Darzi (RA)
Darzi, Chhipe, Chhipi, Damdo, Surjia (UP)
Darzi, Idrisi (WB)
Das or Dangdidas (MR)
Dasari (AP)
Dasari (TN)
Dasari, Desri (KA)
Dasaris (Donga and Gudu) (AP)
Daula, Soni-Braderi (PU)
Davadiga, Devadigar, Moili, Moyili, Devadig, Devaili Sappaliga, Sheregar, Servegar, Suplig, Ambalavasi (KA)
Davendrakulathan (KE)
Deha, Dhaya, Dhea (CH)
Dehuri (OR)
Dekkani Muslims (TN)
Deons (OR)
Deoris (MA)
Depala (MR)
Desali (TR)
Desari (PO)
Deshantri (RA)
Deshwa, Deshwalu (MP)
Deshwali, Dewang, Jandra, Koskati (MP)
Deva-Telikula, Gondla, Teli (AP)
Devadiga (KE)
Devadiga (PO)
Devang, Challiyan, Chilliyan, Koshti, Hutgar, Jed, Winkar, Julahi, Hutkar, Hatgar (KA)
Devanga (AP)
Devanga (KE)
Devanga (MR)
Devanga, Devangan (PO)

Devangar (Sedar) (TN)
Devar (KE)
Devari, Gosavi, Nath Panthi (MR)
Devendra Kulathan (AP)
Devendra Kulathan (OR)
Devhar (BI)
Devig (MR)
Devli (MR)
Dey, Sudra Das (MF)
Dhadi (RA)
Dhai (CH)
Dhakad (RA)
Dhakad, Bhandari, Nagar, Singhavi, Talaya (MP)
Dhakkada (AP)
Dhakkada (KE)
Dhakkada (OR)
Dhakkada (PO)
Dhakkada (TN)
Dhamai (AS)
Dhamin (BI)
Dhaner (OR)
Dhangar (GD)
Dhangar, Bagla, Gadri, Gadaria, Hatgar, Hatkar, Kurmar, Pal (MP)
Dhangar, Kuruba, Kurubar (MR)
Dhanka including Tadvi, Tetaria and Valvi (KA)
Dhankar (BI)
Dhankia, Dhanka (MP)
Dhanohi (RA)
Dhanuk, Purwa (BI)
Dhanwar (AS)
Dhanwar (BI)
Dhanwar (HR)
Dhar (Muslims) (JK)
Dhari (BI)
Dhari (UP)
Dhasa (WB)
Dhaya, Dheya, Daiya (HR)
Dhekaru (BI)
Dhekaru (WB)
Dhemaru (TR)
Dhenuar (WB)
Dhenwar (CH)
Dhenwar (PU)
Dher (AP)
Dher (KA)
Dhimar (BI)
Dhimar (RA)
Dhimar, Dhinwar, Jhinwar, Kahar, Mallah (CH)
Dhimar, Dhivar, Gabit, Harkantra, Mangeli, Mangele, Page, Sanduri (MR)
Dhimar, Dhiwar, Dhinwar, Jheevar, Jhinwar, Kahar, Kashyap-Rajput, Mallah (HP)
Dhimar, Dhiwar, Dhinwar, Jheevar, Jhinwar, Kahar, Kashyap, Rajput, Mallah (PU)
Dhimar, Mallah, Kashyap Rajput (HR)
Dhimen (MP)
Dhimer, Benua, Banawar, Bhorji, Dhimar, Kewat, Raikar, Raikwar, Saimari (MP)
Dhinwar, Jhinwar, Nishad (DE)
Dhirkar (MP)
Dhirwar, Britia, Navada, Ezingabhui (MP)
Dhobi (AN)
Dhobi (CH)
Dhobi (DN)
Dhobi (Excluding those in S/C) (MP)
Dhobi (excluding those in S.C.) (DE)
Dhobi (GD)
Dhobi (GU)
Dhobi (Muslims) (KA)
Dhobi (RA)
Dhobi (Washermen) (JK)
Dhobi, Batham, Chauhan-Bhatti, Khurdania, Monson, Rajpar, Tanwar (HR)
Dhobi, Qasab (PU)
Dhobi, Rajak (excluding those in S.C.) (UP)
Dhobi, Vannan (TN)
Dhobi,Parit, Watts, Madwal, Rajak (MR)
Dhodia (KA)
Dhodia (RA)
Dholi (KA)
Dholi (MP)
Dholi (MR)
Dholi (UP)
Dholwala (JK)
Dhor (GD)
Dhor, Kakkayya, Kankayya (RA)
Dhosali (CH)
Dhosali, Dosali (HR)

Dhosali, Dosali (PU)
Dhosali, Sosal (HP)
Dhunia, Dhumian (BI)
Dhunia, Kathoria, Naddaf (UP)
Dhunia, Mansoori (WB)
Dhunia, Naddaf (MP)
Dhunia, Pinjara, Kadher Dhunnewala (DE)
Dhunkar, Kadore (MP)
Dilpali (WB)
Divachakoli (GU)
Diwan (AR)
Doai (TR)
Dom, Dombara, Paidi or Pano (KE)
Domb-Andhiya Domb, Audiniya Domb, Chonel Domb, Christian Domb, Mirgani Domb, Oriya Domb, Ponaka Domb, Telegaga Domb and Ummia Domb (KE)
Domb-Andhiya Domb, Audiniya Domb, Chonel Domb, Christian Domb, Mirgani Domb, Oriya Domb, Ponaka Domb, Telega Domb and Ummia Domb (OR)
Dombidasa (KA)
Dombo (AP)
Dombo (KE)
Dombo (TN)
Dombs, Andhiya Dombs, Chonel Dombs, Oriya Dombs, Ponaka Dombs, Telaga Dombs and Ummia Dombs (TN)
Dombs-Andhiya, Dombs, Audiniya Dombs, Chonel Dombs, Christian Dombs, Nirgani Dombs, Oriya Dombs, Poraka Dombs, Telaga Dombs, Ummia Dombs (AP)
Dombs-Audhiya, Dombs-Audiniya, Dombs-Christian, Dombs-Chonel, Dombs-Miragani, Dombs-Oriya, Dombs-Ponaka, Domns-Telaga, Dombs-Ummia (KA)
Dommara (AP)
Dommara (MR)
Dommara (PO)
Dommera (TN)
Donga Yatas (TN)
Donga Yerukalas (KA)
Dongayathas (AP)
Doom, Dooma, Ganai/Qusab (excluding those in S.C.) (JK)
Dosadh, Dosad (TR)
Dosali (JK)
Dovalkar (PO)
Drain (PU)
Duari (TR)
Dubla (RA)
Dudekula (TN)
Dudekula, Laddaf, Pinjari or Noor-Bash (AP)
Dudokula, Pinjari (PO)
Dudubi (PO)
Dugla, Dholi (MA)
Dumala, Dumal (OR)
Duraj (WB)
Durgamurga-Burburchal (KA)
Dusad (AS)

Easiija, Daavat (KA)
Ediga, Gowda (Gammalla, Kalalec), Goundla, Settibalija (AP)
Eluvaln (AN)
Enadi (PO)
Enadi (TN)
Eravaliar (PO)
Eravallar (TN)
Ethayar, Idayar, Konar and Udayar (TN)
Exhava (Exhuva, Ezhava Illuvan) (PO)
Exhuthachan (PO)
Ezhavas (KE)
Ezhavathi (KE)
Ezhavathy (TN)
Ezhavathy (Vathi) (PO)
Ezhuthachan (KE)
Ezhuthachans (PO)
Ezhyva (TN)
Ezuthachar (TN)

Fakir (DE)
Fakir Bandarwala (MR)
Fakir or Faquir (Muslims) (GU)
Fakir, Faquir, Sain (MP)
Fakir, Sain (WB)
Fakir-Bandarwala (MP)
Faqir (CH)
Faqir (Muslim) (BI)
Faqir (Muslims) (KA)
Faqir (PU)
Faqir (UP)

Faquir (HP)
Farda (JK)
Fishermen (JK)
Futgudi (MR)

Gaadla, Gaadavars (PO)
Gaalda Konkani (PO)
Gabada or Godba (MR)
Gach, Mandewala (DE)
Gadaba (BI)
Gadaba (WB)
Gadaba, Gadabasboda, Gadaba-Cerilam, Gadaba-Franji, Gadaba Jodia, Gadaba Olaro, Gadaba Pangi (KA)
Gadabas-Boda Gadaba, Cerllam Gadaba, Olarao Gadaba and Pranga Gadaba and Grangi Gadaba, Jodiagadaba (TN)
Gadabas-Bodo Gadaba, Cellan Gadaba, Franji Gadaba, Jodia Gadaba, Olaro Gadaba, Pangi Gadaba and Pranga Gadaba (KE)
Gadalia or Gadiluharia (GU)
Gadaria (CH)
Gadaria (MR)
Gadaria, Banghela, Barela, Biar, Bilra, Hiranwal, Kalanlia, Pondowal, Pal, Shiviya (HR)
Gadaria, Chandalia, Gadaria, Gavala, Ghosi, Kabiria (RA)
Gadaria, Gaddi, Gaderia, Gareria, Pal (UP)
Gadderia, Gadaria (PU)
Gaddi (BI)
Gaddi (CH)
Gaddi (excluding the areas where specified as Scheduled Tribe) (HP)
Gaddi (HR)
Gaddi (JK)
Gaddi, Garri (DE)
Gaddi, Ghosi (WB)
Gaddi, Guddi (PU)
Gaderia (DE)
Gaderia (HP)
Gadhai (Muslims) (GU)
Gadhavi (MR)
Gadheri (DE)
Gadhia (UP)
Gadia-Lohar (RA)
Gadihar (Muslim) (BI)
Gadole, Gaddoli, Langoliha, Lehpita (MP)
Gadolia (RA)
Gadri (CH)
Gadri (MR)
Gadri, Gari (MP)
Gahamandi (MP)
Gain (WB)
Gainey (Nepali) (MA)
Galiara (Muslims) (GU)
Gamit, Gamta, Gavit (including Mavchi, Padvi, Vasava, Vasave and Valvi) (RA)
Ganaka (KE)
Ganali or Gandali (MR)
Ganda (AS)
Ganda (BI)
Ganda (WB)
Gandharap (MR)
Gandharb (BI)
Gandharva, Bhatu (UP)
Gandhila (UP)
Gandia (MP)
Gandla (PO)
Gandla, Teli (KA)
Gandla, Telikula (AP)
Gandwal, Gangwa (HR)
Gangai (Nagesh) (BI)
Gangakule, Gangemakkalu, Gowrimatha, Ambig, Ambiga, Kabbaliga, Kabbili, Kabber, Kabbera, Kharvi, Bhoyi, Boyi, Thoreya, Harakanthra, Harikanthra, Kahar, Meenagar, Kharia, Sunnagar, Siviyar, Bestha, Gangamatha, Gangaputra, Bhoi, Parivara, Eravva, Brudebestaru, Mogaveera (KA)
Gangam Reddi (KE)
Gangani (AP)
Gangani (MR)
Gangani, Gabit, Gabbit, Gapit, Gasbit (KA)
Gangavar (TN)
Gangavars (PO)
Gangin (TR)
Gangota, Gangoth (BI)
Ganiga, Chakkam, Teli (KA)
Ganigredlavaru (AP)
Ganika (including Nagavamasam) (PO)
Ganju (TR)
Gankak in Cachar only (AS)

Ganobha (RA)
Ganshi (AS)
Gaoli, Lingayat-Gaoli (MP)
Gara (Blacksmiths) (JK)
Gara (TR)
Garai (WB)
Gareri (TR)
Garhwal (MP)
Gari (TR)
Gari, Kamlivagan, Phylanwar, Purvia (MP)
Garo (MA)
Garodi (AP)
Garodi, Garudi (MR)
Garpagari (MR)
Garpagri, Nath (MP)
Garwadi, Garradi (MP)
Gatti (KA)
Gatti (KE)
Gatti (PO)
Gauda (GD)
Gauria, Gwar, Gwaria (CH)
Gavandi (MR)
Gavara (AP)
Gavara (PO)
Gavarai (Kavarai) and Vadugar (Vaduvar) other than Kamma, Kapu, Balija and Reddy (TN)
Gawala, Ghosh, Goal, Goala, Gop, Gowala, Ahir (AS)
Gawala, Gowala, Yadav, Yaduvanshi, Ahir, Gwar (PU)
Gawari, Gauria, Gwar (HR)
Gawaria (MP)
Gawaria, Gauria (HP)
Gayari (MP)
Gazula Balija, Gazulasetti (Gajula) (PO)
Ghadi (KA)
Ghadshi (MR)
Ghadsi, Ghadshi (KA)
Ghai (CH)
Ghai (HP)
Ghai (PU)
Ghami (MP)
Ghanchi (Muslims) (GU)
Gharati (JK)
Ghariya (MP)
Ghasi or Haddi, Relli Sachandi (KE)
Ghasi or Haddi, Relli, Sachandi, Ghasi, boda Ghasi and Sanghasi (KA)
Ghasi, Ghasiara, Ghosi (HP)
Ghasi, Ghasiara, Ghosi (PU)
Ghasi, Ghasiyara, Ghosi (HR)
Ghasi, Haddi, Relli and Sachandi (TN)
Ghasiara (CH)
Ghasiara (DE)
Ghasis-Boda Ghasis and San Ghasis (KE)
Ghati, Ghare, Ghatti, Ghasi (MP)
Ghatowar (AS)
Ghatuar (AS)
Ghatwal (WB)
Ghatwar (BI)
Ghatwar (OR)
Ghatwar (WB)
Ghiradh, Ghirath (HR)
Ghirath, Ghrit, Grith-Bahti, Chang (HP)
Ghisadi (KA)
Ghisadi, Ghisadi Lohar, Gadi Lohar, Ghitodi Lohar, Rajput Lohar (MR)
Ghondali, Gondaliga, Gondhali, Gondhalli (KA)
Ghosh, Gopa, Gawala, Yadav (ME)
Ghosi (CH)
Ghosi (DE)
Ghusuria (BI)
Ghusuria (WB)
Giddildki, Pingle, Pingale (KA)
Gidhiya (UP)
Gidigar (KA)
Gingra (OR)
Giri (UP)
Giri, Goswami, Gosain (RA)
Girigiris (OR)
Goala, Gope, Yadav (TR)
Gobba (PO)
Gochaki (MP)
Gochaki (MR)
Godaba (AP)
Godaba (PO)
Godagali (KA)
Godari (KA)
Godari (KE)
Godari (TN)
Godda (AP)
Godda (OR)
Godhi (MP)
Godi (Muslim) (RA)
Godo (Chhavo), Godhi (BI)

Godra (BI)
Godra (WB)
Godri (HP)
Godri (HR)
Godri (PU)
Goggi (GD)
Gogra (KA)
Gokha (BI)
Gokha (WB)
Gola, Golla, Gope, Sadgope, Ahir, Gour, Gouda, Goudo, Mekala Golla, Punnu Golla and Yadav (OR)
Gola-Rana (GU)
Golla, Dhangar, Iddayar, Konar, Kurba, Kurwa, Yadav, Yerragella (AP)
Golla, Gollewar, Goler, Golkar, Goller (MR)
Golla, Gouli, Gopal, Yadava Asthana Golla, Yadava, Advai Golla, Gopala, Gopali, Hanabaru, Krishna Golla, Anubaru, Atanaburu, Hanbar, Hanabar, Dudhigola (KA)
Gond (KE)
Gond (ME)
Gond (RA)
Gond (TN)
Gond-i-Modya Gond & Rajo Gond (OR)
Gonda (AS)
Gonda (TR)
Gonda (WB)
Gondali (KA)
Gondhali (MP)
Gondhali, Gondala (MR)
Gondi, Modya Gond and Rajo, Gondo (PO)
Gondi-Modya Gond and Rajo Gond (KE)
Gondi-Modya Gond and Rajongond (KA)
Gonds (AS)
Gondu-Bato, Bhirthya, Dudho Kouriya, Hato, Jatako & Joria (OR)
Gondus-bato, Bhirithya, Dudho, Kouria, Hato Jatako and Joria (KA)
Goniga, Sadusetty (KA)
Gonrh (UP)
Gonrh, Gorh, Gothahum (BI)
Gonrhi (TR)
Gontia (MP)
Gopal, Gopal Bhorpis, Khelkari (MR)
Gopal, Pangala-Gopal (MP)
Gor (AS)
Gorait (AS)
Gorang (TR)
Gore (WB)
Gore-khans (JK)
Gorkha (HP)
Gorkha (HR)
Gorkha (PU)
Gorkha (WB)
Gorkhali (ME)
Gosain (UP)
Gosain, Bharti, Geria, Gosai, Gowsami, Gosaib (MP)
Gosangi (OR)
Gosangiwar (MP)
Gosavi (GD)
Gosavi Bava, Bairagi, Bharati, Girigosavi, Bharati Gosavi, Saraswati Parbat, Sagar, Ban or Van, Teerth Ashram, Aranya Chadbhan, Sanyasi, Nath Panthi Gosavi (MR)
Gosavi, Gosayi, Gosain, Atit (KA)
Goudu (AP)
Goudus Bato, Bhirithya, Dodhokouria, Hato, Jatako and Joria (PO)
Goudus, Bato, Bhirithya, Dudhokouria, Hato, Tatako and Joria (TN)
Goudus-Bato (Bhirithya, Dudhokuria, Hats, Jatako and Joria) (AP)
Goudus-Bato, Bhivthiya, Dudho Kouria, hato, Jatako and Joria (KE)
Gound (BI)
Gound or Gowdi, Machhus, Pal, Paiko Patra or Patara, Sundi or Telli, tanti, Yeranagollas, Oriya or Veddy Samantho, Oriya Backward Classes Badhai Bhokta, Darji, Gour (PO)
Gounder, Padayachi, Vanniya, Kulaksativa, Vallalar, Vanniar (TN)
Gounder, Pillai (KE)
Goundu (BI)
Gowala, Gwala, Gwar, Yadav, Ahir (HP)
Gowar (WB)
Gowda (including Gammala Kalali and Gounder) (TN)
Gowda (KE)
Gowda, Gouda (including Gamalla or Kalali) (PO)
Gowtia (MP)

Gramani, Shanar, Nadar (TN)
Grammani, Shanan & Nadar (PO)
Gratie (JK)
Gudala (AP)
Gudheri (WB)
Gudia or Guria, Gurja, Gunju (OR)
Gudigara (PO)
Gujar (UP)
Gujar, Bad-Gujar, Dagar-Dahabi, Dasa, Davari, Gawr, Giyar-Gaur, Kansana, Malhli-Gujar, Harbola (MP)
Gujar, Bahar, Barwal, Bhanot, Char, Kalsan, Magria, Padaji, Rawal, Sangi (HR)
Gujar, Bhumla, Gujjar, Ninwalia, Thakur (PU)
Gujar, Gujjar (RA)
Gujar, Gurjar (DE)
Gujar, Guzar (Masons) (KA)
Gujjar (JK)
Gujjar, Gujar (excluding the areas where specified as Scheduled Tribe) (HP)
Gujrath Baori (MR)
Gujree (JK)
Gujula Balija, Dasar, Musoku, Perika Baloa (AP)
Gulgaliya (BI)
Gumtian (HP)
Gunar (TR)
Gundi (TR)
Gurav, Gurou (MR)
Gurav, Gurov, Tambli, Tamballa, Gurava, Gurout, Gurrat (KA)
Guraw (MP)
Guri (TR)
Gurkha (MI)
Gurung (SI)
Gutka jat, Chillon Jat (CH)
Gutka Jat, Chillon Jat (HR)
Gwaria, Gauria, Gwar (PU)

Habra (OR)
Habura (MP)
Habura (MR)
Haddi (KE)
Hadi (CH)
Hadi (TR)
Hadi (WB)
Hajjam (MP)
Hajjam, (Awadhiya, Kanaujia, Kawa, nai, Naiya, Napit, Naya, Thakur) (BI)
Hajjam, Nai (Barbers) (JK)
Hajjam, Nai (CH)
Hajong (MA)
Hajuri Daroga (MP)
Halalkhor (excluding those in Scheduled Caste) (WB)
Halalkhor (TR)
Halalkhor (UP)
Halawakki, Wakkal, Vakkal, Gram Vakkal, Gam-Gowda, Gam-Gawada, Gvada, Karevakkal Kunchavakal, Attevakkal, Shilwakkal, Halakkivakkal (KA)
Halepaik (MR)
Hali (CH)
Halleer (RA)
Hallfee (KA)
Halsar, Haslar, Hulasvar, Halasvar (RA)
Halwai (UP)
Halwai (WB)
Halwai, Halwayee, Kanyakubj, Vaish (MP)
Halwari (WB)
Handervut (KA)
Handevazir (KA)
Hangie (Manjhi Boatmen and rowing class excluding houseboat owners) (JK)
Hankiya (UP)
Hansi (OR)
Haranshikari, Chigaribetegar, Vaghri, Wagiri, Nirshikari, Bagri, Baori, Phasachari, Vagri (KA)
Hari (AS)
Harni (CH)
Harni (DE)
Harni (HP)
Harni (HR)
Harni (MP)
Harni (MR)
Harni (PU)
Hasla (AP)
Hasla (OR)
Hasla (TN)
Hatkar (AP)
Hatkar (MR)
Hazuri (RA)
Hdiga (including Settibalijas of East and

West Godavari Distt.) (PO)
Hedge (PO)
Hegde (KE)
Hegde (TN)
Hela (MP)
Hela (RA)
Hela (WB)
Helava (KA)
Helva (PO)
Helve, Hilav (MR)
Herbi (DE)
Hilka/Mason (JK)
Hill Pulaya (TN)
Hill Reddi (KA)
Hill-reddis (MR)
Hima, Karanjia, Qassar (Muslims) (BI)
Hingora (Hindu & Muslims) (GU)
Hira (MA)
Ho (TR)
Holar, Valhar (RA)
Holaya, Holer (RA)
Holeva (KA)
Holeya (OR)
Holra (AS)
Holva (KE)
Holva (TN)
Holva, Helava, Helavamallur, Helvagolla, Handihelva, Pitchiguntalu, Helvaru (KA)
Honniyar (KA)
Hovadiga, Hugar, Hoogar, Mallgar, Mali, Phoolmali, Phulmali, Phulari, Pholari, Jeer (KA)
Howgar, Hawagar, Howadiga (KA)
Huga, Lohar, Lohpeta, Jadav, Jaga, Jandza (MP)
Hurkiya (UP)

Ibrahimi (WB)
Idiga (including Sett Balija) (PO)
Idiga (TN)
Idiroso or Darzi (Muslim) (BI)
Iilavathi (TN)
Iliga, Halepaik, Billaava, Devar, Malayali-Billava, Deevar, Divaramakkalu, Namdhari, Goondle, Goundla, Thiyar, Tiyan, Idiga-Kalal, Diviga, Eliga, Kommarpaik (KA)
Illathu Pillaimar (Luvar, Ishuvar Illathar) (TN)
Illavan (KE)
Illavathi (KE)
Illuvan (Ezhvan) (PO)
Ilovan (TN)
Irika (BI)
Irika (WB)
Irula (AP)
Irula (OR)
Irulas (PO)
Isai Vallalar or Melakarar (PO)
Isaivallalar (TN)
Izhuven (Illuvan) (KE)

Jadapu (TN)
Jadapus (KA)
jadapus (KE)
Jadapus (OR)
Jadapus (PO)
Jadup (BI)
Jaggal (KA)
Jaggali (KE)
Jagiasi (MR)
Jaintrapans (OR)
Jajak (MR)
Jakkala (AP)
Jakkulas (PO)
Jalarlu (PO)
Jallad (DE)
Jambuvandondai (PO)
Jambuvanodai (TN)
Jambuvulu (KE)
Jambuvulu (OR)
Jamoria (UP)
Jandara (PO)
Jandra, Kuruvina Setty (AP)
Jangalla (AP)
Jangam (AP)
Jangam (MP)
Jangam (MR)
Jangam (PO)
Jangama, Jangam (TN)
Jangra, Jasondhi, Janms-Lodhi (MP)
Janira (AP)
Janwa (RA)
Jat (Gutka and Chillon) (PU)
Jat (Muslims) (GU)
Jatapu (TN)
Jatapus (KA)

Jatapus (KE)
Jatigar (MR)
Jatiya (MR)
Javeri, Jawari, Johari (KA)
Javeri, Johari (MR)
Jeoni (WB)
Jetty (AP)
Jetty (PO)
Jhadi (MR)
Jhadi, Sonar (MP)
Jhala, Malo (MA)
Jhalo, Malo (TR)
Jhamral (MP)
Jhangara Brahmin, Khati, Viswakarma (PU)
Jhangra-Brahman, Khati (CH)
Jhara (TR)
Jhari (MP)
Jhatkia-Sikh (DE)
Jheevar (AN)
Jheevar (TN)
Jheewar (JK)
Jhetty (TN)
Jhimar, Atlas, Bidran, Bire, Dhinwar, Duglan, Dora, Chitre, Jhewar, Jhinwar, Jimar, Kahar, Kirnal, Lamsar, Malri, Radhav, Tala (HR)
Jhodia (OR)
Jhojha (UP)
Jingar (AP)
Jingar (MP)
Jingar (MR)
Jogde (MP)
Jogi (AP)
Jogi (JK)
Jogi (KE)
Jogi (MP)
Jogi (PO)
Jogi (TN)
Jogi (UP)
Jogi or Yogi (OR)
Jogi, Bans, Chillar, Faqir, Gandi, Galiya, Nath, Padha, Powar, Riwal, Ruel, Tanwar, Toor, Sihag (HR)
Jogi, Goswami (DE)
Jogi, Jogar, Sanjogi, Joger, Sanyasi (KA)
Jogi, Jogo, Jugi (BI)
Jogi, Jugi, Nath, Yogi (AS)
Jogi, Nath (CH)
Jogi, Nath (PU)
Jogi, Nath (RA)
Jogi, Nath, Nathjogi, Gosai, Devori (MR)
Jogin (MR)
Joginath (MP)
Jogulas (TN)
Jolha (AS)
Jori (HP)
Joshi, Bududki, Damruwale, Kudmude, Medhangi, Sarode, Sahadev Joshi, Sarvade, Saroda (MR)
Joshinandiwalas (AP)
Juang (BI)
Juang (WB)
Julaha (BI)
Julaha (excluding those in S.C.) (CH)
Julaha (Hindu and Muslim) (RA)
Julaha (Weaver) (HR)
Julaha, Dhaver, Dhuna, Kabirpanthi (excluding those in S/C) (PU)
Julaha, Momin (excluding those in S.C.) (DE)
Julaha, Momin (MP)
Julaha, Winkar, Vankar, Vanya, Vankar (MR)
Julaya, Garana. Taria & Tari (Muslims) (GU)
Jullaha (JK)
Jyotish, Grahbipra Brahman, Sakaldarpee Brahman (OR)

Kabar, Kaleari, Kabari (MP)
Kabari (BI)
Kabaria (UP)
Kabbara (PO)
Kabbora (TN)
Kabirpanthi (RA)
Kabirpanthi, Ramdasiya, Ravidasia (MP)
Kachari (MA)
Kachari (TR)
Kachari (WB)
Kacher (MP)
Kachera, Lakhera (MP)
Kachhi (RA)
Kachhi, Koeri, Murai, Murao (DE)
Kachhi, Kouri, Kushwa, mauriya, Murar, Naldih, Nardiha (UP)
Kachhi, Kushwoha, Kshatriya-Kadore (MP)

Kachi (AP)
Kachi, Kachhia (MR)
Kachora (MR)
Kadaiyan (PO)
Kadan (AP)
Kadan (KA)
Kadan (OR)
Kadan (PO)
Kadan (TN)
Kadar (BI)
Kadar (KA)
Kadar (TR)
Kadera (MR)
Kadera, Kamwal (MP)
Kadore (MP)
Kadu-Konkani (KA)
Kadupattan (KE)
Kadupattan (PO)
Kadupattar (Malabar) (TN)
Kaghzi (BI)
Kaghzi (WB)
Kahar (MP)
Kahar (WB)
Kahar, Bhoi (RA)
Kahar, Chandraborai, Chatrapati, Chotra Bansi, Ramani, Rawani, Paneri (BI)
Kahar, Dhadhan, Dhimer, Dhiver, Dhuru, Godia, Kashyap, Mehra (UP)
Kahar, Kashyap (DE)
Kahar, Kumbhar (DN)
Kaibartta (BI)
Kaibartta, Jaliya (MA)
Kaikadi (AP)
Kaikadi (or Korva) (AP)
Kaikadi (where they are not Sch. Castes), Korach, Dhontle, Korva or Kochi Korva, Makadwale, Padlor, Korvi (MR)
Kaikadi or Korach (GU)
Kaikadi, Korach (RA)
Kaikadi, Koragar, Yerkala, Erakala, Kunchi, Korva, Koramasetty, Yerukala (KA)
Kaikala (AP)
Kaikari (MP)
Kaikolan Kammara (excluding the areas comprising old Malabar District) (KE)
Kaikolan, Kaikolar, Sengunthar (TN)
Kaira (TR)
Kaira (WB)
Kakhera, Manihar (DE)
Kakkalan (where they are not Sch. Castes) (TN)
Kaladis (TN)
Kalahandi (AS)
Kalai (TR)
Kalal, Kalar, Kapdi (MP)
Kalal, Kalar, Lad, Ladwak, Gond Kalal, Shivhare (MR)
Kalal, Kalwar (DE)
Kalandar (BI)
Kalandar (UP)
Kalar (UP)
Kalari Kurup (Kalari Panich) (TN)
Kalarikurups (Kairal Panicker) (PO)
Kalavanthula (PO)
Kalavanthulu, Baggala, Ganika (AP)
Kalel (RA)
Kalhodia (GU)
Kalihandi (AS)
kalingi (PO)
Kalingi (TN)
Kalladi (OR)
Kalladi, Kalwar (AP)
Kallan (PO)
Kallar (PO)
Kallar, Vellalar (TN)
Kalloda (KA)
Kallundar (MP)
Kalota (MP)
Kalu (TR)
Kalu, Teli, Garai, Mondal, Sadhukhan, Pal, Patra, Sadhu, Barik (WB)
Kalveli Gounder (TN)
Kalwar (BI)
Kalwar (OR)
Kalwar (TR)
Kalwar (WB)
Kamalas (Viswakarmala) (PO)
Kamar (WB)
Kamar, Barhai, Kakit, Maggia, Maghaiya, Mistri, Nagbansi, Viswakarma (BI)
Kamati (MR)
Kamati, Kanian (KA)
Kambadia Bhagat (GU)
Kambar (TN)
Kamboj, Bala, Kamboh, Masok, Nande, Thand (PU)

Kamboj, Bangwa, Bangwai, Chimde, Gadhi, Gagwaik, Jangla, Kamboth, Lagle, Padhe, Pradhan (HR)
Kamboj, Kamboh (CH)
Kami (Nepali) (MA)
Kamkar (BI)
Kammalana (Kamsalas, Viswav-Brahman and Viswa Karma, Karuvaw) (PO)
Kammalar Kamsala-Viswa Brahmin and Viswakarmala (including Thattar or Porkollar, Kannar, Karumar or Kollar Thacher and Kalthacher) (TN)
Kammalas, Viswa Karmalas (Viswa Karma Karuvan Agari, Moosari, Thattan Vilkurup or Villasan, Viswabrahmanar, Viswam) (KE)
Kammara (excluding Kollegal taluk of Mysore Distt.) (KA)
Kammara, Kamara, Kamar, Kammaro, Muli, Lohuru, Loharo (OR)
Kammi (MR)
Kamriya (MP)
Kan, Kanu (WB)
Kanakkan (AP)
Kanakkan (OR)
Kanate (KA)
Kanbi, Kulwadi, Kunbi (KA)
Kanchan (CH)
Kandarpa (OR)
Kandel (MR)
Kandera (MP)
Kandera (RA)
Kandh (TR)
Kandh (WB)
Kandhal (AS)
Kandra (AP)
Kandra (BI)
Kandra (PO)
Kandra (TR)
Kandu (WB)
Kandu, Kanu (MA)
Kaner (MP)
Kangar (DE)
Kangar, Batwalo (MP)
Kangasia (GU)
Kangh (TR)
Kanghara (CH)
Kanghera (HP)
Kangi, Kangiwala (RA)
Kani or Kanisu or Kaniyar Panikkar (TN)
Kani, Kanian or Kaniyan and Kanisu or Kaniyar Panik kar, Ganka, Kanisy (PO)
Kanikaran, Kannikar (where they are not Sch. Tribes) (TN)
Kanisan (KE)
Kanisan, Kaniyan, Kanyan (excluding Kollegal Taluk of Mysore Distt.), Kaniyar (KA)
Kanisu or Kaniyar Panicher, Kani or Kaniyan (Ganaka) (KE)
Kaniyan (KE)
Kaniyan (OR)
Kanjar (AP)
Kanjar (CH)
Kanjar (KE)
Kanjar (OR)
Kanjar (TN)
Kanjar, Kanchan (HP)
Kanjar, Kanchan (PU)
Kanjar, Kanjari, Kanjir, Khanjarbhat (KA)
Kanjara-Bhatta (AP)
Kanjra (BI)
Kanmaeli (DE)
Kannada Saineegar, Kannadiyar and Dasapalanjika (TN)
Kannadiyan (KE)
Kannakan, Padanna (where they are not Sch. Castes) (TN)
Kannatia (MP)
Kansari, Kansyakar (WB)
Kanu (BI)
Kanvi (RA)
Kanwar (Jaiswal) (AP)
Kaora (TR)
Kapadia (BI)
Kapadia (MP)
Kapali (TR)
Kapali (WB)
Kapdi (DN)
Kapdi (MR)
Kapmare or Reddika (Redika) (AP)
Kapudia (OR)
Kapumaries (AP)
Kapumaries (KA)
Kapumaries (KE)
Kapumaries (TN)
Kapuria (TR)

Kapuria (WB)
Karan (MP)
Karani (WB)
Karar, Keer (MP)
Karbi (AS)
Karenga (TR)
Karha (WB)
Karhara (OR)
Kari (TR)
Karikalabhakthulu, Kaikala or Kaikolan (Sengundam or Sangunther) (AP)
Karikudumbi (KA)
Karimpalan (AP)
Karimpalan (KA)
Karimpalan (OR)
Karmakar (WB)
Karmakar, Kamar (TR)
Karmali (AS)
Karmali (OR)
Karnabhakthulu (AP)
Karnaveegar (Karnam), Kanaka Pillais (AP)
Karneegar, Karnam (TN)
Karuneegar (Seer Karuneegar, Srikaruneegar, Satrattu Karuneegar, Kaikatti Karuneegar, mathu Vazhi Kanakkar, Sozhi Kanakkar and Sunnambu Karuneegar) (TN)
Karuva (KA)
Karwalnat, Karwalnuts (WB)
Karwalnut (BI)
Kasab, Kassab, Kasai, Quraishi, Qussab, Qassab (MP)
Kasai (UP)
Kasai, Katik, Khatik, Katuka, Katuga, Kasab, Aray, Kulal (KA)
Kasai, Khatik, Kasab (MR)
Kasai, Qassab, Quraishi (DE)
Kasai-Maji (WB)
Kasar (GD)
Kasar, Kansar, Kancheri, Kanchara, Kanchugara, Bogar (KA)
Kasar, Kasera (MR)
Kasbi (MP)
Kasbi (MR)
Kasbin (KA)
Kasera, Jamera, Kasar (MP)
Kasera, Temara, Thathera, Thathiar (DE)
Kasgar (UP)
Kashan (AS)
Kashikappi, Kashi Kapadi, Tirumali (KA)
Kasikapadi (MR)
Kassab (CH)
Kassab (Kasai) (Muslim) (BI)
Kasta (WB)
Kasta, Kastha (TR)
Kastha (WB)
Katabu (MR)
Katabu, Katabar (KA)
Katesar or Pattamkatti (TN)
Kathar Katharwani, Kanthaharwani (Lingayatwani or Ladwani excluded) (MR)
Kathi-Khati (MR)
Kathikkaran (KE)
Kathikkaran (TN)
Kathputli-Nachanewala (DE)
Katika, Kasai (AP)
Katipamula (AP)
Katipamula (MR)
Katipapala (AP)
Katipaula (KA)
Katri-Rajulu (AP)
Kattunayakan (OR)
Kauathi (KE)
Kaura (BI)
Kauri, Kori, Kodar (MP)
Kavadi (KA)
Kavara (where they are not Scheduled Castes) (TN)
Kavathi (TN)
Kavatiyan (KA)
Kavudiyaru (KE)
Kavuthiyan (KE)
Kavuthiyan (PO)
Kavuthiyar (TN)
Kawar (AS)
Kawar (BI)
Kayasth-Kaiti Brahmin (AP)
Kayastha (Bengali) (AS)
Kechai (TR)
Keer (RA)
Kehal (CH)
Kehal (HP)
Kehal (HR)
Kehal (PU)
Kela (BI)
Kela (WB)

Kelasi (Kalasi Panicker) (KE)
Kelasi (PO)
Kelkari, Khelkari (KA)
Keot (AS)
Keot (BI)
Kerala Kudeli (TN)
Kerala Mudali, Kerala Muthali (PO)
Kerala Mudalis (KE)
Kerala Muthali (TN)
Kesar (JK)
Kewat, Bansi, Chai, Jalehar, Kharsa, Majhi, Mallah, Nishad (UP)
Kewat, Mallah (DE)
Khadwar (BI)
Khaira (OR)
Khaira (TR)
Khairwa (UP)
Khamgara (MP)
Khami (TR)
Khami (WB)
Khampti, Khamti (MA)
Khamti (AS)
Khamti (ME)
Khandait (TR)
Khandait (WB)
Khandnals (OR)
Khangar (BI)
Khangar (UP)
Khanghera (HR)
Khanghera (PU)
Khanjiman (OR)
Khant (GU)
Khant (RA)
Kharag (WB)
Kharia (AN)
Kharia (AS)
Kharia (WB)
Kherol (RA)
Kharol, Telugu-Munar, Kapu (MP)
Kharot (UP)
Kharvi (PO)
Kharvi (TN)
Kharwa or Kharwi (MR)
Kharwa-Bhardela (GU)
Kharwar (MP)
Khasi (MA)
Khatana (JK)
Khatgune (DE)
Khatik (BI)
Khatik (excluding those in S.C.) (DE)
Khatik (GU)
Khatik (TR)
Khatka (RA)
Khatka, Khatia (MP)
Khatki or Kasai, Chamadia-Khatki, Halarikhatki (Muslims) (GU)
Khatri (TN)
Khatti-Khatti (OR)
Khattia-Khatti, Kommarao and Lohara (TN)
Khattis, Khatti, Kommorao and Lohara (KE)
Khattis-Khatti, Kammarao and Lohara (PO)
Khattis-Khatti, Kommarao and Lohara (AP)
Khatua (OR)
Khatwa (BI)
Khatwe (BI)
Khelta (BI)
Khemcha (TR)
Khen (TR)
Khen (WB)
Kherwar (AS)
Kherwar (WB)
Khetauri (BI)
Khetauri (OR)
Khetauri (WB)
Khodal (AS)
Khodra (OR)
Kholie (JK)
Khond (AP)
Khond (AS)
Khond (KA)
Khond (KE)
Khond (ME)
Khond (TN)
Khondal (OR)
Khonyor (AS)
Khristi Gujarati Christian (Converts from Scheduled Castes only) (GU)
Khuangsai (MA)
Khyang (TR)
Khyang (WB)
Khyara (WB)
Kichagara (KA)
Kichak (TR)
Kichak (WB)

Kingharia (UP)
Kintali Kalinga (TN)
Kinthala Kalinga (AP)
Kintoli Kalinga (AP)
Kir (MP)
Kirad (MP)
Kirar (MR)
Kirar (RA)
Kirar, Dhakar (MP)
Kirar, Kirad (MP)
Kisan (UP)
Kisarwaki (WB)
Kishar (BI)
Kitara (PO)
Kitaran (KE)
Knowar (TR)
Koch (ME)
Kochh (BI)
Kochi (AP)
Koda (TR)
Koda (WB)
Koda, Kuda (OR)
Kodalo (AP)
Kodalo (KA)
Kodalo (KE)
Kodalo (TN)
Kodar (MP)
Kodu (KA)
Kodu (KE)
Kodu (PO)
Kodu (TN)
Koeri, Koiri (WB)
Kohdala (PO)
Kohli (CH)
Kohor (AS)
Koikolan or Koikola (Sengunthar, Sengundar) (PO)
Koilar (OR)
Koiri (AS)
Koiri (TR)
Koiri, Koeri (UP)
Kol (AS)
Kol (RA)
Kol (WB)
Kolaga (HP)
Kolaga (Misal) (DN)
Kolalar, Davar, Thevar (TN)
Kolam (OR)
Kolarios or Munivanies (PO)
Kolayanurali (KA)
Kolayiri, Kolari (KA)
Kolhati, Dombari (MR)
Koli (BI)
Koli (DN)
Koli (GD)
Koli (UP)
Koli (WB)
Koli Mahadeo (KA)
Koli, Koli Malhar, Koli Mahadev or Dongar Koli, Ghedia Koli, Idaria Koli, Kharwa Koli, Rathwa Koli, Baria Koli, Dhebaria Koli, Talpada Koli (where they are not Scheduled Tribes) (GU)
Koli, Koli-Suryawanshi, Malhar Koli, Christian Koli (MR)
Koli-Mahadev (RA)
Kolinga, Baragana Kalinga (AP)
Kolla, Kollahab (KA)
Kolta (UP)
Kolthati, Kolhatigi (KA)
Kolu (WB)
Komakapu (AP)
Komakapu (MR)
Komakpu (KA)
Komar (OR)
Komer (TR)
Kommar (AP)
Kommar (KA)
Kommar (KE)
Kommar (PO)
Kommar, Kommara (TN)
Konai (TR)
Kond (Kui) (AP)
Kond (Kui) (KA)
Kond (Kui) (KE)
Kond (Kul) (OR)
Kond Danoars (KE)
Konda Dhera, Kond (Kui) (TN)
Konda Dhora, Konda Reddis (KA)
Konda Dora (KE)
Konda Kapu (OR)
Konda Reddi (OR)
Kondh, Desaya, Kondhs, Dongria, Kondhs, Kuttiya, Kondhs, Tikiria (KA)
Kondh-Desaya Kondh, Dongria Kondh, Kuttiya Kondh. Tikiria Kondh and Yamity Kondh (TN)
Kondh-Desaya Kondh, Dongriya Kondh,

Kuttiya Kondh, Tikiria Kondh and Yanity Kondh (OR)
Kondhs-Desaya Kondh, Dongria Kondhs, Kuttiya Mondhs, Tikiria Kondhs and Yemity Kondhs (KE)
Kondpan (AS)
Kondu (MR)
Konga, Kongadi (KA)
Kongadi (MR)
Kongu Chettiar (TN)
Kongu Malayan (KE)
Kongu Vellalar (including Anupa Vellala Gounder, Chendalai Gounder, Harambukatti Gounder, Kurumba Gounder, Nattu Gounder, Padaithalaj. Poosari, Paualankatti Vellala Gounder, Pala Gounder, Rathinagiri Gounder, Sanku Vellala Gounder, Tirumudi Vellala, Thondu Vellalar, Vellala Gounder (TN)
Konkna Yenity (KA)
Koosa (AP)
Koosa (OR)
Kootan, Koodan (where they are not Scheduled Castes) (TN)
Koppala Velama (TN)
Kopplavalamas (PO)
Koppulavelama (AP)
Koracha (Keravars) (AP)
Koracha (PO)
Koracha Koravar, Yerukala (TN)
Korachas (or Koravar or Yerukala) (KE)
Korachas or Yerkula or Korvay (MR)
Koraga (AP)
Koraga (OR)
Korchar (MR)
Koria (MP)
Korku (BI)
Korku (RA)
Kormakar (AS)
Korwa (AS)
Korwa (TR)
Korwa including Kodaku (MR)
Kosalya Coudus, Bosotheriya Goudus, Chiti Goudus, Dangayath Goudus, Doddu Kamariya, Dudu Kamaro, Ladiya Goudus & Pullo Soriya Goudus (OR)
Kosalya Goudus Bosothoriya Goudus, Chitti Goudus, Dangayath Goundus, Doddu, Kamariya, Dudu Komaro, Ladiya Goudus & Pullosoriya Goudus (PO)
Kosalya Goudus, Bosothoriya Goudus, Chitti Goudus, Dangayath Goudus, Dodukamariya, Dodukamaro, Adiya Goudus & Pullosariya Goudus (KA)
Kosalya Goudus, Bosothoriya Goudus, Chitti Goudus, Dangayath Goudus, Doddu Kamariya, Dudu Kamarok, Ladiya Gouds and Pullsoriya Goudus (KE)
Kosalya Goudus, Bosothoriya Goudus, Chith Goudus, Dangayath Goudus, Doddu Kammariya, Dudu Kamaro, Laddiya Goudus and Fullo Soriya Goudus (TN)
Kosalyagoudus — (Bass Theriya Groundus, Chitti Groundus, Dangayath Goundus Doddu, Dudu Kamaro Ludiya, Komariya Goundus and Pullo Sariya Goundus) (AP)
Kosavans, Kuyauar (PO)
Koshta (BI)
Koshta (UP)
Koshti (AP)
Koshti (MP)
Koshti (RA)
Koshti, Kashkoti-Devanga (MR)
Kosti, Chaudhry, Kusata, Koli-Keskati (MP)
Kota (AP)
Kota (OR)
Kota (TN)
Kotari, Kottari (KA)
Kotayar (Shoragara Kushatriya) (PO)
Kotekshatriya (KA)
Koteyar (KE)
Koteyar (TN)
Kotia-Bartika, Bantho Oriya, Dhulia or Dulia, Holva, Paiko, Putiya Sanrona and Sidho Paiko (TN)
Kotia-Bartika, Bentho Oriya Dhulia or Dulia, Holva Paiko, Putiya, Sahrona and Sidho Paiko (KE)
Kotia-Bartika, Benthooriya, Dhulia or Dulia, Holva Paiko, Putiya, Sanrona and Sidho Paiko (KA)

Kotil (MP)
Kotwal (AS)
Kotwal (RA)
Kotwal or Kotwalia (GU)
Kotwar (UP)
Koya (AS)
Koya or Goud (with its subsects Raj or Rasha Koyas, Linga Dhari Koya (ordinary) and Kottukoya (TN)
Koya or Goud, with its subsects Raj or Rasha Koya, Kottu Koya and Lingadhari Koya (KE)
Koyava (KA)
Koyi (AP)
Koyi (KE)
Koyi (OR)
Koyi (TN)
Krishnabalija (Dasari Bakka) (AP)
Krishnanyaka (KE)
Krishnavaka (PO)
Krishnavaka (TN)
Kritiria (BI)
Kshatriya (AR)
Kshattriya (AS)
Kshattriya (ME)
Kubbora (TN)
Kuchband (CH)
Kuchband (HR)
Kuchband, Kuchhband (PU)
Kuchbandh (MR)
Kuchhria (MR)
Kudiya (AP)
Kudiya (OR)
Kudubi (AP)
Kudubi (OR)
Kudubi (TN)
Kudubi, Kudubi-Koyi (KA)
Kudubi, Kudumbis (KE)
Kudumban (AP)
Kudumban (OR)
Kudumbi (PO)
Kudumbi (TN)
Kuki (MA)
Kuki (WB)
Kul-Faqir (JK)
Kulait (CH)
Kulala (including Kumbarar and Kyyavar) (TN)
Kulbandhiya, Kumavat (MP)
Kulela, Kulala, Kummari (PO)
Kulta (OR)
Kumahari, Kumbhar, Kumhar (excluding those in S/C) (MP)
Kumar (MP)
Kumar, Rudra Paul (ME)
Kumar, Rudra Paul of Cachar (AS)
Kumarbhag Pahadia (BI)
Kumbar-Kulla, Salivahana (AP)
Kumbara, Kummara, Khumbhar, Kambhar, Kulala, Kulalar, Moolya, Kusavan (KA)
Kumbaran (PO)
Kumbhakar, Kumbhar (TR)
Kumbhakshatriya (AP)
Kumbhar (Biyar, Kadra Patel, Lathiya, Potmaker, Prajapati, Sakariya Variya, Varia) (GU)
Kumbhar, Kulal, Kumhar, Kumbharo (OR)
Kumbhar, Kumar, Kumbhakar, Kumhar, Kumrakar, Rudra (WB)
Kumbhar, Kumhar (MR)
Kumbi, Kumar (MP)
Kumhar (AS)
Kumhar (Potters) (JK)
Kumhar (RA)
Kumhar, Ahitan, Ghamar, Ghumar, Hansanwal, Jopa, Keer, Langotra, Lehri, Narhia, Prajapat, Sanmare, Sohal, Talephail, Zalaf (PU)
Kumhar, Chakbya, Chakire, Kohar, Kumbhar, Prajapati (UP)
Kumhar, Chotrapati, Kobhalkar, Kumbhar, Kumbhakar, Prajapati (BI)
Kumhar, Prajapati (CH)
Kumhar, Prajapati (DE)
Kumhar, Prajapati (HP)
Kumhar, Prajapati (HR)
Kummara or Kulala (AP)
Kunapili (AP)
Kunbi (GD)
Kunbi (MR)
Kunchetigara (AP)
Kunchi Korwa (KA)
Kunchidigar (TN)
Kundamatia (OR)
Kunduma/Kuduma (OR)
Kunjra (MP)

Kunjra, Rayeen (UP)
Kunjra, Rayeen (WB)
Kunnuvar Mannadi (PO)
Kunnuvar Monnadi (TN)
Kupadhar, Kushiar, Rarh (ME)
Kupadhar, Kushiari, Rarh (AS)
Kuraban, Kurumban, Kurumba, Hulumatha, Dhangar Bharwad, Gorava (KA)
Kurakula (AP)
Kurariar (OR)
Kurariar (TR)
Kuravan (AP)
Kuravan (OR)
Kuravar (TN)
Kurhini Chetty (TN)
Kurhinshetty (MR)
Kurichchan (AP)
Kurichchan (KA)
Kurichchan (OR)
Kurma, Kurmi (KA)
Kurmar (MR)
Kurmi (AR)
Kurmi (AS)
Kurmi (BI)
Kurmi (CH)
Kurmi (DE)
Kurmi (HP)
Kurmi (HR)
Kurmi (OR)
Kurmi (PU)
Kurmi (TR)
Kurmi (UP)
Kurmi (WB)
Kuruba or Kuruma, Hegde (AP)
Kuruman (Kurumba) (AP)
Kuruman (Kurumba) (OR)
Kurumans (AP)
Kurumba (where are no Scheduled Tribes) (TN)
Kurumba, Kuruba, Kurubar, Kuruva (PO)
Kurumbaravas (TN)
Kuruva, Kurub, Kurab, Kurubar (KA)
Kusavan (Kulala, Andhra Nair or Anthuru Nair) (KE)
Kusavan (PO)
Kushwaha (Koeri) (BI)
Kuta (UP)
Kutuma (KA)
Kutwar, Kotwal (excluding those in S/C) (MP)

Labana (HP)
Labana, Mahravat, Goti, Hadkashi, Zod, Dhinga, Pelya, Shatbai, Baman (GU)
Labana, Vanzara, Lobana Banjara (CH)
Labbai (PO)
Labbai (TN)
Labera (RA)
Labha (MR)
Ladaff. Laddaf (MR)
Ladar, Lad, Ladaru, Yelegar (KA)
Ladha-Lohar (RA)
Ladia, Ladhia, Laria (MP)
Ladia, Ladhia, Laria (MR)
Lahana (DE)
Lahar (AS)
Lahara (AS)
Laher (OR)
Laheri (BI)
Lakar (WB)
Lakhera (RA)
Lakhera, Chhan, Manihar, Panihar, Paniar (HR)
Lakhera, Kanihar, Manihar (PU)
Lakhera, Lakhari (MR)
Lakhera, Manihar (CH)
Lakhra (OR)
Lakra (WB)
Lalbegi (MA)
Lalbegi (TR)
Lalbegi, Bhangi (Muslim) (BI)
Lalung (MA)
Lambadi (OR)
Lambadi (PO)
Lambadi, Banjara, Sugadi (TN)
Lambadi, Banjara, Sugali, Gavara (KE)
Lambana, Bhagtava, Ghotra, Kaknia, Khasrin, Labana, Lohana, Lobana, Vanzara, Lavana, Pelia (PU)
Langoliha (MP)
Lanzad (MR)
Larhia (MP)
Laskar, Lashkar (TR)
Latin Catholics (KE)
Latin Catholics (TN)
Lek (RA)
Liamei-Naga (MA)

Limbo, Limbu (ME)
Limboo, Limbu (SI)
Lingabalija (AP)
Lingader (RA)
Lingayat Sections namely Shimpi, Shivashimpi, Neelagar, Koshti, Hatagar, Jeda, Bilijeda, Neygi, Kumhinashetty, Bilimagga, Nayinda, Navi, Kshonrada, Kelasi, Hadapad, Nadig, Mangala, Kummar Badagi, Agasa, Modivala, Rajaka, Gurav, Tambli, Kumbar, Kambhar, Kulal, Banagar, Nagalika, Gowli, (Cowherd), Hugar, Jeer, Malagar, Teligar, Pujar, Mathapatis amongst Jangams, Ganigar, Shuddhashiva Shivarechka, Jhammadi (KA)
Lippara (KA)
Lobana, Labana, (Same as in S.No. 5) (HR)
Lodha (AS)
Lodha (BI)
Lodha (GU)
Lodha (TR)
Lodha, Lodh (UP)
Lodhi (AS)
Lodhi (RA)
Lodhi, Hardha, Parihar, Lodha (MP)
Lodhi, Lodha, Lodh, Maha Lodh (DE)
Lohar (BI)
Lohar (JK)
Lohar (MA)
Lohar (MP)
Lohar (TR)
Lohar, Abangar, Luhar, Mistri, Ruriya (UP)
Lohar, Bakhon, Bamsa, Bhati, Bhuhi, Birdi, Channa, Jhita, Luhar, Phul, Roopra, Sandhu, Sehami, Virdi (PU)
Lohar, Jaradi, Khuadi, Khutwal, Lohargiri, Malvi, Panchal, Pancholi, Thurawar, Zaradi (RA)
Lohar, Lohar-Gada, Dodi, Khatwali, Panchal (MR)
Loi (AS)
Loi (ME)
Lome (MP)
Lonari (KA)
Lonari, Chunari (MR)
Lone (JK)
Lonia, Lunia, Nunia, Nonia (MP)
Luhar (DE)
Luhar, Gahelot, Jeva, Kariyar, Kawigar, Luckman, Madwar, Vishwakarma (MP)
Luhar, Lohar (HR)
Luhura (OR)
Luniya, Lonia (UP)
Lushei (WB)

Machhi (Hindu), Bitna, Dhimar, Dhivar, Kahar, Khalas, Khalasi, Kharwal, Mangela, Sarang, Tandel (GU)
Machhi, Machhera (DE)
Machhi, Mali, Marar (MP)
Machhi, Tandel (MR)
Machhua (WB)
Machi, Aaribharatbhara, Bharatbhara, Chamadia, Chandlia, Dasania, Jansali, Jingar, Myangar, Sonari, Sivania (GU)
Machua (OR)
Madar (BI)
Madara (KE)
Madari (AS)
Madari (CH)
Madari (HP)
Madari (HR)
Madari (JK)
Madari (KE)
Madari (Muslim) (BI)
Madari (PU)
Madari, Bharathari, Nath (GU)
Madgi (MP)
Madiga (KE)
Madivala (KE)
Madri (AP)
Madugar or Modavar or Vethakkara (PO)
Maga (MR)
Magadhi Goral (OR)
Magatha Goudu, Bernia Goudu, Boodu Magatha, Dongayath Goudu, Ponna Magatha, Sana Magatha and yadya Goudu (TN)
Magatha Goudus, Bermia Goudus, Boodo, Magatha, Dongayath Goudu, Ladya Goudu, Poona Magatha and Sana Magatha (OR)
Magatha Goudus, Bernia-Goudus, Boodo Magatha, Dongayath Goudu, Lady

Goudu Pona Magatha and Sana Magatha (KA)
Magatha, Goudus-Bernia, Goudus Boodo, Magatha, Dongayath Goudus Ladya Goudu, Ponna Magatha and Sanna Magatha (KE)
Maghaiya-Dome (TR)
Maghi or Meghia (OR)
Maghya (HR)
Magura (OR)
Maha-Brahman (RA)
Mahadarda (WB)
Mahaedra, Mahandra, Medara (PO)
Mahali, Mahli (MR)
Mahandra, Medara (TN)
Mahapatra (DE)
Mahar (TR)
Mahara (MA)
Mahasari (AP)
Mahasari (KA)
Mahasha, Bajgal, Sahunta (PU)
Mahata (WB)
Mahatam (CH)
Mahatam (HP)
Mahatam (HR)
Mahatam (PU)
Mahatar (Muslims) (AP)
Mahato (AS)
Mahato (WB)
Mahigir (JK)
Mahil (MR)
Mahishtya (WB)
Mahishya (BI)
Mahisya Das, Mahisya (ME)
Mahisya-Das, Mahisya (AS)
Mahli (AS)
Mahli (TR)
Mahratta (non-Brahmin) (including Namdev Mahratta) (TN)
Mahto (BI)
Mahunta (OR)
Mahuria (BI)
Mahuria (WB)
Maidhasi (KA)
Maidhasi (MR)
Maila (AP)
Maila (OR)
Maimals (Muslim fishermen) (AS)
Mairal, Dangat, Vir (MR)
Maiti (AR)
Majhabi (MP)
Majhi, Deshwali-Majhi (WB)
majhiara (AR)
Majhwar (BI)
Majhwar (MR)
Majothi Kumbhar, Darbar or Darban Majothi (Muslims) (GU)
Majwar (AS)
Makrana (Muslim) (DN)
Makrani (Muslims) (GU)
Mal (TR)
Mal Paharia (OR)
Mala (MP)
Mala Dasu (KE)
Mala Dasu (TN)
Mala Pantaram (KE)
Mala Pulayan, Karavali Pulayan, Kurumba Pulayan, and Paubu Pulayan (KE)
Maladasu (OR)
Malakar (WB)
Malapantaram (TN)
Malapulayan, Kurumbapulayan, Keravalipulayan, Pambupulayan (TN)
Malar (Malhor) (BI)
Malas or Agency Malas, Valmikies (KE)
Malasar (AP)
Malasar (OR)
Malayali (where they are not Scheduled Tribes) (TN)
Malayan, Malayar (TN)
Malayavayan (TN)
Malayekandi (KE)
Male (PO)
Male (TN)
Malhar (RA)
Mali (Malakar) (BI)
Mali (RA)
Mali (WB)
Mali (where they are not Scheduled Tribes) (AP)
Mali, Bhuimali, Bhuinmali (MA)
Mali, Phoolmali (MR)
Mali, Phoolmali, Saini (CH)
Mali, Phuli, Sagbaria, Bhajemali (OR)
Mali, Saini (UP)
Mali, Saini, Southia, Sagarwanshi-Mali, Nayak (DE)

Mali/Mondi Patta (AP)
Malia-Korchia Malis, Paiko Malis and Pedda Malis (TN)
Malis, Korchiamalis, Paiko Malis and Pedda Malis (KA)
Malis-Korchia Malis, Paido Malis & Pedda Malis (OR)
Mali — Kerchia Mali, Paiko Mali and Peddamali (AP)
Malla Malasar (KE)
Mallah (MP)
Mallah (TR)
Mallah, Birhar, Gayotri, Ghetwel, Jalwar, Kewat, Kurwaha, Maheta, Majhi, Muriyoni, Masuria, Phutant, Purhia, Nisad, Goshi, Dhiwar, Jhiwar, Jhimar (BI)
Mallik (TR)
Malpaharia (AS)
Malphariya (TR)
Malyar (JK)
Manavans (KE)
Manbhav (MR)
Mandula (AP)
Manga (MP)
Mangala (AP)
Mangala (MR)
Mangala (Nayee-Brahman) (PO)
Mangali — Nayi Brahmin (AP)
Mangan (BI)
Mangan (WB)
Mangar (Magar) (BI)
Mangar (WB)
Mangli (OR)
Mangtha Goundus, Bana Megatha, Beraia Goundu, Boodo Magatha, Gongayath Goundu, Ladya Gounda, and Pennagagatha (AP)
Manihar (MP)
Manihar, Lakhera (UP)
Manipuri (including Manipuri Brahmins, Manipuri Muslims & Meteis) (AS)
Manipuri (MI)
Manipuri (TR)
Maniyan (AP)
Maniyani, Muniyani (KA)
Manjar, Mara, Mathwaddar (MP)
Manjhi (UP)
Mankar (MP)
Mankar Khalu (MR)
Manki (AS)
Manna Dhora (KA)
Manna Dhora (KE)
Manna Dhora (OR)
Manna Dhora (TN)
Mannan (KA)
Mannan, Vannan, Pathiyar (where they are not Scheduled Castes) (TN)
Mannus (PO)
Mansari (Muslims) (GU)
Manula (AP)
Manurukapu (Telangana), Munnor — Kapu (AP)
Mapilla (TN)
Mappila (KE)
Mappila (PO)
Marakkan (KE)
Marakkan (TN)
Marameri, Gramani (TN)
Marar (TN)
Marar (TR)
Marasi (HP)
Marathi (AP)
Marathi (excluding South Kanara Distt.) (KA)
Marathi (OR)
Marathi (PO)
Marathi (TN)
Marathi, Marati (KE)
Marauan (KE)
Maravan (TN)
Maravans (KE)
Maravar, Maravaw (PO)
Maravars (Sembanad and Appanad Kondayankottai) (TN)
Marayan, Maravanr (KA)
Marchha (UP)
Maria (AS)
Markande (BI)
Marta (KA)
Maru Sotiya (MP)
Maruar, Marumaravar (TN)
Maruthuvar (PO)
Maruthuvar, Navithar (TN)
Marwar Baori (MR)
Marwari, Budhiya (TN)
Masania-Jogi (DE)
Masaniayogi (KA)

Masanjogi, Sudga-Dsiddha, Mapanjogi (MR)
Matangi (KE)
Matangi (OR)
Matangi (TN)
Mathura (AP)
Mathura (MR)
Matial (WB)
Matiara, Matihara (MR)
Matwa or Matwa-Kureshi (Muslims), Gavli (Hindus) (GU)
Maulik (BI)
Maune (AP)
Maune (KE)
Maune (OR)
Maune (TN)
Mauria (MP)
Mauriaro (BI)
Mavi (MP)
Mavilan (AP)
Mavilan (OR)
Mawati (HR)
Mdivla, Madivala (PO)
Me (MR)
Me or Meta (GU)
Mech (MA)Changar (PU)
Mech (TR)
Medara (KE)
Medara (TN)
Medara, Medari, Burud, Gauriga, Medara (KA)
Medari or Mahendra (AP)
Meena, Mina (CH)
Meena, Mina (HR)
Meena, Mina (PU)
Meenavar, Parvatha, Rajakulam, Sembadaran, Patanavan (TN)
Meghaiya-Domes (WB)
Mehra (HP)
Mehra (RA)
Mehtar, Bhungi (MA)
Meitei and Meitei Pangal (MA)
Melakudi or Kudiyan (PO)
Memar, Raj (DE)
Mena (Bhil) (GU)
Meo, Mewati (DE)
Mer (GU)
Mer (RA)
Merasi, Mirasi (DE)
Merasi, Mirasi (RA)
Merat (RA)
Merat-Gorat (RA)
Merat-Kathat (RA)
Merh-Rajpoot (CH)
Meru (MP)
Mewati (CH)
Mewati (MP)
Mewati (PU)
Mewati (UP)
Mhali, Nai, Navi, Nhavi (MP)
Miana, Miyana (Hindus & Muslims) (GU)
Michi (CH)
Mikir (MA)
Mina (DE)
Mina (MR)
Minka (OR)
Mir (JK)
Mir, Dhadhi, Langha, Mirasi (Muslims) (GU)
Mirasi (CH)
Mirasi (JK)
Mirasi (MP)
Mirasi (PU)
Mirasi, Gathala, Halwe, Kuchra, Simrachhukar (HR)
Mirasi, Merasi (UP)
Mirhdar (AS)
Miri (MA)
Miriasin (Muslim) (BI)
Mirshikar (Muslim) (BI)
Mirshikar (WB)
Mishmi (MA)
Mistri, Gujar, Mistri Rathod, Mistri Suthar (GU)
Mitha (MR)
Mitha Ayyalvar (KA)
Mitna (GD)
Mochi (excluding those in S.C.) (PU)
Mochi (excluding those in S.C.) (UP)
Mochi (excluding those in S.C.) (DE)
Mochi (HR)
Mochi, Saraj (Shoe-repairers) (JK)
Modi (AS)
Modi Bans (PO)
Modiga, Modikara, Modikar (KA)
Modugar or Muduvan (KA)
Mogaveera (KE)

Mogaveera (PO)
Moger (AP)
Moger (OR)
Moger, Morgau (WB)
Moghia (RA)
Mogia (RA)
Mohli (AS)
Moili, Moli (PO)
Momin (Asar) (UP)
Momin (Muslim) (BI)
Momin (WB)
Momin (Weaver) (MR)
Mon (Drum-beaters) (JK)
Mondgolla (PO)
Mondivaru, Mondi Banda, Banda (AP)
Mondiwar (AP)
Mondiwar, Mondi waru (KA)
Mondiwar, Mondiwaru (MR)
Mongar (SI)
MOngola (PO)
Moniagar (PO)
Moniagar (TN)
Moopar (TN)
Moran, Matak (AS)
Moran, Matak (ME)
Morapora-Brahmin (WB)
Moundadan (PO)
Moundadan Chetty (TN)
Mro (TR)
Muchhia (MP)
Mudava/Muduga (PO)
Mudhar (KA)
Mudiraj, Mutrasi, Tenugollu (AP)
Mug (WB)
Mukha Dhora or Nooka-Dhora (KA)
Mukha Dhora, Nooka Dhora (TN)
Mukhadora-Mokka Dhora (OR)
Mukhari (PO)
Mukhi (AS)
Mukhi (ME)
Mukkavan (KA)
Mukkuvan Mukkuvar (TN)
Mukkuvan or Kukayan, Mogayan, Logavan (including Bovis) (PO)
Mukkuvan, Mukaya (KE)
Mukri (RA)
Mukro (Mukero) (Muslim) (BI)
Muliya (AP)
Muliya (KE)
Muliya (OR)
Muliya (TN)
Muliya, Muria (KA)
Munda (AN)
Munda (AS)
Munda (MA)
Munda (ME)
Munda (MR)
Mundala (OR)
Mundas (AS)
Mura (AS)
Murao, Murai (UP)
Muria (AP)
Muria (KE)
Muria (OR)
Muria (PO)
Muria (TN)
Muria Bhottada (KE)
Murraha, Murha (MP)
Murrari (KA)
Musavar (CH)
Muslim Banjara (UP)
Muslim-Kayastha (UP)
Mutherachas (AP)
Muthuraja (Muthuracha, Muthiriyar and Muttiriyar) (TN)
Muthuraja (PO)
Muthursi — Bania, Ganga Putra, Mudiraj, Muthuraja, Telenga, Tenugu (AP)
Mutlakampatti (PO)
Mutlakampatti (TN)
Muttiriyan/Muthiriyar (PO)

Naar (CH)
Naar (HR)
Nadafs, Ladafs, Dhunya, Mansuri, Pinjar or Pinjari (Muslims) (KA)
Nadar (KE)
Nadar (PO)
Naddaf, Pinja (CH)
Nadia, Hadi (RA)
Nadkal (UP)
Nadora, Nadar, Uppunador, Troke Nador (KA)
Nag Bansi (AS)
Naga (MA)
Nagar (TR)
Nagar (WB)

Nagaralu (AP)
Nagaralu (PO)
Nagaram (PO)
Nagaram (TN)
Nagarchi (RA)
Nagasia (AS)
Nagatha Goudus-Bemia Goudub, Boodo Magatha, Dengoyath Goudo, Ladya Goudu. Ponna Magatha and Sanâ Magatha (PO)
Nagavaddilu (AP)
Nagavaddily (PO)
Nagavasam (Nagavamsa), Nagbansh (AP)
Nagesia (TR)
Nahar (OR)
Nai (RA)
Nai (Valand) (DN)
Nai, Amrewal, Banbiro, Didhia, Hajjam, Mandi, Jadowal, Japi, Juvwa, Kaikan, Kaila, Kaith, Kuleen-Brahman, Matwal, Napit, Navki, Neogi, Panwar, Rajwan, Thakur (HR)
Nai, Bamneru, Hajam Kuleen-Brahman, Patiyal (HP)
Nai, Banvaru, Dhanwal, Dhari Ghangas, Ghiri, Hajjam, Hazam, Hergun, Jallan, Lekha, Nagi, Naisikh, Palan, Panju, Patara, Raja (PU)
Nai, Bij, Hajjam, Napit (AS)
Nai, Hajjam, Naiya, Napit (WB)
Nai, Hazzam, Nai (Sabita) (DE)
Nai, Jakur, Hajjam, Khawe, Napit, Nau, Orrey, Sarivas, Savita (UP)
Naidu (GD)
Naidu (Vadulu, Karare, Naicker, thayya, Nambiar) (AN)
Naidu Balija Gouda, Vadugan (KE)
Naidu Gavara (PO)
Naik (AP)
Naik (RA)
Naik, Nayak, Nayaka, (Non-Brahmin) (MP)
Naikapu (AP)
Naiker, Vanniya (PO)
Naikkans (KE)
Naikkans, Naicken (PO)
Naikkar (TN)
Naiko (TR)
Naita, Nayata, Nata, Navta (MP)
Naiya (TR)
Nakkala (PO)
Nakkalas (AP)
Nakkalas (TN)
Nal Band (JK)
Nalakeyava (OR)
Nalakodaya (PO)
Nalband (BI)
Nalband (CH)
Nalband (DE)
Nalband (HP)
Nalband (HR)
Nalband (Muslims) (KA)
Nalband (PU)
Nalband (WB)
Nalis, Korchia Malis, Paikonalis and Pedda Malis (KE)
Nalki (KA)
Namasudra, Adhikari, Sarkar, Dhati, Bala, Hira, Baidai, Maji, Daligbi, Bodoi, Diskas, Poddar, Hindal, Roy, Das, Hadder, Manji, Basi, manser, Biri, Nag, bairagi, Bhatra, (Baidya) (AN)
Namdev (MP)
Namdev, Simpi (PO)
Namdhari, Paik (MR)
Namshudra (BI)
Namsudra (MP)
Nandiwala, Fullmali (KA)
Nandiwala, Tirmal (MR)
Naniar (PO)
Nanijil Mudali (TN)
Napit (ME)
Napit (TR)
Napit, Nai (MA)
Naqashi (MR)
Naqqal (DE)
Nar (HP)
Nar (PU)
Narikoravan (PO)
Narikoravar (TN)
Nat (Muslim) (BI)
Nat (OR)
Nat, Nat-Bajania, Natada, Bajigar (GU)
Nat, Nattadas (TR)
Nat, Natuva (KA)
Nath (AS)
Nath (MP)
Nath, Jogi (GD)

Nath, Yogi (WB)
Nathpanthi, Dauri Gosavi (KA)
Nattu Malayans (KE)
Nav-Buddhists, Neo-Buddhists (KA)
Nav-Buddhists, Neo-Buddhists (TN)
Nav-Buddhists, Neo-Buddhists (UP)
Nav-Buddhists, Neo-Buddhists (WB)
Nav-Buddhists, Neo-Buddhists (BI)
Nav-Budhhist, Neo-Buddhists (GU)
Nav-Budhists, Neo-Budhists (PU)
Nav-Budhists, Neo-Budhists (RA)
Navda (MP)
Navi, Nhavi, Hajam, Kalseru Navaliga, Kelashi, Nabhik, Nai (MR)
Navundian (PO)
Nayadi (AP)
Nayadi (OR)
Nayak (AP)
Nayak (AS)
Nayak (TR)
Nayinda, Nayanaja Kshatriya, Hajjam Nhavi, Nadig Ambettam Mangala, Kelasi, Kshowrad, Ksihowrik, Chouriya, Navaliga Napitha, Bhandari (KA)
Nayor (AR)
Neelakanthi (AP)
Neeli (MR)
Neelkanti (MR)
Nekar, Jada (MR)
Nelakanavaru (KA)
Neo Buddhists, Nav Buddhists (MR)
Neo-Buddhists, Nav-Buddhists (MP)
Nepali (Chatri, Chhetri, Dami, Gaine, Gurung, Lama, Lihu, Lohar, Magar, Rai, Sarki, i.e. Cobbler, Thapa) (AS)
Nepali (Damai, Gaine, Gurung, Lama, Lohar, Newar, Rai, Sarki, i.e. Cobbler, Thapa) (ME)
Nepali (Limbo, Matwali, Rai) (TR)
Nepali Lama (AR)
Nerali (MP)
Neria (MP)
Neriya (RA)
Nessi or Kurni (AP)
Nethura (MR)
New Buddhists, Nav-Buddhists (PO)
Newar (WB)
Neygi, Kuruhingsetti, Bilimagga, Thogata, Soniga, Jamkhana, Ayiri, Avir, Sale, Saale, Kaikolan Neikar, Jadar, Jandra Swakulasale (KA)
Neyyala (AP)
Nhavi (AP)
Nhavi, Nai (GD)
Nilgar (MP)
Nilgar, Nirali (MR)
Nirshikari (MR)
Nirshikaris (AP)
Nirshikaris (TN)
Nokka (PO)
Nokkar (AP)
Nokkars (TN)
Nolakeyava (AP)
Nolia (OR)
Nolli (AP)
Nonia (MR)
Nonia, Kharwat, Nunia (BI)
Nonia, Nunia (AS)
Noongar (CH)
Noongar, Mungar (HR)
Noongar, Nungar (PU)
Nuhura, Nuhuraj (OR)
Nulayan (KE)
Nulayan (TN)
Nuniya (OR)
Nuniya, Nunia (TR)
Nut (excluding those in S.C.) (UP)

Od (GU)
Odans (Andhra Nair or Anthuru Nair) (KE)
Odans, Odde, Voddoo or Vadda or Veddai, Odon (Donga), Odiya (PO)
Odar, Oddar, Woddar, Odiya (TN)
Odd (RA)
Oddar (or Weddars), Odde, Odder, Vadde, Oddilu, Vaddi, Vadde (AP)
Ode, Wader, Waddar, Odiya (MP)
Odhia (UP)
Oinlu (PO)
Ojulu or Metta, Kamasalie (OR)
Ojulus or Metta Komsalies (KE)
Ojulus or Motta, Komsalis (AP)
Ojulus, Metall Komasalies (TN)
Omanaito (KE)
Omanaito (PO)
Omeyita (OR)

Ommaite (AP)
Oraon (AS)
Oraon (MA)
Oraon (ME)
Oraon (TR)
Orh. Od (UP)
Ostha (KA)
Otari (KA)
Otari, Otankar, Otkar, Vatari, Ojhari (MR)
Ottanaickan (PO)
Ovachar (TN)

Pacha Bhotla (AP)
Pacha Bhotla, Pacha Botla (KA)
Pachabhotla, Pachabotla (MR)
Pachabotla (AP)
Padampari (AP)
Padampari (KA)
Padampari (MR)
Padamsali-Margude, Setty, Devanga (KA)
Padannan (where they are not Scheduled Castes) (TN)
Padaria, Pamaria, Pandara (OR)
Padarti (KA)
Padayachi (PO)
Pademsali, Salewar, Sali/Sutsali (MP)
Padhar (where they are not Scheduled Tribes) (GU)
Padharia (MR)
Padia, Padiyar (KA)
Padiar (MR)
Padit (KA)
Padka (MP)
Padmasali (Pattusali, Sali, Salivan, Seanapathulu, Thogata Sali) (AP)
Padmasali (PO)
Padmashali-Pattushali (GU)
Pagadai (AP)
Pagadai (KA)
Pagadai (KE)
Pagadai (OR)
Pahar (MP)
Pahira (BI)
Pahri (UP)
Paidi (AS)
Paidi (KE)
Paidi (TN)
Paigarapu (AP)
Paigarapu (KA)
Paigarapu (KE)
Paigarapu (OR)
Paigarapu (PO)
Paigarapu (TN)
Paiko (OR)
Painda (AP)
Painda (KA)
Painda (KE)
Painda (PO)
Painda (TN)
Paite (MI)
Pakhali, Bhisti (MR)
Pakhiwara (CH)
Pakhiwara (DE)
Pakhiwara (HP)
Pakhiwara (HR)
Pakhiwara (PU)
Paky (KA)
Paky (KE)
Paky (OR)
Paky (TN)
Pal (Bherihar-Gaderi), Gaderia (BI)
Pal (OR)
Pal Pardhi (MR)
Palaekari (PO)
Palakari (AP)
Palanwadia (GU)
Palasi (KA)
Palasi (KE)
Palasi (OR)
Palasi (PO)
Palasi (TN)
Palhari (MP)
Paliyan (OR)
Paliye (TR)
Palk (TR)
Palla, Pallikari, Pallikarullu, Agnikela (AP)
Pallan (AP)
Pallan (OR)
Palli (AP)
Palli (KA)
Palli (OR)
Palli (PO)
Palli (TN)
Palli — Vada Balika, Gangavar, Goondla Valari, Vanyakulak — Shatriya

(Vannokapu, Venneredd Nayyala and Pattapu) (AP)
Palwadia (GU)
Pamaria (Muslim) (BI)
Pambada (OR)
Pambala (AP)
Pamidi (KA)
Pamidi (KE)
Pamidi (TN)
Pamula (AP)
Pamula (KA)
Pamula (PO)
Pamula, Panchal (MR)
Pamulu (TN)
Pan (ME)
Pan (TR)
Pan Davakulan (KA)
Panaba (KA)
Panan (KA)
Panan (where they are not Scheduled Castes) (TN)
Panar (TN)
Panasa, Panssa (KA)
Panchama (MR)
Panda (MR)
Pandara (AP)
Pandaram, Pandar, Pandara (KA)
Pandaran, Maniakar (KE)
Pandi (BI)
Pandi Thattan (PO)
Pandithar (Anpattan, Pranopkari and Nasivan) (PO)
Pandithavs (KE)
Pangul (MR)
Panika (AS)
Panika, Panikkar (KA)
Panikkan (KE)
Panikkan (TN)
Paniyan (AP)
Paniyan (OR)
Panjira (OR)
Panka (MR)
Panki (TR)
Pannagadikara (PO)
Pannaiyar or Pannayar (PO)
Pannan Vettuva Goundor (PO)
Pannayar (TN)
Panniandi (AP)
Panniandi (KE)
Panniandi (OR)
Pannirandam Chettiar or Uthama Chettiar (TN)
Panniyar (KE)
Pano (KE)
Pano (TN)
Pans (AS)
Panthi (WB)
Panwari (MP)
Papmelara Konkani (KA)
Para (JK)
Paradhi, Pardhi, Pardhi-Raj, Advichincher, Phase Pardhi (where they are not Scheduled Tribes) (GU)
Paraiyan (OR)
Paralayan (AP)
Paramban (PO)
Parashar (MP)
Paravan (AP)
Paravan (Christians) (PO)
Paravan (OR)
Paravan, Paravar (where they are not Scheduled Castes) (TN)
Pardhan (KA)
Pardhi (including Advichincher and Phanse-Pardhi) (RA)
Pardhi (Nirshikari) (AP)
Pardies (AP)
Parhaiya (OR)
Pariki Muggula (AP)
Pariyas (Vengur and Vappur) (TN)
Parja (AS)
Parkavakulam Suruthinar, Malayamar, Nathamar (TN)
Parna, Perna (JK)
Parol Madivala (PO)
Parrakavakulam (Surithinaman) Malayanan, Nathaman, Moopanar & Nainar (PO)
Parthi (MP)
Parya (BI)
Pasi (AS)
Pasi (KA)
Pasi (TR)
Passi (AP)
Pathar Chera, Sangtarash (DE)
Patherkut, Bachigolia (BI)
Pathir (JK)
Pathiyan (where they are not Scheduled

Castes) (TN)
Pathukudi (PO)
Pathuria (OR)
Patka, Patki (MP)
Patkar (Khatri) (AP)
Patkar (MR)
Patnaik (BI)
Patnulkaran (PO)
Patra (AP)
Patra (KA)
Patradaveru (MR)
Patramela (KA)
Patratanti (AS)
Patrikulam, Patrakulam (PO)
Patro (OR)
Patta avam (PO)
Pattariya (KE)
Pattariyas or Pattarias (PO)
Pattulakaran (PO)
Patua (WB)
Patvekari, Pategar, Pattegar (KA)
Patwa (BI)
Patwa (DE)
Patwa (Phadal) (RA)
Patwa, Namdev, Pathakar, Sipiya (MP)
Pauan (AP)
Pauri (UP)
Pawariya (UP)
Payak (MP)
Peddammavandlu, Davaravandlu, Yellamma Vandlu, Mutyalamma Vandlu (AP)
Peer (JK)
Pengua (OR)
Pentia (KA)
Pentia (KE)
Pentias (PO)
Perika (Perike Balija, Puragiri Kshatriya) (AP)
Perikalu, Reddy (AP)
Perike (Perike Balija) (TN)
Perike, Perike balija, Piragiri Kshatriya (PO)
Perki (MP)
Perki (MR)
Perumannan (TN)
Perumbadlan (PO)
Perumkollans (KE)
Perumkollans (PO)
Perumkollar (TN)
Peruvannan (PO)
Peruvannan (Vearanacvar) (KE)
Petias (AP)
Petias (TN)
Phar (MR)
Phasechari (MR)
Phudgi (MR)
Phulari (MR)
Phutdhar (BI)
Picchigunta (PO)
Picharis (AP)
Pichati, Pichari (KA)
Pichgunta, Picchiguntala, Pichuguntala (KA)
Pielai (PO)
Pillai (KE)
Pillai, Vilaler, Vellalar, Karabhattu, Karanbattu (AN)
Pillava (PO)
Pindara (MP)
Pindaras or Pendaris (Muslims) (KA)
Pinganiya (BI)
Pinja, Penja (HP)
Pinja, Penja (PU)
Pinjali, Pinja (HR)
Pinjara (RA)
Pinjara, Ghanchi, Mansuri-Panjara (Muslims) (GU)
Pinjara, Pinjari (MR)
Pinjare (MP)
Pirali (WB)
Pita (OR)
Pitchiguntala (AP)
Pod (TR)
Poligars (AP)
Polinativalma of Srikakulam & Visakhapatanam Distt (PO)
Polinativelamas (AP)
Pomla (KA)
Pomla (RA)
Pomnala (PO)
Pony-Men-Mule-Men (JK)
Poosala (AP)
Poraya (PO)
Poraya (TN)
Porja-Bado, Bonda, Daruva, Didva, Jodia, Mundil, Sano, Pengu, Pydi, Saliya, Sodia and Pareng (OR)

Porja-Bodo, Bonda, Daruva, Diduva, Jodia, Mundili Pengiyi, Pydi and Proja (KE)
Porjas or Porajas-Bodo, Bonda, Daruva, Didua, Jodia, Mundili, Pareng, Pydi, Salliya, Sano and Sodia (TN)
Porjas, Bonda, Daruva, Didua, Mundili, Pengu, Pundi and Saliya (KA)
Poroja (KE)
Poroja-Boda, Poroja, Sodia Poroja, Sano Poroja, Joddia Poroja and Parenga Poroja (KA)
Porojas-Bodo Poroja or Sodia, Sano Poroja, Jodia Poroja and Pareng Saliya (KE)
Poroja —— Bado Peroja or Sodia, Jodia Perjoa, Pareng Peroja and Sona Paroja (AP)
Powar (MP)
Powara (KA)
Powara (RA)
Powra (GU)
Pradhan (AS)
Pradhan (BI)
Pradhan (OR)
Praravatharajakulam (PO)
Pukhali (MR)
Pulaya (KE)
Pulayan (AP)
Pulayan (KA)
Pulayan (OR)
Pullavan (KA)
Pulluvan (KE)
Pulluvan (PO)
Pulluvan, Pulluvar (TN)
Pundari (TR)
Pundari (WB)
Punnan Vettuva Gounder (TN)
Pusala, Pusalavaan, Pusalvandlu (PO)
Pusale (TN)
Puthirai Vannan (KA)
Puthiraj Vannan (AP)
Putligar (MP)
Putligar (MR)
Puttnul, Karan (AP)

Qureshi (Kassab) Muslims (KA)

Rabari, Sorthia, Charalia, Charmta, Luni, Kushar, Tank, Muchhal Kadiyakumbhar (where they are not Scheduled Tribes) (GU)
Rabha (MA)
Rabha (ME)
Rabha (TR)
Rachband (CH)
Rachband (HR)
Rachband, Rechband (PU)
Rachbandhia (MR)
Rachevar (MR)
Rachkoya (AP)
Rachkoya (MR)
Radhi or Niari (OR)
Raghavi (MR)
Raghavi, Raghvanshi (MP)
Rai (SI)
Rai-Sikh (CH)
Rai-Sikh (HR)
Rai-Sikh (PU)
Raighatwal (TR)
Raika (RA)
Raikari (MR)
Raj (UP)
Raj Pardhi, Gaon Pardhi, Haran Shikari (MR)
Rajaka (PO)
Rajamuria, Rangari (MP)
Rajapow (KE)
Rajapuri (TN)
Rajapuri, Rajpur, Balavalikar (KA)
Rajapuri, Raju (PO)
Rajbanshi (ME)
Rajbanshi, Koch (AS)
Rajbanshi, Rajbansi (TR)
Rajbhar (BI)
Rajboshi (Risiya and Poliya) (BI)
Rajdhobi (BI)
Rajgir (MP)
Rajgond (MP)
Rajput (AS)
Rajput (KA)
Rajput Bhamta, Pardeshi Bhamta, Pardeshi Bhamti (MR)
Raju (TR)
Raju (WB)
Rajwar (AS)
Rajwar (OR)
Rajwar (TR)

Rakhal (WB)
Ralte (MI)
Ramgharia, Bimra, Brar, Bumral, Chan, Dhiman, Kalsi, Matharoo, Murway, Ramgarhia, Saggu, Sahota, san, Saran, Tarkhan (PU)
Ramoshi (MR)
Rana (WB)
Ranbari (RA)
Raneyar (AP)
Raneyar (OR)
Rangari, Rangrez, Bhawsar (MR)
Rangrez (DE)
Rangrez (Muslim) (BI)
Rangrez (UP)
Rangrez (WB)
Rangrez, Rangarej, Rangraz, Ramgari, Rangredh (MP)
Rangwa (BI)
Rao (AN)
Rao (MP)
Rao (RA)
Raot, Rautia, Rawt (MR)
Raot, Rawt, Raoti (MP)
Rasali (WB)
Rathawa (RA)
Rathodia (GU)
Raulo (AP)
Rauther (PO)
Rautia (MP)
Rautia (MR)
Rauttiya (BI)
Raval, Raval or Raval Yogi (MR)
Raval, Ravalia Raul, (KA)
Raval-Ravalia, Jati or Raval Yogi, Rawal Jati, Jagaria, Padat, Ravar Rawalia (GU)
Ravana-Rajput (RA)
Rawal (MP)
Rawat (RA)
Rawat, Beder, Gahira, Rast, Rawar, Thethwar (MP)
Rawat, Raya, Rewath (KA)
Rayakwar (DE)
Rayeen (BI)
Rebari (RA)
Rechband (HP)
Reddi Dhokas (OR)
Reddi Dhora (KA)
Reddi Dhoras (TN)
Reddian (KE)
Reddikas (AP)
Reddiyar (Reddiyar, Jhothi, Reddyar) (AN)
Reddy Dhora (KE)
Rehar, Behara, Rer, Rihar (CH)
Rehar, Rehara, Rihar, Rea (HR)
Reinudas (KA)
Relli or Sachandi (KE)
Relli Orsachandi (KA)
Relli, Sachndi (TN)
Rhar (MP)
Riaigar (PU)
Rihar, Rehar, Rehare (PU)
Rohade, Sujharia (MP)
Rohangia, Roshangia (WB)
Rohar (MP)
Rohit (GU)
Rona (KA)
Rona (KE)
Rona (PO)
Rona (TN)
Ronas (OR)
Roniaur (UP)
Routia (OR)
Ruchhandhia (MP)
Rupai (TR)

S.C. (Converted to Christianity) (KA)
S.I.U.C (KE)
Sad-Sausi (Sehar) (RA)
Sadajoshi (KA)
Sadan, Dedan (PO)
Sadhu (RA)
Sadhu Chetty (including Telugu Chetty, Telugupatty Chetty, Twenty four Mani Telugu Chetty) (TN)
Sadhuchetty (AP)
Sagalis (PO)
Sagar (GD)
Sagarpasha (OR)
Sagra (HP)
Saha (WB)
Sahabar (OR)
Sahis, Sais, Shis (MR)
Sahora (AS)
Sahte (MA)
Sain (MP)
Saini (HR)
Saini (PU)

Sais, Sayees, Shis (MP)
Saiva vellalan (PO)
Saiz (DE)
Sajalang (AR)
Sakaravar (Kavathi) (KE)
Sakkarvar (Kavathi) (TN)
Sakravar (Kavathi) (PO)
Salat (where they are not Scheduled Tribes) (GU)
Sali, Padamshali, Swakulsali (MR)
Salian (Pattarayan), Saliyas, Saliyan, Pattusali, Senapathulu, Kamithoktulu, Sale, Jhogata Sali (PO)
Salivahana, Salivagana (TN)
Saliyar (Padmasaliyar, Adhaviyar, Pattariyar) (TN)
Saliyas (KE)
Salói (AS)
Saloi (ME)
Salvi, Sali (MP)
Samban (OR)
Sambavan (Tamil) (KE)
Sanaithalaivar (Senaikudiyan) (PO)
Sandhi (Hindus & Muslims) (GU)
Sangar (MR)
Sangari (AP)
Sangari (KA)
Sangari (MR)
Sangatrash (BI)
Sangheda (GU)
Sangtrash (JK)
Saniyar (KA)
Sanjogi (MR)
Sankhakar, Sarkheru (WB)
Sankhari (OR)
Sanoria (MP)
Sansi (GU)
Sansi (JK)
Sansi (KA)
Sansia (KA)
Santal (KA)
Santal (MA)
Santal (MR)
Santhal (ME)
Santhal, Santal (AS)
Sanyasi, Mambram (OR)
Sao-Teli (MR)
Saonta or Saunta (MR)
Saora (AP)
Saora (KA)
Saora (KE)
Saora (TN)
Sapari (AP)
Sapari (KE)
Sapera (MR)
Sapera, Kalbelia (UP)
Sarabara (RA)
Saraj (JK)
Sarania (GU)
Sarania (KA)
Sarania (MR)
Saranjia (MP)
Sarbhangi (MP)
Sare (AP)
Sare (KA)
Sare (MR)
Sargara (GU)
Sarki (Nepali) (MA)
Sarodi, Saroda (KA)
Satani (Chattada Srivaishnava Chatadi) (AP)
Satani, Chattada, Srivaishnava (KA)
Satarkar (KA)
Sathatha Srivaishnava (including Sathani Chattadi Chattada) (TN)
Satiya-Sindhi (RA)
Saun (UP)
Sauria Paharia (OR)
Sausashtra (Pathulkarar) (TN)
Sauta (Sota) (BI)
Savalakarar (TN)
Savara (KE)
Savara-Kapu, Savara, Khutto Savara, Mallya Savara (OR)
Savaras-Kapusavaras, Khotto Savaras and Maliya Savaras (KE)
Savaras-Kopu Savaras, Khutto Savaras and Maliya Savaras (TN)
Savare (ME)
Savarsa, Kapusavara, Khuttosavara, Maliya Savara (KA)
Saya Pillaimar (TN)
Sayar (WB)
Sayee (Muslim) (BI)
Scheduled Caste converted Christianity (WB)
Scheduled Caste converted to Christianity (CH)
Scheduled Caste converts to Christianity and their children (AP)

Scheduled Castes converted to Christianity (KE)
Scheduled Castes converted to Christianity (MP)
Seela-Ventham (AP)
Seerithi Goudu (KA)
Seerithi Goudu (OR)
Seerithi Goudus (AP)
Seerithi Goudus (KE)
Seerithi Goudus (TN)
Semman (AP)
Semman (KA)
Semman (OR)
Senai Thalavar (Elavaniar) (KE)
Senai Thalvivar (Elavabanias) (PO)
Senaithalaivar, Illaivaniar and Senaikudiyar (TN)
Senatal (AP)
Server, Agamudyar (AN)
Sestakarnam (AP)
Setti Balija (PO)
Shagird Pesha (WB)
Shagirdpesha (TR)
Shaksaz (JK)
Shanan (KA)
Sharia (MP)
Shenva, Chenva, Sedma, Ravat, Shindhaya (RA)
Shikkaligar of Sikkaligar (KA)
Shikligar (GU)
Shilavat (MR)
Shimpi, Bhavgar, Shiv Shimpi, Namdeo (MR)
Shin (JK)
Shingdav or Shingadya (GU)
Shingdav or Shingadya (KA)
Shingdav or Shingadya (MR)
Shingdev, Shingadya (RA)
Shivhari (BI)
Sholaga (AP)
Sholaga (KE)
Sholagar (AP)
Sholagar (KA)
Sholagar (KE)
Sholagar (OR)
Shorgir (CH)
Shorgir (HR)
Shorgir (PU)
Shrawan, Sarwan (GU)
Shupri Wattal (excluding those in S.C.) (JK)
Siddi (where they are not Scheduled Tribes) (GU)
Sikkalgar, Kotari (MR)
Sikligar (JK)
Sikligha (RA)
Silkigar (MP)
Sindhor (AP)
Sindhor (KA)
Sindhor (MR)
Singalu (AP)
Singhikat, Singhiwala (PU)
Singhiwala, Singhikaut (CH)
Singikant, Singiwala (HR)
Singiwala (MP)
Singiwala (MR)
Singpho (MA)
Sinke (OR)
Sipai, Patni Jamat or Turk Jamat (Muslims) (GU)
Sirkiwal (RA)
Sistakkaranm (PO)
Sithuria, Sitaria, Situlia (OR)
Siyal (BI)
Siyal (WB)
Siyane (MP)
Sochi (GU)
Sochi (KA)
Sochi (RA)
Sochies (JK)
Sodhi (MP)
Soi (CH)
Soi (PU)
Soir, Soyer (BI)
Soliga (KA)
Sollar (PO)
Sonar (MR)
Sonar, Arya (Koli) (KA)
Sonar, Sunar (MA)
Sonar, Sunar, Swarnakar (UP)
Sonar, Swarnakar (WB)
Sondhiya, Chandel (MP)
Sondi, Soundika (AP)
Sore (AP)
Sore (KA)
Sore (MR)
Sorollo (Somavansha Kshatriya) (AP)
Sourashtras (KE)
Soveras (AS)
Sozhia Chetty (TN)

Sozhia Vellalar (including Keerakarar, Kodikalarar, Sozhia Vellalar and Vatrilaikaran) (TN)
Srehde (AR)
Sri Sayama, Segidi (AP)
Srisayana (PO)
Srisayar (TN)
Sthai (DE)
Suba (SI)
Suda (OR)
Sudha Salva Shivarchka (AP)
Sudir, Sudra (KA)
Sudra Das, Dey (AS)
Sukli (TR)
Sukli (WB)
Sukuli, Tanti (OR)
Sulia (OR)
Sumra (GU)
Sunar (AR)
Sunar (DE)
Sunar (SI)
Sunar, Ashta, Chaganara, Dawar, Kangra, Karod, Katcviriya, Lamba, Mahij, Mandwa, Saraf, Shirisiwan, Sirsohal, Sona, Soni, Swarnkar, Thingo, Urwal (HR)
Sunar, Ashtat, Bhatti, Dhume, Jure, Kande, Karwar, Sheen, Suniara, Sur, Swarnkar (PU)
Sunar, Bakwar, Sonar, Swarnkar (BI)
Sunar, Jargar, Kapila, Soni, Swarnkar, Tonk (HP)
Sunar, Sonar (MP)
Sunna (AP)
Sunna (MR)
Sunna, Sunnai (KA)
Sunnai (AP)
Sunnai, Sutharia (MR)
Sunri (BI)
Sunri (TR)
Sunri/Sundi (OR)
Suppalig (MR)
Surava (KA)
Surehra (HP)
Sut (ME)
Sut, Soot (AS)
Sutar, Bhadai, Wadai (MR)
Sutari (AP)
Sutradhar (TR)
Sutsali (KA)
Swakulasali (AP)
Swami (RA)
Swarankar (RA)
Sweepers (Muslims) (KA)
Synteng (MA)

Tachavire (KA)
Tadavi (MP)
Taga (CH)
Taga (HR)
Taga (PU)
Taga, Tagah (DE)
Taga-Bhat (UP)
Tak (RA)
Takankar (KA)
Takankar (MR)
Takaras (Muslims) (KA)
Takari (MR)
Talabia (GU)
Talavia (KA)
Talayari (AP)
Talwar Kanade (MR)
Tamang (SI)
Tamang (WB)
Tamariya (BI)
Tambat (MR)
Tamboli (AP)
Tamboli (BI)
Tamboli (MR)
Tamboli, Jamboli, Kumavat, Purabia (MP)
Tamboli, Tamali, Tamuli (WB)
Tamboli, Tamuli (MA)
Tameli (UP)
Tamera, Tambatkar, Thatera (MP)
Tammali (AP)
Tamoli (BI)
Tamta (UP)
Tana (OR)
Tankar (GU)
Tanti, Tantubaya (WB)
Tanti, Tati (TR)
Tanti, Tati, Tatin, Tatwa, Swati (BI)
Tanti, Tatwa, Tantripal, Patwa (UP)
Tantripal, Tanti, Tantri (AS)
Tantripal, Tanti, Tantri (ME)
Tantubai (AS)
Tapoli (BI)
Tarakan (PO)
Targala (MR)

Targala, Bhayiya, Bhojak, Nayak (GU)
Tarkhan (CH)
Tatapux (PO)
Tausa (AS)
Tei, Modh Ganchi (GU)
Telaga (KA)
Telaga Pamula (OR)
Telaga Pamula, Peddati Gollas (TN)
Telega, Kamma (AP)
Telenga (AS)
Teli (AS)
Teli (BI)
Teli (CH)
Teli (DE)
Teli (JK)
Teli (MA)
Teli (ME)
Teli (PU)
Teli (RA)
Teli (TR)
Teli, Badbaik, Balu, Rathore (MP)
Teli, Ganiga, Ghanchi (MR)
Teli, Hansarti, Kanala (HR)
Teli, Sahu (Hindu and Muslim both) (UP)
Teli, Telli, Kubara, Talakar, Sahu, Bahaldia (OR)
Tellunga, Palatti Chattis (TN)
Teruvan, Chillya (KA)
Thai-Chanhari (AS)
Thakaroa, Baria, Dharala, Patanwadia, Thakore (GU)
Thakkar (MR)
Thakur (Nai) (AN)
Thakur (Non-Rajputs) (GU)
Thakurai (Muslim) (BI)
Thami (MP)
Thandal Vannan (PO)
Thandan (where they are not Scheduled Castes) (TN)
Thanta Pulayan (KE)
Thantapulayan (TN)
Thanu (OR)
Thanwar (MP)
Thanwin (CH)
Thapa (WB)
Tharu (BI)
Tharu (WB)
Thatari (OR)
Thathera (BI)
Thathera (RA)
Thathera, Kasera (CH)
Thathera, Tamera (PU)
Thathera, Tamera, Thater, Kasera, Tamkar (HR)
Thathers, Kasera (UP)
Thawin (HP)
Theba (Muslims) (GU)
Thelari (MR)
Thetwar (MR)
Thevar (TN)
Thiya, Elhura, Thiyyas (PO)
Thiyya (TN)
Thiyyas (KE)
Thogata Veerakashatriya (TN)
Thogata, Thogati or Thogataveera Kshatriya (AP)
Thogatta Veerakshatriya (PO)
Thogti, Thogati (MR)
Tholko Lans (KE)
Tholkollans (PO)
Tholkollar (TN)
Tholuva Naicker and Vetalakara Naicker (TN)
Tholuva Naicker and Vettalakara Nairko (PO)
Thondaiman (PO)
Thondaman (TN)
Thontaman (KE)
Thoraiyan (PO)
Thori (MP)
Thori, Turi (CH)
Thoria (MR)
Thoriyar (TN)
Thotewadu (KA)
Thotewadu (MR)
Thoti (OR)
Thoti, Burad (MP)
Thottai Naicks (TN)
Thottia Naick (KE)
Thottia Naicken (including Rajakambalam, Gollavar, Sillayar, Thokalavar and Tholuva Naikar) (PO)
Thottia Naicks (AP)
Thottia-Naicks (KA)
Thottian (KE)
Thottiya Naicker (including Gollavar, Silavar, Rajakambalam, Thockalavar and Tholuva Naicker) (TN)
Thottiyar (PO)
Thulva — Vellala, Agamu — Daiyan

(AP)
Thunnan (PO)
Thuria (MP)
Thuria (OR)
Thurpur Kapus, Casula Kapus (PO)
Tigala (Tigla) (PO)
Tigala, Thigala, Tigler, Vannikula Kshatriya, Shanbhukula, Kshatriya, Dharmaraja, Kapu, Kuravana, Pallai Agnikula Kshatriya (KA)
Tikulhar (BI)
Tilari, Tirali (KA)
Tili (WB)
Tilvi (KA)
Timali (GU)
Timali (KA)
Timali (MR)
Timali (RA)
Tipara (ME)
Tipara (TR)
Tipara (WB)
Tipara, Tipera (AS)
Tipera (MA)
Tippera (WB)
Tirgar (MP)
Tirmale (MP)
Tiruvalluvan (KA)
Tiruvalluvar (AP)
Tiruvalluvar (KE)
Tiruvalluvar (OR)
Tirwa (UP)
Tirwalli (MP)
Tivoro (OR)
Tiyar (BI)
Tiyar (OR)
Tiyar (TR)
Toda (AP)
Toda (KE)
Toda (OR)
Toda (TN)
Tolikula (PO)
Tonla Gaud (OR)
Toto (TR)
Tsong (SI)
Turha (MP)
Turha (WB)
Turha, Sao (BI)
Turi (AS)
Turi (KA)
Turi (TR)
Turi (UP)
Turupukapus (AP)

Ulladan (TN)
Ullatan (TN)
Upasara (AP)
Uppaliga Settey-Reey (KA)
Uppara (PO)
Uppara (Upplillia Sagara) (TN)
Uppara or Sagara (AP)
Uppara, Uppear, Uppiliyan, Beldar, Sagara, Chunar, Gavandi, Govandi, Govadi, Goundi, Melusakkare (KA)
Urali Goundan (PO)
Urali Gounders (TN)
Urao, Bandot, Haro, Karkata, Luidu, Shitheo, Tigga, Tirki (WB)

Vada Balija, Vadava (Golla or Kondri) (PO)
Vadder-Bevi, Upparilu (AP)
Vadi (GU)
Vadi (KA)
Vadra or Vaddara (PO)
Vadugan (AP)
Vadukan, Vadagan, Vadugan, Vaduvan (PO)
Vaduvan (KE)
Vaghri, Vaghari, Salat, Salat Vaghri (MR)
Vaghri-Gamicho, Vedva Churalia, Jakhudia (where they are not Scheduled Tribes) (GU)
Vagri, Vaghri, Pradhan (MP)
Vaidu (KA)
Vaidu (MR)
Vaidyanai (MP)
Vaiti (MR)
Vajluthedan (KA)
Vakkaliga (KE)
Valaiyars (TN)
Valakatalavan (PO)
Valan (TN)
Valans (PO)
Valayar (KA)
Vale, Valand, Nai (Hindus), Hajjam, Khalipha (Muslims) (GU)
Vallamber (TN)
Valluvan (AP)
Valluvan (OR)

Valmiki (AP)
Valmiki (KE)
Valmiki (PO)
Valmiki (TN)
Valmiki Boya (Boya, Bedar, Kirataka, Nishadi, Vellapi Pedda Boya), Talayari and Chundu Vallu (AP)
Valvai (KA)
Valvai (MR)
Vanadi (MR)
Vanian (Vanika, Vanika Vaisya, Vanikha Chetty, Vaniya Chetty, Ayiravar, Nagarthar and Vaniyan) (KE)
Vaniar (KE)
Vaniyan or Vaniar (Vanika, Vanika-Vaisya, Vaisyachetty, Vanibaacherry, Ayiravar and nagarathar) (PO)
Vaniyar (PO)
Vaniyar, Vania Chettiar (including Gandala, Ganika, Chekkalar and Telugula) (TN)
Vanjara (Vanjari) (AP)
Vanjara, Banjara, Charan Banjara, Mathura Banjara, Maru Banjara, Bagora Banjara, Kangashiya Banjara, Bamania Banjara, Ladonia Banjara, Gavaria or Gawalia, Rohidas Banjara (GU)
Vanjari, Vanjar (MR)
Vanjari, Vanjara (MP)
Vankar Sadhu (GU)
Vannan (Mannan, Pathiyan) (TN)
Vannan (OR)
Vannan, Vannar (PO)
Vannar, Rajakula Veluthadar (where the community is not a Scheduled Caste) (TN)
Vanniyakula Kshatriya (including Vanniya Vanniyar, Vannia Gounder, Gounder or Kander, Pidayachi Palli, Agniguia Kshatriya) (TN)
Vanniyakula Kshatriya, including Vanniar or Vanniyar Gounder, Kondar or Vannia Gounder and Vannikandar (other than Vella Gounder belonging to Vanni Vanniyakula Kshatriya Caste) (PO)
Vans-Foda, Vansfodia or Vanza, Wansfoda (GU)
Varala, Thogra, Bholla, Baliga (AP)
Varli (RA)
Varnavar (KE)
Varnavar (TN)
Vasawa (MR)
Vasudeo (MR)
Vasudev (KA)
Vathiriyan (KA)
Vathis (PO)
Vedar (TN)
Veeramushti (Nettikotala) (AP)
Veerasaivas (Yogeeswara and Yogis) (KE)
Veerassiva (Fandaram, Matapathi, Vairagi, Vairavi, Yogiswarar) (PO)
Veetasaiva (TN)
Velaan (KE)
Velaiyar (TN)
Velakkithalanayar (TN)
Velan, Vollan (PO)
Vellala Pillai, (Nanjinad Vellala) (PO)
Vellan Chettiar (TN)
Vellayan-Kuppam Pandayaochis (TN)
Veluthadanayar, Veluthonathunayar (TN)
Veluthedathu Nair (Veluthedan and Vannathan) (KE)
Veluthsdan, Veluthedathu Nair (PO)
Vetan (where they are not Scheduled Castes) (TN)
Vettai Karans, Vettaikarar (TN)
Vettaikaran (PO)
Vettakkaran (KE)
Vettakkaran (TN)
Vetturan (PO)
Vettuva Goundar (PO)
Vettuva Goundus (TN)
Vettuvan (AP)
Vettuvan (KA)
Vettuvan (OR)
Vettuvan (PO)
Vidiki, Niyogi (AP)
Vikurup (PO)
Vilakkathala Nairs (Velakkathalavan) (PO)
Vilakkethal Nair (Vilakkithalavan) (KE)
Vina Tulavina (OR)
Vir, Veer, Veeramasti (KA)
Virakadi Veklalar (PO)
Virakod Vellaa-la (TN)
Virasivalingayat (AP)

Vishavan (KE)
Vishavan (Malankudi) (TN)
Vishavan (TN)
Vishnoi (MP)
Vishwa Brahman, Sarpa, Daivagnya-Brahman, Kammar, Ausala, Kammalan, Kamsal, Kamsala, Panchal, Panchala, Sutar, Badagi, Badiwadli, Soni, Pattar, Gejjigar, Silipi (KA)
Vishwakarma-Luhar, Akkasale, Achari, Sivachar, Ahru (KA)
Vishya (MP)
Viswabrahmin (Ausula or Kamsali, Kammari, Kanchari, Vedia or Vadra or Vadrangi and Silpis) (AP)
Vitholia (KA)
Vitholia (MR)
Vitholia (RA)
Vitolia, Kotwalia, Barodia (RA)
Vizhavan (Malankhdi) (KE)
Vokkaliga (Rural areas only) (KA)
Vokkaligar (including Gounder, Gowda, Kappiliyr, Kappliyar, Oklaligar, Okkaliya, Vakkaligar) (TN)
Vyasokta (WB)

Waddar or Kala Waddars or Pathrods (AP)
Wadder, Wadder (Kalawader or Patharod), beldar, Od, Girni Waddar, Vaddar, Gaddi Vaddar, Jati Vaddar, Mati Vaddar, Patharvat (MR)
Wadi (MR)
Wadla (AP)
Wadwa Waghari (GU)
Waghari, Dataniya, Waghari, Vodu Waghari, Talapada, Waghari, Gamachia Waghari, Godadia Waghari, Chibhadia Waghari (GU)
Wagher (Hindus & Muslims) (GU)
Wandhara (GU)
Wanha (MP)
Wanjari, Wanjara (MR)
Wansfoda (MR)
Warthi (MR)
Wasdeo (MP)
Wynad Chetty (TN)

Yadav (Gwala, Ahir, Gope, Sadgope, Ghasi) (BI)
Yadav, Gavli (GD)
Yadav, Rolal, Kollubhatti, Konar (AN)
Yadava (Iruman, Kolaya, Muniyani, Ayar) (KE)
Yadava (Konar, Kolaya, Ayar, Mayar, Muniyan, Eruman) (PO)
Yadavan (Idayan) (KE)
Yadavan (Idayan) or Yadava (including Idaiyar, Telugu speaking Idaiyar known as Vaduga Ayar or Vaduga Idaiyar or Golla, Mond Golla Asthanthra Golla) (TN)
Yakthungba (SI)
Yanadi (KE)
Yanady, Yenadi (TN)
Yandi (KA)
Yandi (OR)
Yaras (AP)
Yashkun (JK)
Yata (AP)
Yavane (TN)
Yedu Kulam (AP)
Yeklar, Yaklar, Yekkali, Egalika (KA)
Yenadiwads (MR)
Yenadiwaos (KA)
Yenadiwards (AP)
Yeragolawad of Thella Pamalwads (MR)
Yeragolawad or Thella Pamalwada (KA)
Yeralu (KA)
Yerkilwar, Yerkula (MP)
Yerna Golta (OR)
Yerukula (KE)
Yerukula (OR)
Yerukula (TN)
Yetla (AP)
Yogeswaran (TN)
Yoggeswaran. (PO)
Yogi, Jogi, Nath (TR)
Yogi, Jugi, Nath (MA)
Yogi, Jugi, Nath (ME)
Yorukula (PO)
Yuarulau (AP)

Zamral (RA)
Zargars/(Muslims) (KA)

16

The List of Depressed Backward Classes Enumerated in the Second Backward Classes Commission (Mandal)

Alphabatical list to facilitate users to identify the backward class in respective States.

ABBREVIATIONS USED FOR THE STATES

ANDAMAN & NICOBAR ISLANDS	AN
ANDHRA PRADESH	AP
ARUNACHAL PRADESH	AR
ASSAM	AS
BIHAR	BI
CHANDIGARH	CH
DADRA AND NAGAR HAVELI	DN
DELHI	DE
GOA, DAMAN & DIU	GD
GUJARAT	GU
HARYANA	HR
HIMACHAL PRADESH	HP
JAMMU & KASHMIR	JK
KARNATAKA	KA
KERALA	KE
MADHYA PRADESH	MP
MAHARASHTRA	MR
MANIPUR	MA
MEGHALAYA	ME
MIZORAM	MI
ORISSA	OR
PUNJAB	PU
RAJASTHAN	RA
SIKKIM	SI
TAMIL NADU AND PONDICHERRY	TP
TRIPURA	TR
UTTAR PRADESH	UP
WEST BENGAL	WB

Abbasi, Bhisti, Sakka (DE)
Abdal (BI)
Achukatalavandhu (AP)
Adhiri (BI)
Adhori (MP)
Adi Karnatak (AP)
Adi-Dravida (OR)
Adi-Karnataka (OR)
Adidharmi (MP)
Adikari (WB)
Adiya (excluding Coorg District) (KA)
Adodia (GU)
Agaria, Agariya (TR)
Agaria, Agariya (WB)
Agariya (BI)
Agasa (KE)
Agasa, Madivala, Tsakala, Sakalavadu, Shakala, Vannan, Mannan, Dhobi, Parit, Rajaka, Puthirajvannan, Velluthedan (KA)
Ager (RA)
Agharia, Agaria, Aghria (OR)
Aghore (WB)
Aghore, Karkarmunda (KA)
Agri (DN)
Agri (GU)
Agri (UP)
Agri Kherwal (DE)
Agri, Agala or Kalan (MR)
Aheri (MP)
Aheria, Aheri, Heri, Naik, Thori, Turi (HP)
Aheria, Aheri, Heri, Naik, Thori, Turi (PU)
Aheria, Aheriya (UP)
Aheria, Ahiria, Heri, Aheri, Naik, Thori, Turi (HR)
Ahir (DN)
Ahir, Yadav (CH) (CH)
Ajila (OR)
Alavan (KE)
Alitkar (MR)
Amaat (BI)
Amant, Amat, Amath (WB)
Ambalakkaran (KE)
Amblar. Ambathan, Ambithan, Eshavatory, Kalrrikurup, Maruthuver Naiken, Pandithar Villakkithatanavi (KE)
Ampattan (TP)
Apatani (MI)
Arakh (UP)
Aranadan (KA)
Aranedan (OR)
Arayan (KE)
Arayan, Arayar (Nulayar) (TP)
Arayavathis (KE)
Ard-Pop (HP)
Arematharti (KE)
Arundatilu (H) (AN)
Arunthuthiyar (OR)
Arupatun (KE)
Aruthuthiyar (KA)
Arya Mala (AS)
Aryakshatriya, Chittari, Chitrakara, Giniyar, Nkha (AP)
Asada (RA)
Asara (MP)
Asur (AS)
Asur (OR)
Asur (TR)
Ataari (KA)
Atar (KA)
Atar (MR)
Athiya (MP)
Audhie, Avadhi (MP)
Audhiya (MP)
Audhiya (MR)
Auji (UP)

Badabukkala (AP)
Badaga (KA)
Badaga (OR)
Badaga (TP)
Badagar (TP)
Badak (MP)
Badak (UP)
Badaka (MP)
Badasuda (OR)
Badera, Baoria (RA)
Badi (MP)
Badi, Chinsoras, Meloris, Odmata, Uramamara (HP)
Badia (HP)

Badia (MR)
Badia (UP)
Badia (WB)
Badia, Sapera (MP)
Badyakar, Dhuli, Nagarchi, Sabdakar (TR)
Bag (WB)
Bagad-Bogadi, Bagodi, Bagadi, Bogodi (KA)
Bagalu (KA)
Bagalu (MR)
Bagari, Bedar, Borad, Beldar (MR)
Bagari, Byageri (KA)
Bagaria (CH) (CH)
Bagaria (HR)
Bagata (KA)
Bagata (KE)
Bagata (KE)
Bagata (TP)
Bagdi (Gujarati Boori, Marwar Boori, Marwar Waghri, Salat Waghri) (MR)
Bagdiya, Bawaria (RA)
Bagdo (BI)
Baghta, Baree, Bawar, Payak, Vaidyanai (MP)
Bagria (HP)
Bagria, Bagaria (PU)
Bahari (CH) (CH)
Bahelia (TR)
Bahti (HP)
Bahurupi (MP)
Bahurupi (MR)
Baiga (AS)
Baijara (AS)
bailapatar, Bailaptar, Bikapatar (KA)
Baira (KA)
Baira (OR)
Bairagi (MP)
Bairi (UP)
Baishnab (TR)
Baiti (TR)
Bajadar, Bajania, Bedey (WB)
Bajania (MR)
Bajania, Bajonia (KA)
Bajania, Kannatia (MP)
Bajel (SI)
Bajgar, Bajigar (MP)
Bajigar (BI)
Bajigar (HP)
Bajigar (MR)
Bajigar (UP)
Bajikar (CH) (CH)
Baked, Bant (RA)
Bakuda (OR)
Balasanthanam (MR)
Balasanthu, Bahurupi (AP)
Balasantoshi (KA)
Balpari (OR)
Banchada (RA)
Banda (AP)
Bandara (AP)
Bandara (AP)
Bandi (MR)
Bandi (OR)
Bandi (UP)
Bangala (JK)
Bangalo (BI)
Bangela, Badia, Perna Sapera (DE)
Banjara (WB)
Banjara badi Lobana (JK)
Banjara, Banjari, Labana, Bamania Banjara, Mathura Banjara (MP)
Banjara, Banjari, Vanjara, Mathura Banjaras(A) Goar Banjars, Lambada/Lambara, Lambhani, Charan Bangarao, Labhan, Mathura Labhan, Kachikiwale, Sanjaros, Laman Banjaras, Laman/Lamani, Laban, Dhali/Dhaia, Dhadi/Dhari, Singaris, Navi Banjaras, Jogi Banjaras, Banjari (MR)
Banjara, Gawaria, Kangiwala, Kangi, Baladia, Sirkiwala, Labana, Labhana, Maru Banjara, Bamama Banjara, Bayora, Digora (RA)
Banjara, Gor, Ladenia, Gamalia, Osaria, Mathura, Labana, Labhana, Dhanakuta Banjora, Brajawasi Banjara, Banjara nut Gwar, Banjara Sikh (UP)
Banjara, Lambadi, Lamani, Sugali (GD)
Banjara, Vanjara, Gwar, Badi (HR)
Banjara, Vanraja, Charan Banjara, Mathura Banjarah, Maru Banjara, Bagora Banjara, Kangashia Banjara, Bamania Banjara, Gavaria, Gavalia, Rohidas Banjara (GU)
Banjogi (TR)
Banjogi (WB)

Banka (OR)
Banpar (BI)
Bansphor (MR)
Bant (excluding Belgaum, Bijapur, Dharwar and North Kanara Distt.) (KA)
Bantu (KA)
Bantu (MR)
Banus, Buna, Bunna, Buno (WB)
Baoria (MP)
Baoria, (MR)
Bara, Barra (HR)
Barad (JK)
Barad (MP)
Baragiri (WB)
Barahar, Basod (RA)
Barai, Tarboli, Tamboli (PU)
Barar (RA)
Barar (Umati) (AN)
Barasa, Labana, Labhan, Lamame, Mathura, Nayakda (MP)
Barchain, Chai, Chain (WB)
Barda (KA)
Barda, Dhia (RA)
Barer (PU)
Bargi (MP)
Bargunda (RA)
Bari (BI)
Bari (MP)
Bari (UP)
Baria (AS)
Baria (MP)
Baria, Koli Bari (MR)
Barika, Bhandari, Beja, Napit and Nai (OR)
Bariki (KE)
Bariki (TP)
Barjubi (AS)
Barlur (KA)
Barma (HR)
Baro (WB)
Barot, Vahivancha, Charan Gadhvi (GU)
Barra (CH) (CH)
Barthunda (MP)
Barwar (CH) (CH)
Barwar (HR)
Barwar (PU)
Basigar (KA)
Basor (AS)
Basor (RA)
Basphor (AS)
Basphor (BI)
Bastar, Sanchaluwaddar (MR)
Batahini (KA)
Bateri (PU)
Bathai, Battal, Batler, Battar (KA)
Bathi (CH) (CH)
Bathini (AP)
Bathini (MR)
Bathudi (WB)
Battada (AP)
Battada (KA)
Battada (KE)
Battada (OR)
Battera (HR)
Batterha (CH) (CH)
Batterha (HP)
Baura (UP)
Bauri (AS)
Bauri (TR)
Bauria (DE)
Bauriah (UP)
Bavcha (MR)
Baver (MP)
Bavri or Baori (GU)
Bavuri (KA)
Bavuri (KE)
Bavuri (TP)
Bawaria (MP)
Bawrtar (KA)
Bayar (UP)
Bazigar, Nat, Kalendar (excluding those in S.C.) (DE)
Beda (HP)
Beda, Bedaru, Bedar, Naik, Bedar Nayaka, Naika Makkalu, Naikwara, Palegar, Talwar, Valmiki, Valmikimakkalu, Boya, Vedan, Berad, Ramoshi (KA)
Bedak (MR)
Bedia (AS)
Bedia (JK)
Bedia (UP)
Bedia, Bediya (TR)
Beetha, Siviar (TP)
Begal (WB)
Begari (AP)
Bekewal, Bakkarwal (JK)
Bekhada (BI)

Beldar (AS)
Beldar (TR)
Beldar, Bachgotra, Sapera (BI)
Beldar/OD (MR)
Beldiya (BI)
Bellara (AP)
Bellara (KA)
Bellara (OR)
Bemariha (MP)
Bendari (KE)
Bentkar (BI)
Bentkar (OR)
Bentkar (WB)
Beri (DE)
Beria (CH) (CH)
Beria (HR)
Beria (KA)
Beria (MP)
Beria (PU)
Beriah (UP)
Berua (TR)
Berua (WB)
Bestha, Gangamatha, Gangaputra Bhoi, Parivara, Kabbera Kabbaligar, Bariki, Bariker, Mogaverra, Besthar, Bunde, Besthar, Gangamakkalu, Gowari Matha, Ambiga, Ambig, Kharvi, Bhoi Boyi, Thoreya, Harakantra, Kahar, Meenagar, Sunnagar, Koli, Gabit, Daavat, Kanet (KA)
Bestna, Jelare, Vade-Balaji, Neyyalu, Agnikula-Kshatriya, Palli, gangaputragoondla, Parvatharajakulam, Gangavar (AP)
Beta, Hensi, Hesi (CH) (CH)
Beta, Hensi, Hesi (PU)
Beta, Hensi, Hosi (HP)
Beta, Herai or Hesi (HR)
Betere or Betra (OR)
Bettada (TP)
Bezigar (JK)
Bhadbhunja (MR)
Bhadre (MP)
Bhadre (MP)
Bhaduja (MP)
Bhaduria (MP)
Bhakta (TR)
Bhalia (GU)
Bhampta or Ghantichote or Pardesi Pong, Baser Uchale (MR)
Bhampta, Ghantichor, Pardasi-Bhampt (RA)
Bhamta (AP)
Bhamta, Bhampta, Paradesi, Bhampata, Takari, Uchillian, Rajaput, Bhampta (KA)
Bhamta, Bhamti, Bhanmate, Bhanta, Bhammate (MP)
Bhamta, Pardeshi Bhamta (GU)
Bhand (CH) (CH)
Bhand (DE)
Bhand (JK)
Bhand (MP)
Bhand (MR)
Bhandari (GD)
Bhangi (excluding those in Scheduled caste) (WB)
Bhangi, Khokrob, (Sweepers) (excluding those in S.C.) (JK)
Bhant (WB)
Bhanta (MR)
Bhantu, Sansi (MP)
Bhanumati (RA)
Bhaot, Bhatraj, Bhatraju (KA)
Bhar (BI)
Bhar (TR)
Bhar (UP)
Bhar (WB)
Bhar (WB)
Bharadi, Balasantoshi, Kinggriwale, Nathbava, Nath Jogi, Nath Panthi (MR)
Bharai-Bharibar (MP)
Bharaik (AS)
Bharari (MP)
Bharatar (TP)
Bharbhooja (DE)
Bharbhuja (BI)
Bharbhuja (MP)
Bharbhuja, Bharbhunja, Kalanera (HR)
Bharbhunja (CH) (CH)
Bharbhunja, Bharbhuja (HP)
Bharbunja, Bharbhuja (PU)
Bhardi, Bharagi (KA)
Bharewa (MP)
Bhari, Rode (PU)
Bharud (MP)
Bharud (RA)
Bharunja (JK)

Bharwad (DN)
Bharwad (excluding Nesses of forest of Alech Barada & Gir) (GU)
Bhathiara (UP)
Bhatiara, Basgaqi (WB)
Bhatraju (other than Kshatriya Raju) (TP)
Bhatua (OR)
Bhavaiya or Targala (MR)
Bhettadas-Bodo, Bhottads, Muriabhattada and Sano Bhottads (AP)
Bhil (AS)
Bhil (UP)
Bhilava (KE)
Bhina Koya (MR)
Bhinbar (TR)
Bhisti or Pakhali (MR)
Bhogta (OR)
Bhoi (MP)
Bhoi, Bhoiraj, Dhimar, Zingabhoi, Kevat, Bhoi, Bhanara Bhoi, Manchhindra Bhoi, Palewar Bhoi, Kirat Bhoi, Keher Bhoi, Pardesh Bhoi, Shrimali Bhoi (GU)
Bhoi, Kharvi, Dhiwar Bhoi, Zinga Bhoi, Pardeshi Bhoi, Raj Bhoi, Bhoi, Kahar, Tadia Kahar, Kirat, Machwa, Manzi, Jatia, Kewat, Dhiwar, Dheewar, Dhimar, Palowar, Mechhendra, Navadi, Malhar, Malhav, Gadhav Bhoi, Khadi Bhoi, Khare Bhoi, Dhevra, Dhuria Kabar (MR)
Bhokta (AS)
Bhokta (OR)
Bhotia (WB)
Bhottadas-Boda-Bottada, Muria-Bhottada and Sano Bhottada (KE)
Bhottadash-Bodo Bhettada, Muria Bhottada & Sane Bhottada (TP)
Bhottads, Boto Bhattad, Muria Bhottada, Sano Bhatatda (KA)
Bhoyar (MP)
Bhoyar (Pawra) (MR)
Bhubhalia (DE)
Bhugal (WB)
Bhuhalia (HP)
Bhuhalia (PU)
Bhuihar, Bhuiyar, Bhubhalia (BI)
Bhujan (OR)
Bhujru (CH) (CH)
Bhujwa (MP)
Bhul (UP)
Bhuliya (OR)
Bhumaao-Bhuri, Bhumia Bodo-Bhumia (KA)
Bhumias-Bhumia and Bodo Bhumia (KE)
Bhumias-Bhuri Bhumia and Bodo Bhumia (TP)
Bhumij (AS)
Bhumij (AS)
Bhumij (MR)
Bhumij, Bhmij (TR)
Bhumji (ME)
Bhurji, Bharbjuja, Bharbhunja, Bhunj, Bhunjia, Kandu, Kashodhay (UP)
Bhurtiya (MP)
Bhuta, Bhopa (MR)
Bhutia (MP)
Bhuyan (AS)
Bhuyan (AS)
Bidarkia (MP)
Bijoria (MP)
Billava (TP)
Bin (TR)
Bin (WB)
Binapatta (KA)
Bind (BI)
Bind (TR)
Bind (UP)
Bindili (KA)
Binedhany (OR)
Bingi (KA)
Binjhawar (WB)
Binjhia (TR)
Binjhia (WB)
Binjia (AS)
Binjina (BI)
Binjina (WB)
Birhor (AS)
Birjhia (OR)
Birjia (AS)
Bissey, Barangi Jodia, Bennagi, Dadus, Frangi, Bollar, Theoriya, Kollal, Konde, Paranga Jodia, Sodo and Takora (KA)
Bissoy-Barangi Jodia, Bannangi, Daduva, Godo Jodia, Hollar, Jheriya, Kollai, Konde, Paranga, Pergajodia, Prangi, Takora (AP)

Bissoy-Barangi Jodia, Bannagi, Daduva, Frangi, Mollar, Jheriya, Kollai, Konde, Paranga, Panga-Jodia, Sodo Jodia and Takore (TP)
Bissoy-Barangi Jodia, Bennangi, Daduva, Frangi, Hollar, Jhoriya, Kollai, Konde, Paranga, Pengajodia, Sodo Jodia and Takoara (OR)
Bissoy-Barangi, Jodia, Bennangi, Bollar, Daduva. Frangi. Jhoriya Kollai, Konda Pranga, Ponga, Jodia, Sodo Jodia and Takora (KE)
Bogada (OR)
Bolodhia (OR)
Bondil (TP)
Bondo (AS)
Boro, Bore Kachari (MR)
Boro-Kachari (ME)
Botehra (CH) (CH)
Bowri (AS)
Boya (TP)
Boya, Valmiki (AP)
Boyar, Oddar (TP)
Brahmi (DN)
Brijia (WB)
Budabukhala (TP)
Budbukhi, Bubdkala, Devari (KA)
Budbukk (AP)
Bududki, Damruwale, Kudmude, Madhangi, Sarodo, Sahdev Joshi, Sarvade, Sarode (MR)
Bukadra (KA)
Bukka (AP)
Burbook (AP)
Burbook (MR)
Buruashankar/Barna Suarkar, Beja (OR)
Burud (GU)
Burud, Madar (MR)
Butakusuda (OR)
Buttal (MR)
Byagari (KE)
Byagari (TP)

Chaak (WB)
Chachati (KE)
Chackaravar (KE)
Chadar (MR)
Chahang (PU)
Chain, Chayeen (BI)
Chak (DE)
Chakala, Chawla, Dhobi, Rajaka, Chakali, Vannar (AP)
Chakkala (KE)
Chakkiliyan (OR)
Chakrawadya Dasar (GU)
Chakrawadya Dasar (KA)
Chakrawadya-Dasar (RA)
Chalavadi (OR)
Chalavdi (KE)
Chalvadi, Chamnayya (RA)
Chamana (RA)
Chamar (AS)
Chamlong (WB)
Chamtha (MR)
Chanal (UP)
Chanchati (TP)
Chandal (MR)
Chandalagade (MR)
Chandrabhanshi (Kahar) (BI)
Chang, Chahang (HP)
Changar (HP)
Chanou (BI)
Chaparband (Muslim) (KA)
Chapota (BI)
Charg (CH) (CH)
Chasadhoba, Haladhar, Halari, Satchasi (WB)
Chatri-Agnikulaksatryya, Bombili (AP)
Chatwal (BI)
Chavalakkaran (KE)
Chavalakkaran, Chavalakkarer (TP)
Checta (RA)
Chelopa (HP)
Chemchu or Chanchwar (MR)
Chenchu (KE)
Chenchu (TP)
Chene-Dasaru (RA)
Chenna-Dasar, Holaya (RA)
Chere (AS)
Chero (OR)
Cheruman (AP)
Cheruman (OR)
Chhara, Adodia, Sansi (GU)
Chick Banik (AS)
Chidar (RA)
Chik (OR)
Chik (UP)
Chik, Chikwa, Kasai, Kassab (WB)

Chikbaraik (OR)
Chintala (AP)
Chintala (KA)
Chintala (MR)
Chirimar (CH) (CH)
Chirimar (DE)
Chirimar (WB)
Chitra, Chitrakar (KA)
Chitra, Chitrakar (OR)
Chitrakar (WB)
Chitrakathi-Joshi (KA)
Choongar (MP)
Chopemari (AP)
Choudang (AS)
Choudang (ME)
Chouhan (TR)
Christian Chamar (GD)
Christian Mahar (GD)
Chuhar or Chuhra (KA)
Chumpa (UP)
Chunal (UP)
Chunara (GU)
Chunkar (MP)
Churia (OR)
Churihara, Lakhera, Lahera (WB)
Churima (HR)
Chutia, Chutiya (AS)
Chutiya (ME)
Chuvalia Koli (GU)

Dabgar (GU)
Dabgar (MP)
Dabgar (MR)
Dafali, Dholi (MP)
Dafla (MR)
Dahalia (OR)
Dahez (MP)
Daiya (CH) (CH)
Daiya (PU)
Dakalaru (RA)
Dakaleru (MR)
Dakaut (CH) (CH)
Dakaut, Dahkaut (PU)
Dakaut, Dakot, Jyotshi (HR)
Dakot, Garo, Gakudia (RA)
Dalera (UP)
Dalu (TR)
Dalu (WB)
Damai (Nepali) (MR)
Damai (TR)
Damal (OR)
Damala (AP)
Damami (RA)
Dana (MP)
Danasi (KE)
Dandari (AS)
Dandasi (AS)
Dandasi (KA)
Dandasi (TP)
Dandesa (KE)
Dang-Dasar (KA)
Dangua (OR)
Daoli, Daola (HR)
Daoli, Deola (PU)
Daoli, Doala (CH) (CH)
Dapala (MR)
Dasari (AP)
Dasari (Donga & Gudu) (AP)
Dasari (TP)
Dasari, Desari (KA)
Dasir Dangdidas (MR)
Daula, Soni-Braderi (PU)
Daya, Dhaiya, Jallad (DE)
Deha, Dhaya, Dhea (CH) (CH)
Dehuri (OR)
Dekaleru (GU)
Deons (OR)
Deoria (MR)
Desali (TR)
Devari, Gosavi, Nath, Panthi (MR)
Devhar (BI)
Devli (MR)
Dey, Sudra Das (ME)
Dhadi (RA)
Dhai (CH) (CH)
Dhakad Dhanak Dhanaka, Dhanuk Gokhi (RA)
Dhakad, Bhandari, Nagar Singhavi, Talaya (MP)
Dhakaru (WB)
Dhakkada (AP)
Dhakkada (OR)
Dhakkada (TP)
Dhamai (AS)
Dhamin (BI)
Dhanchi (RA)
Dhaner (OR)
Dhangar (GD)

Dhangar, Gadri, Gadaraia, Hatgar, Hatkar, Kurmar, Pal Bagala (MP)
Dhangar, Kruba, Kurubar (MR)
Dhanka including Tadvi, Tataria and Valvi (KA)
Dhankar (BI)
Dhankia (MP)
Dhanwar (AS)
Dhanwar (BI)
Dhanwar (HR)
Dhaon (WB)
Dhar (MR)
Dhari (BI)
Dhari (UP)
Dheevara (KE)
Dheha (BI)
Dheha (JK)
Dheha (JK)
Dhekaru (BI)
Dhemaru (TR)
Dhenuar (WB)
Dhenwar (CH) (CH)
Dhenwar (PU)
Dher (AP)
Dher (KA)
Dhimar (BI)
Dhimar (RA)
Dhimar, Dhinwar, Jhinwar, Kahar, Mallah (CH) (CH)
Dhimar, Dhivar, Gabit, Harkantra, Mangali, Mangale, Page, Sankuri (MR)
Dhimar, Dhiwar, Dhinwar, Jheevar, Jhinwar, Kahar, Mallah, Kashyap, Rajput (HP)
Dhimar, Dhiwar, Dhinwar, Jheevar, Jhinwar, Kahar, Kashyap, Rajput, Mallah (PU)
Dhimar, Mallah, Kaashyap Rajput (HR)
Dhimer, Benmu, Banawar, Bhorji, Dhimar, Kewat, Raikar, Raikwar Saimari (MP)
Dhinwar, Jhinwar, Nishad (DE)
Dhirkar (MP)
Dhiwar, Britia, Navada, Ezingabhui (MP)
Dhobi (AN)
Dhobi (CH) (CH)
Dhobi (DN)
Dhobi (excluding those in S.C.) (DE)
Dhobi (GD)
Dhobi (GU)
Dhobi (including those in S.C.) (MP)
Dhobi (RA)
Dhobi (Washermen) (JK)
Dhobi, Batham, Chauhan-Bhatti, Khurdania, Monson, Rajpar, Tanwar (HR)
Dhobi, Parit, Watts, Madwal, Rajak (MR)
Dhobi, Quasab (PU)
Dhobi, Rajak (excluding those in S.C.) (UP)
Dhobi, Vannan (TP)
Dhodia (KA)
Dhodia (RA)
Dholi (Dholi) (UP)
Dholi (KA)
Dholi (MR)
Dholi (RA)
Dholwala (JK)
Dhor (GD)
Dhor, Kakkayya, Kankayya (RA)
Dhosali (CH) (CH)
Dhosali, Dosali (HR)
Dhosali, Dosali (PU)
Dhosali, Sosal (HP)
Dhunia, Dhumian (BI)
Dhunia, Katheria, Naddaf (UP)
Dhunkar, Kadore (MP)
Dibbipuria (HR)
Digwan, Jinger (KA)
Dilpali (WB)
Divachakoli (GU)
Diwan (AR)
Dom, Dombara, Paidi or Pano (KE)
Domb-Andhiya Dombs, Audiniya Dombs, Chonel Dombs, Christian Dombs, Mirgani Dombs, Oriya Dombs, Ponaka Dombs, Telgaga Dombs and Ummia Dombs (KE)
Domb-Andhiya Dombs, Audiniya Dombs, Chonel Dombs, Christian Dombs, Mirgani Dombs, Oriya Dombs, Ponaka Dombs, Telega Dombs and Ummia Dombs (OR)
Domba (TP)
Domba, Dommara, Domba-Audhiya, Domba-Audiniya, Domba-Christian, Domba-Chonal, Domba-Nirgani, Domba-Oriya, Domba-Ponaka,

Domba-Telaga, Domba (KA)
Domba-Adhiya Domba, Chonel Domba, Oriya, Domba, Poneka Domba, Telaga Domba and Ummia Domba (TP)
Dombidasa (KA)
Dombo (AP)
Dombo (KE)
Dombs-Andhiya Dombs, Audiniya Dombs, Chonel Dombs, Christian Dombs, Nirgani Dombs, Oriya Dombs, Ponaka Dombs, Telaga Dombs, Ummia Dombs (AP)
Dommara (AP)
Dommara (AP)
Dommara (MR)
Dommara (TP)
Donga Vata (TP)
Donga Yerukala (KA)
Dongayatha (AP)
Doom, Dooma Gansi/Quash (excluding those in S.C.) (JK)
Dosali (JK)
Dubla (RA)
Dudakula (TP)
Dugla, Dholi (MR)
Dumala, Dumal (OR)
Duraj (WB)
Durgamurga, Burburchal (KA)
Dusad (AS)

Eakkarauar (Kavathi) (TP)
Eluvain (AN)
Enadi (TP)
Eravallar (TP)
Eshavathi (KE)
Eshuthachan (KE)
Ezhava (KE)
Ezhavathy (TP)
Ezhuthachar (TP)
Ezhyva (TP)

Faqir (UP)
Fishermen (JK)

Gadaba (BI)
Gadaba (WB)
Gadaba or Godba (MR)
Gadaba, Gadababoda, Gadaba-Garilum, Gadaba-Franji, Gadaba Jodia, Gadaba Olaro, Gadaba Pangi (KA)
Gadabas, Boda Gadaba, Garlas Gadaba, Olarao Gadaba and Frangi Gadaba, Jodia Gadaba (TP)
Gadabas-Boda Gadaba, Cellan Gadaba, Franji Gadaba, Jodia Gadaba, Olaro Gadaba, Pangi Gadaba, Pranga Gadaba (KE)
Gadaria (CH) (CH)
Gadaria (MR)
Gadaria, Baghela, Berela, Biar, Hiranwal, Kalanlia, Padnowal, Pal, Shiviya (HR)
Gadaria, Chandalia, Gadaria, Gavala, Ghosi, Kabiria (RA)
Gadaria, Geddi, Gaderia, Gaerria (UP)
Gadderia, Gadaria (PU)
Gaddi (CH) (CH)
Gaddi (HR)
Gaddi (JK)
Gaddi, Garri (DE)
Gaddi, Guddi (PU)
Gaderia (DE)
Gaderria (HP)
Gadhavi (MR)
Gadheri, Ghandila (DE)
Gadhia (UP)
Gadi (KA)
Gadilohar (DE)
Gadolia (RA)
Gadri (CH) (CH)
Gadri (MR)
Gadri, Gari (MP)
Gahamandi (MP)
Gahtowar (AS)
Gain (WB)
Gamit, Gamta, Gavit (including Mavchi, Padvi, Vassva, Vasava and Valvi) (RA)
Ganali or Gandali (MR)
Ganda (AS)
Ganda (WB)
Gandharap (MR)
Gandharb (BI)
Gandharva, Bhatu Sausi (UP)
Gandhila (UP)
Gandia (MP)
Gangani (AP)
Gangani (KA)
Gangani (MR)
Gangavar (TP)

Gangin (TR)
Ganju (TR)
Gara (MR)
Gara (TR)
Garai (WB)
Gareri (TR)
Garodi (AP)
Garodi (MR)
Garpageri (MR)
Garudi, Garudiga, Modiga, Modikara, Modikar, (KA)
Garvdi (MR)
Gatti (KE)
Gaude (GD)
Gaudhila (JK)
Gavandi (MR)
Gavara (AP)
Geddi (excleding the araes where specified as S.T.) (HP)
Ghadi-Waddar, Matti-Waddar, Waddar, Ode, Odiya (MP)
Ghadsi, Ghadshi (KA)
Ghagi, haddi, Relli and Sachandi (TP)
Ghandshi (MR)
Ghansi (AS)
Ghantia (GU)
Ghariya (MP)
Ghasi or Haddi, Relli, Sachandi (KE)
Ghasi, Ghasiara, Ghosi (PU)
Ghasi, Ghasiyara, Ghosi (HR)
Ghasi, Haddi, Relli, Sachhandi, Boda, Ghasia & Sanghasia (KA)
Ghasiara (DE)
Ghasis-Boda Ghasis and Sen Ghasis (KE)
Ghassi, Ghasiara, Ghosi (HP)
Ghati, Ghare (MP)
Ghatuar (AS)
Ghatwal (WB)
Ghatwar (BI)
Ghatwar (OR)
Ghatwar (WB)
Ghiradh, Ghirath (HR)
Ghisadi (KA)
Ghondali, Gondaliga, Ghondali, Gondahalli (KA)
Ghosi (CH) (CH)
Ghusuria (BI)
Ghusuria (WB)
Giddibidki, Pingle, Pingale (KA)
Gidhiya (UP)
Gingra (OR)
Giri (UP)
Girigiri (OR)
Gisadi, Ghisadi, Lohar Gadi Lohar, Chitodi Lohar, Rajput Lohar (MR)
Goala (TR)
Godabs (AP)
Godala (AP)
Godali (KA)
Godari (KA)
Godari (KE)
Godari (TP)
Godda (OR)
Godhi (MP)
Godo (Chhavo), Godhi (BI)
Godra (BI)
Godra (WB)
Godri (HP)
Godri (HR)
Goehaki (MP)
Goggi (GD)
Gogra (KA)
Gokha (WB)
Golla, Hawu Golla, Dudi Golla, Adavi Golla, Kishna Golla, Handi Golla (KA)
Gond (KE)
Gond (RA)
Gond (TP)
Gonda (AS)
Gonda (TR)
Gonda (WB)
Gondali (KA)
Gondhali (MP)
Gondi-Modya Gond & Rajo Gond (OR)
Gondi-Modya Gond and Rajo Gond (KE)
Gonds (AS)
Gondu-Bato, Bhirtiya Dubho, Kouria, Bato Jatako & Joria (KA)
Gondu-Rato, Bhirthya, Dudho Kouriya, Hato, Jatako & Joria (OR)
Goniga (KA)
Gonrh (UP)
Gonrh, Gorh, Godh, Gothahum (BI)
Gonrhi (TR)
Gontia (MP)
Gor (AS)
Gora (WB)
Gorait (AS)

Gorang (TR)
Gorkha (HR)
Gorkhali (ME)
Gosavi (GD)
Gosavi Bava, Dairgai, Bharati, Girigosavi, Bharati Gosavi Saraswati Parbat, Sagar, Ben or Ven (MR)
Goskha (BI)
Goud (BI)
Goudu, Bato, Bhirithya, Dudhokouria, Hato, Tatake & Jori (TP)
Goudus-Bato (Bhirithya) Dudhokuria, Hats, Jatako and Joria (AP)
Gowtia (MP)
Gramani, Sahnar, Nadar (TP)
Gudala (AP)
Gudheri (WB)
Gudigar (KA)
Gujarath Baori (MR)
Gulgaliya (BI)
Gumtian (HP)
Gunar (TR)
Gundi (TR)
Guri (TR)
Gurjamar (JK)
Gurjamar (JK)
Gurkha (MI)
Gurung (SI)
Gutgudi (MR)

Habra (OR)
Habura (MP)
Habura (MR)
Hadi (CH) (CH)
Hadi (TR)
Hadi (WB)
Hajjam (MP)
Hajjam, Nai (CH) (CH)
Hajong (MR)
Halalkhor (excluding those in Scheduled Caste) (WB)
Halalkhor (RA)
Halalkhor (TR)
Halalkhor (UP)
Halavakki Vakkal, Gramvakkal, Gam-Gowda, Gavada, Karevakkal Attevakkal, Halakkivakkal (North Canara, Distt) (KA)
Halepaik, Deevar, Namadhari, Billava, Kalal, Kumarpaik (KA)
Hali (CH) (CH)
Halleer (RA)
Hallpaik (MR)
Halsar, Haslar, Hulasvar, Halssvar (RA)
Halve, Hilav (MR)
Hangie (Manjhi Boatmen and rowing class excluding house-boat owners) (JK)
Hankiya (UP)
Hansi (OR)
Haranshikari, Chigaribetegar, Vaghri, Wagriri, Nirshikaro, Bagri, Baori, Phasa Chard, Vagri (KA)
hari (AS)
Hari (TR)
Harni (CH) (CH)
Harni (DE)
Harni (HP)
Harni (PU)
Hasla (AP)
Hasla (OR)
Hasla (TP)
Hawari (WB)
Hela (WB)
Helar (RA)
Helva, Helava, Helava Mallar, Hevagolla, Handi Helva, Helvaru, Pitchosuntala (KA)
Herbi, Hori (DE)
Hika/Mason (JK)
Hill Puleya (TP)
Hingora (GU)
Hira (MR)
Hirhor (TR)
Ho (TR)
Holar, Valhar (RA)
Holaya, Holer (RA)
Holeya (OR)
Holra (AS)
Holve (TP)
Honniyar (KA)
Hoobhudish (WB)
Hovan (TP)
Howgar, Hawagar, Howadiya (KA)
Hurkiya (UP)

Irika (BI)
Irika (WB)

Irula (AP)
Irula (OR)

Jadapu (KA)
Jadapus (OR)
Jadup (BI)
Jaggale (KA)
Jaintrapans (OR)
Jambuvanodai (TP)
Jambuvulu (OR)
Jatapua (TP)
Jatgar (KA)
Jatigar (MR)
Jatiya (MR)
Javeri, Jawari (KA)
Jhadi (MR)
Jhala, Malo (MR)
Jhamral (MP)
Jhari (MP)
Jheewar (JK)
Jhimar, Atlas, Bidran, Bire, Bhinwar, Duglan, Dora, Ghitra, Jhewar, Jhinwar, Jimar, Kahar, Kimal, Lamsar, Malri, Radhav, Tala (HR)
Jhodia (OR)
Jingar (MP)
Jingar (MR)
Jodapue (TP)
Jogde (MP)
Jogi (AP)
Jogi (DE)
Jogi (MP)
Jogi (TP)
Jogi (UP)
Jogi or Yogi (OR)
Jogi, Joger, Sanjogi (KA)
Jogi, Jogo, Jugi (BI)
Jogi, Nath (CH) (CH)
Jogi, Nath (PU)
Jogi, Nath, Nathjogi (MR)
Jogin (MR)
Joginath (MP)
Jogula (TP)
Joshinadidala (AP)
Juang (BI)
Juang (WB)

Kabari (BI)
Kabbore (TP)
Kadan (AP)
Kadan (KA)
Kadan (OR)
Kadan (TP)
Kadar (BI)
Kadera (MR)
Kadera, Kamwal (MP)
Kadore (MP)
Kadupattar (Malabar) (TP)
Kahar (DN)
Kahar (HP)
Kahar (MP)
Kahar (WB)
Kahar, Chandraborai, Chatrapati, Chotra-Bansi, Ramani, Rawani, Paneri (BI)
Kahar, Dhiver, Dhuru, Godia, Kashyap (UP)
Kahar, Kashyap (DE)
Kahar, Shoi (RA)
Kaibartta, Jaliya (MR)
Kaikadi (GU)
Kaikadi (or Korach), Dhontle, Korve or Kochi Korva, Makadwale, Padler Korvi, Kuchbauda, Gharo (MR)
Kaikadi (or Koracha or Korvav) (AP)
Kaikadi, Korech (RA)
Kaikari (MP)
Kaira (WB)
Kakkalan (TP)
Kala (WB)
kaladi (OR)
Kaladi (TP)
Kalahandi (AS)
Kalar (MP)
Kalbodia (GU)
Kalihandi (AS)
Kalladi, Kalwar (AP)
Kalloda (KA)
Kalwar (BI)
Kalwar (BI)
Kalwar (OR)
Kalwar (Wb)
Kamkar (BI)
Kammar Kumbhar (where they are not S.T.) (KA)
Kampmare or Reddika (AP)
Kamriya (MP)
Kanakkan (AP)

Kanchan (CH) (CH)
Kandarpa (OR)
Kandel (MR)
Kandera (MP)
Kanders (RA)
Kandh (WB)
Kandhai (AS)
Kandra (AP)
Kandra (BI)
Kaner (MP)
Kangasia (GU)
Kanghera (CH) (CH)
Kanghera (HP)
Kani or Kanisu or Kaniyar Panikker (TP)
Kanikaran, Kanaikar (TP)
Kaniyan (AP)
Kaniyan (OR)
Kanjar (AP)
Kanjar (CH) (CH)
Kanjar (OR)
Kanjar (TP)
Kanjar Bhat, Chhera, Kanjar, Nat (MR)
Kanjar, Ghair Kuchbanda, Singikat (DE)
Kanjar, Kanchan (PU)
Kanjar, Knajari, Kanjir, Khangarbhat (KA)
Kanjara-Bhatta (AP)
Kanjra Ghara (BI)
Kannakan, Padanna (TP)
Kanvi (RA)
Kapadi (DN)
Kapadia (BI)
Kapdi (MR)
Kapudia (OR)
Kapumari (KA)
Kapumarie (TP)
Kapumaries (AP)
Kapuria (WB)
Karani (WB)
Karawal (DE)
Karbi (AS)
Karha (WB)
Karhara (OR)
Kari Kudumbi (KA)
karimpalan (AP)
Karimpalan (KA)
Karimpalan (OR)
Karmali (OR)
Karwalant, Karwalnut (WB)
Karwalnut (BI)
Kasar (GD)
Kashan (AS)
Kashikaffi, Kashi-Kapadi, Tirmali (KA)
Kastha (WB)
Katabu (MR)
Katabu, Katabar (KA)
Katesar or Pattamkatti (TP)
Katipamul (MR)
Katipamula (AP)
Katipaula (KA)
Kattunayakan (OR)
Kauri, Kori (MP)
Kavadi (KA)
Kavara (TP)
Kavathi (TP)
Kavuthiyar (TP)
Kawar (AS)
Keer (RA)
Keet (BI)
Kehal (CH) (CH)
Kehal (HP)
Kehal (HR)
Kehal (PU)
Kela (BI)
Kelkari, Khelkari (KA)
Kenchoro (MR)
Keot (AS)
Kerala Muthali (TP)
Kewat (DE)
Kewat, Bansi, Chai, Jalehar, Kharsa, Majhi, Mallah, Bishad (UP)
Khadwar (BI)
Khaia (OR)
Khairwa (UP)
Khamgara (MP)
Khandait (TR)
Khandnals (OR)
Khangar (BI)
Khanghera (HR)
Khanjiman (OR)
Khant (GU)
Khant (RA)
Kharag (WB)
Kharia (AN)
Kharia (AS)
Kharia (WB)
Kharol (RA)
Kharol, Telugu-Munar, Beldar, Ghara

(MP)
Kharot (UP)
Kharvi (TP)
Kharwa Bhadela (GU)
Kharwa or Kharwi (MR)
Kharwar (MP)
Khasi (MR)
Khatgune (DE)
Khatik (BI)
Khatik (excluding those in S.C.) (DE)
Khatik (GU)
Khatik (TR)
Khatti (OR)
Khatua (OR)
Khemcha (TR)
Khen (TR)
Khen (WB)
Kherwar (AS)
Kherwar (WB)
Khilarger, Marathi Dhanagar (KA)
Khodal (AS)
Khodra (OR)
Kholie (JK)
Khond (AP)
Khond (AS)
Khond (KE)
Khond (TP)
Khondal (OR)
Khonyor (AS)
Khuangsal (MR)
Khyang (TR)
Khyang (WB)
Khyara, Ghara (WB)
Kichak (TR)
Kichak (WB)
Kingharia (UP)
Kinisan (KA)
Kirad (MP)
Kirar (RA)
Kitaran (KE)
Kochi (AP)
Koda (TR)
Koda (WB)
Kodalo (AP)
Kodalo (KE)
Kodar (MP)
Kodu (KE)
Kodu (TP)
Kohli (CH) (CH)
Kohor (AS)
Koilar (OR)
Koiri (TR)
Kol (AS)
Kol (WB)
Kolaga (HP)
Kolaga (Muslim) (DN)
Kolalar, Devar, Thevar (TP)
Kolam (OR)
Kolhari, Dombari (MR)
Koli (BI)
Koli (DN)
Koli (GD)
Koli (UP)
Koli (WB)
Koli-Mahadev (RA)
Kolla, Kollah (KA)
Kolthats, Kolthating (KA)
Kolu (WB)
Komakapu (KA)
Komakapu (MR)
Komar (OR)
Kond (Kui) (AP)
Kond (Kui) (KE)
Kond (Kul) (OR)
Kond Danogara (KE)
Konda (Kui) (TP)
Konda Dhera (TP)
Konda Dhora, Kondh Desaya, Kondh Dongria, Kondh Dongria, Kondh Kuttiya, Kond Tikiriya, Nokka Dhora Manna-Dhora, Makka Dhora (KA)
Konda Dora (KE)
Kondalo (TP)
Kondha-Besaya Kondha, Dangria Kondha, Kuttiya, Kondha, Tikiria Kondha and Yamity Kondha (TP)
Kondha-Dessya Kondha. Kongria Kondha, Kuttiya Kondha, Tikiria Kondha and Venity Kondha (KE)
Kondhs-Desaya Kondhs, Dongriya Kondhs, Kuttiya Kondhs, Tikiria Konds and Yanity Kondhs (OR)
Kondpan (AS)
Kongadi (MR)
Kongu Malayan (KE)
Konkna Yenity (KA)
Koosa (AP)
Koosa (OR)

Kora, Juda (OR)
Koracha, Koravar, Yerukale (TP)
Korachas (or Koravar or Yerukala.) (KE)
Koraga (AP)
Koraga (OR)
Koraoha or Yerkula or Korva (MR)
Korchar (MR)
Koria (MP)
Korku (BI)
Korku (RA)
Kormakar (AS)
Korwa (AS)
Korwa (TR)
Korwa including Kodaku (MR)
Kosalya Goudu, Bosothoriya Goudu Chitti Goudui, Dangayath Goudus, Doddu Kamariya, Dudu Kamaro, Kadiya Gouds and Pullseriya Goudus (KE)
Kosalya Goudus, Bosothe Riya Goudus, Chiti Goudus, Dangayath Goudus, Doddu Kamariya, Dudu Kamaro, Ladiya, Goudus & Pullo Soriya Goudus (OR)
Koselya Goudu, Bosotholya Goudu, Chith Goudu, Dangayath Goudu, Doddu Kammariya, Dudu Kamaro, Laddiya Goudu & Fullo Soriya Goudu (TP)
Kota (AP)
Kota (OR)
Kotari, Kottari (KA)
Kote (TP)
Koteyar (TP)
Koti (AP)
Kotia-Bartika, Bantho, Oriya, Dhulia or Dulia, Holva Paiko, Putiya, Sanrona & Sindho Paiko (TP)
Kotia-Bartika, Beatho Oriya Dhulia or Dulla, Holva Paiko, Putiya, Senrona and Sidho Paiko (KE)
Kotia-Bartika, Bonth-Oriya, Dhulia, Dulia, Holva Paiko, Putiya, Sanrona and Sidho-Paiko (KA)
Kotil (MP)
Kotoyar (KE)
Kottan, Koodan (TP)
Kotwal (AS)
Kotwal or Kotwalia (GU)
Kotwar (UP)
Koya (AS)
Koya or Goud (with its subsects Raj or Resha Koya, Linga Dhari Koya (ordinary) and Kottukoya) (TP)
Koya or Goud, with its sub-sacts Raj or Rasha Koyas, Kottu Koyas and Limgadhari Koyas (KE)
Koyava (KA)
Koyi (KE)
Koyi (OR)
Koyi (TP)
Kramali (AS)
Krar, Dhakar (MP)
Krishnabalija (Dasari Bukka) (AP)
Krishnanyoka (KE)
Krishnaveka (TP)
Kritiria (BI)
Kshatriya (AR)
Kubbora, Kukuvan (TP)
Kuchband, Kuchhband (PU)
Kuchhria (MR)
Kudiya (AP)
Kudiya (OR)
Kudubi (AP)
Kudubi (KA)
Kudubi (KE)
Kudubi (OR)
Kudubi (TP)
kudubi Koyi (KA)
Kudumban (AP)
Kudumban (OR)
Kudumbi (KE)
Kudumbi (TP)
Kuki (MR)
Kuki (WB)
Kul (RA)
Kulbandhiya (MP)
Kuli, Koli (OR)
Kulta (OR)
Kumarbhag Pahadia (BI)
Kumbhar (DN)
Kunbi (CD)
Kunchi Korwar, Kaidadi, Koraggar, Yerkala, Erakala, Kunchi Korva, Koramasetty, Yerukala (KA)
Kundamatia (OR)
Kunduma/Kuduma (OR)
Kunjra (MP)

Kunjra, Rayeen (UP)
Kunjra, Rayeen (WB)
Kurakula (AP)
Kurariar (OR)
Kuravan (AP)
Kuravan (OR)
Kuravar (TP)
Kurichchan (AP)
Kurichchan (KA)
Kurichchan (OR)
Kurmar (MR)
Kurmi (AR)
Kurubar, Kurub, Kurab, Kuruba (KA)
Kurul Kuruboru, Halamath (KA)
Kuruman (Kurumba) (OR)
Kurumba (TP)
Kurumbarava (TP)
Kutwar (MP)

Labana (HP)
Labana (HR)
Labana, Lobana, Vanzara, Banjara, Banjari (CH) (CH)
Ladar, Lad, Ladaru, Yelyar (KA)
Laher (OR)
Lakhra (OR)
Lakra (WB)
Lalbagi (MR)
Lalbegi (TR)
Lalbegi, Bhangi (Muslim) (BI)
Lalli (DE)
Lalli (HP)
Lalli (HR)
Lalli (JK)
Lalung (MR)
Lambadi (OR)
Lambadi, Bajara, Lambadi Sugali (TP)
Lambodi, Banjara, Subali (KE)
Liamei-Naga (MR)
Limboo, Limbu (SI)
Lippara (KA)
Lobana, Banjara, Vanjara (PU)
Lohar (TR)
Lonari, Chunari (MR)
Lonia, Lunia, Nunia, Nonia (MP)
Luhura (OR)
Luniya, Lonia (UP)
Lushei (WB)

Machhi (Hindu), Bitna, Dhimar, Dhivar, Kahar, Khalas Khalasi, Kharawl, Mangela, Sarang, Tendal (GU)
Machhi, Machhera, Mali, Saini, Southia, Sagarwanshi-Mali, Nayak (DE)
Machhi, Tandel (MR)
Machhu (WB)
Machi, Aaribharatbhara, Bharatbhara, Ghamadia, Chamadia, Chandilia, Dasania, Jansali, Jingar, Myangar, Sonari, Sivania (GU)
Machua (OR)
Madar (BI)
Madara (KE)
Madara (TP)
Madari (AS)
Madari (CH) (CH)
Madari (HP)
Madari (HR)
Madari (JK)
Madari (KE)
Madari (PU)
Madari, Bharsthari, Nath (GU)
Madgi (MP)
Madiga (KE)
Madivala (KE)
Madri (AP)
Magatha Goddus-Bemia Goudus Boodo Magatha. Dongayath Goudus Ladya Goudu, Poana Magatha and Sama Magatha (KE)
Magatha Goudo, Bamia Goudu, Boodu Magatha, Dongayath Goudu, Ponne Magetha, Sana Magetha and Yadya Goudu (TP)
Magaveera (KE)
Magha Doom (WB)
Maghaiya-Domes (TR)
Maghaiya-Domes (WB)
Maghi or Meghia (OR)
Maghya (HR)
Magura (OR)
Mahadarda (WB)
Mahali, Mahli (MR)
Mahandra, Medara (TP)
Mahar (TR)
Mahara (MR)
Mahasari (KA)
Mahigir (JK)

Mahil (MR)
Mahli (AS)
Mahli (TR)
Mahravat, Goti, Hadkashi, Zod, Dhingq, Pelya, Shatbai, Baman (GU)
Mahunta (OR)
Mahuria (BI)
Maidhasi (KA)
maila (AP)
Maila (OR)
Mairal, Dangat, Vir (MR)
Maiti (AR)
Majhabi (MP)
Majhiara (AR)
Majhwar (BI)
Majhwar (MR)
Majwar (AS)
Makrana (Muslim) (DN)
Mal (TR)
Mal Paharia (OR)
Mala (MP)
Mala Dasu (KE)
Mala Dasu (TP)
Mala Pantaram (KE)
Mala Pulayan, Kravali, Pulayan Kurumba Pulayam and Panbu Pulayan (KE)
Maladasu (OR)
Malapantaram (TP)
Malapulayan, Kurumbapulayan, Koravalipulayan, Pambupulayan (TP)
Malas or Agency Malas Valmikies (KE)
Malasar (AP)
Malasar (OR)
Malayakandi (KE)
Malayali (TP)
Male (TP)
Malhar (RA)
Mali (excluding the areas where treated as Scheduled Tribe) (AP)
Mali (Malakar) (BI)
Mali, Bhuimali, Bhuinmali (MR)
Mali, Korchia Mali, Paiko Mali and Padda Mali (TP)
mali, Korchimale, Paikomali and Pedda Mali (KA)
Mali, Marar (MP)
Malis, Korchis Malis, Palkomolis and Pedda Malis (KE)
Malis-Kerchia Malis, Paiko Malis and Peddamali (AP)
Malis-Korchia Malis, Paido Malis & Pedda Mal (OR)
Malla Malasar (KE)
Mallah (MP)
Mallah (TR)
Mallah (WB)
Mallah, Birha, Goyatri, Ghetwel, Jalwar, Kewat, Kurwaha Maheta, Majhi Muriyoni, Masuria, Phutant, Purhia, Nisad, Goshi, Dhiwar, Jhiwar, Jhimar (BI)
Malnar (Malhor) (BI)
Malpaharia (AS)
Malyar (JK)
mandula (AP)
Manga (MP)
Mangan (BI)
Mangan (WB)
Mangar (Magar) (BI)
Mangar (WB)
Mangar Batwal (MP)
Mangli (OR)
Manipuri (MI)
Maniyani, Muniyani (KA)
Manjar (MP)
Manki (AS)
Manna Dhora (KE)
Mannan, Vannan, Pathiyar (TP)
Manne Dhora (TP)
Manula (AP)
Marakkan (KE)
Marakkan (TP)
Maramori, Gramani (TP)
Marathi (TP)
Marathi, Marati (KE)
Maria (AS)
Mariya (RA)
Markande (BI)
Marni (HR)
Maru Sotiya (MP)
Maruthuvar, Navithar (TP)
Marwar Bouria (MR)
Marwari Bauria (BI)
Marwari Bauria (WB)
Masania-Jogi (DE)
Masanjogi, Sadgadsiddha, Mapanjogi (MR)
Matangi (OR)

Matial (WB)
Maugala (AP)
Mauna (TP)
Mauria (MP)
Mavi (MP)
Me or Meta (GU)
Mech (MR)
Medara (KE)
Medari or Mahendra (AP)
Medu Medar, Buruk (KA)
Meena, Mina (CH) (CH)
Meena, Mina (HR)
Mehara (RA)
Mehra (HP)
Mehtar, Bhungi (MR)
Mena (Bhil) (GU)
Meo, Mewati (DE)
Mer (GU)
Merasi, Miras (RA)
Meriasi, Mirasi (DE)
Meru (MP)
Mewati (CH) (CH)
Mewati (MP)
Mhali, Naim Navi, Nhavi (MP)
Mikir (MR)
Mina (MR)
Minka (OR)
Mir (JK)
Mirasi (HP)
Mirasi (HR)
Mirasi (JK)
Mirasi (MR)
Mirasi (PU)
Mirdhar (AS)
Miri (MR)
Mirshikar (WB)
Mishmi (MR)
Mitha (MR)
Mitha Dyyalvar (KA)
Mitna (GD)
Mochi (CH) (CH)
Mochi (excluding those in S.C.) (PU)
Mochi (excluding those in S.C.) (DE)
Mochi (excluding those in S.C.) (UP)
Mochi (HR)
Mochi, Saraj (JK)
Moger (AP)
Moger (OR)
Moghia (RA)
Mogia (RA)
Mohli (AS)
Mondi Patta (AP)
Mondivaru, Mondi Banda, Banda (AP)
Mondiwar (AP)
Mondiwar, Mondiwaru (KA)
Mondiwar, Mondiwaru (MR)
Monduvar, Muduvan (KA)
Mongar (SI)
Moniagar (TP)
Moran, Matak (AS)
Moran, Matak (ME)
Mug (WB)
Mukha Dhora, Nooka Dhora (TP)
Mukhadora-Mokka Dhora (OR)
Mukhi (AS)
Mukhi (ME)
Mukkuvan, Mukkuvar (TP)
Mukkuven, Mukaya (KE)
Mukri (RA)
Muliya (AP)
Muliya (KA)
Muliya (KE)
Muliya (OR)
Muliya (TP)
Munda (AN)
Munda (AS)
Munda (MR)
Munda (MR)
Mundala (OR)
Mundas (AS)
Mura (AS)
Muria (AP)
Muria (KA)
Muria (KE)
Muria (OR)
Muria (TP)
Muria Bhottada (KE)
Muriaro (BI)
Musavar (CH) (CH)
Muslim Banjara (UP)
Muslim Banjara, Muslim Gujar (HP)

Naar (CH) (CH)
Naar (HR)
Nadar (KE)
Nadia, Hadi (RA)
Nadkal (UP)
Naga (MR)

Nagasia (AS)
Nagavaddilu (AP)
Nahvi (AP)
Nai (DE)
Nai Thakur (AN)
Nai, Banvaru, Dhanwal, Dhari, Ghangas, Ghiri, Hajjam, Hazam, Hergun, Jallan, Lekha, Nagi, Naisikh, Palan, Panju, Patara, Raja (PU)
Nai, Bij, Hajjam, Napit (AS)
Nai, Valand (DN)
Naidu (GD)
Naik (AP)
Naik (RA)
Naik, Heri, Aheri (CH) (CH)
Naik, Nom (MP)
Naikappu (AP)
Naikawadi, Talwar, Walmiki (MR)
Naikkan (KE)
Naikkar (TP)
Naita, Nayata (MP)
Naiya (TR)
Nakkala (TP)
Nakkalas (AP)
Nalband (DE)
Nalki (KA)
Namasudra, Adhikari, Sarkar, Dhati, Bala, Hira, Baidal, Maji, Daligbi, Bodoi, Diskas, Poddar, Hindal, Roy, Dass, Hadder, Manji, Basi, manser, Biri, Nag, Bairagi, Bhatra (Badiya) (AN)
Namdhari, Paik (MR)
Namshudra (BI)
Namsudra (MP)
Napit (TR)
Napit, Nai (MR)
Narikeravar (TP)
Nat (OR)
Nat, Nat-Banjania, Natada, Bajigar (GU)
Nat, Natsansi (RA)
Nat, Nattadas (TR)
Nat, Natuvan (KA)
Nath (AS)
Nath (MP)
Nath, Jogi (GD)
Nath, Jogi (RA)
Nattu Malayana (KE)
Navda (MP)
Navi, Nhavi, Hajam, Kalaseru Navaliga, Kalashi, Nambik, Nai, Narrbhllish (MR)
Navilan (OR)
Nayadi (AP)
Nayadi (OR)
Nayak (TR)
Nayak, Naik (UP)
Nayinda, Nayanaja-Kshatriya, Hajjam, Nhavi, Nadig, Ambattan, Mangala, Kelasi, Kshowrad, Kshowrik, Navaliga, Napitha, Bhandari, Panikkan, Kavathiyan (KA)
Nayor (AR)
Neelakanthi (AP)
Neeli (MR)
Nelakanvaru (KA)
Nepali (Limbo, Matwali, Rai) (TR)
Nepali, (Damai, Gaine, Gurung, Lama, Limbu, Lohar, Newar, Rai, Sarki, *i.e.*, Cobbler, Thapa) (ME)
Nerali (MP)
Neria (MP)
Newati (UP)
Neyyala (AP)
Nhavi, Nai (GD)
Nilgar (MP)
Nirshikari (MR)
Nirshikaris (AP)
Nokkar (AP)
Nokkare (TP)
Nolakeyava (AP)
Nolia (OR)
Nolli (AP)
Nonia (MR)
Nonia, Kharwat, Nunia (BI)
Nonia, Nunia (AS)
Noongar (CH) (CH)
Noongar, Nungar (HR)
Nuhura, Nuhuraj (OR)
Nulayan (KE)
Nulayan (TP)
Nuniya (OR)
Nuniya, Nunia (TR)
Nut (excluding those in S.C.) (UP)

Od (GU)
Odd (RA)
Oddars (or Weddars) (AP)

Odde, Odder, Vadde, Oddilu, Vaddi, Vadde (AP)
Odhia (UP)
Omanaito (AP)
Omeyita (OR)
Onamsica (KE)
Oraon (AS)
Oraon (AS)
Oraon (MR)
Oraon (TR)
Orh, Od (UP)
Otare (KA)
Otari (MP)

Pacha Bhatla, Pacha Botla (KA)
Pacha Bhotala (AP)
Pachabhotla, Pachabotla (MR)
Pachabotla (AP)
Pachbandhia (MR)
Padampari (AP)
Padampari (KA)
Padampari (MR)
Padaria, Pamaria, Pandara (OR)
Padarti (KA)
Padhar (GU)
Padharia (MR)
Padia, Padiyar (KA)
Padiar (MR)
Pagadai (AP)
Pagadai (KA)
Pagadai (OR)
Pagadi (KE)
Pahar (MP)
Pahira (BI)
Pahri (UP)
Pahy (KE)
Paidi (AS)
Paidi (KE)
Paidi (TP)
Paigarapu (AP)
Paigarapu (KA)
Paigarapu (KE)
Paigarapu (OR)
Paigarapu (TP)
Paik (TR)
Paiko (OR)
Painda (AP)
Painda (KA)
Painda (KE)
Paite (MI)
Pakhali, Bhisti (MR)
Paky (KA)
Paky (OR)
Paky (TP)
Pal (Bherihar-Gaderi) (BI)
Pal Pardhi (MR)
Palakari (AP)
Palasi (KA)
Palasi (KE)
Palasi (OR)
Palasi (TP)
Palhari (MP)
Paliyan (OR)
Paliye (TR)
Paliye (TR)
Pallan (AP)
Pallan (OR)
Palluvaw (KE)
Pambada (OR)
Pambala (AP)
Pamide (KA)
Pamidi (TP)
Pamula (AP)
Pamula (KA)
Pamulu (TP)
Pan (TR)
Panabas (KA)
Panan (AP)
Panan (TP)
Panar (TP)
Panasa, Pansa, (KA)
Panchama (MR)
Pangul (MR)
Panidi (KE)
Panika (AS)
Panika (KA)
Panikkan (TP)
Paniyan (AP)
Paniyan (OR)
Panjira (OR)
Panka (MR)
Panki (TR)
Pannan (KA)
Panniandi (AP)
Panniandi (OR)
Panniyar (KE)
pano (KE)
Pario (TP)

Pans (AS)
pantias (KE)
Panwari (MP)
Para (JK)
Paradhi (excluding Kutch District) (GU)
Paraiyan (OR)
Parashar (MP)
Paravan (AP)
Paravan (OR)
Paravan, paravar, Kabbora, Parvatharajakulani, Pattanavan (TP)
Pardhi (including Adwishincher and Phase-Pardhi) (RA)
Pardhi (Nirshikari) (AP)
Pardhi Advichincher (In districts of Amerali, Bhavnagar, Jamnagar, Junagarh, Kutch, Rajkot, Surendra Nagar) (GU)
Pareiyan (AP)
Parhaiya (OR)
Pariki Muggula (AP)
Pariyas (Vengur and Vappur) (TP)
Parja (AS)
Parjas, Bonda, Daruba, Mundile, Pengu Pundi and Saliya, Poroja, Bodo-Porc , Sodia Poroja, Jodia Poroja and Parei ;a poroja (KA)
Parkavakulam Suruthinar, Malayama Nathamar (TP)
Parki (MR)
Parthi (MP)
Parya (BI)
Pasi (AS)
Pasi (TR)
Passi (AP)
Pathekut, Bachigolia (BI)
Patherphers, Sangtarash (DE)
Pathira (OR)
Pathiyan (TP)
Patia (TP)
Patka, Patki (MP)
Patra, Patramela (KA)
Pattariyas (KE)
Patua (WB)
Patwa (BI)
Patwa (DE)
Patwa (Phadal) (RA)
Patwa, Pathakar, Sipiya (MP)
Pauri (UP)
Pawariya (UP)
Payak (MP)
Pengua (OR)
Pentia (KA)
Perika (AP)
Perki (MP)
Perunkollons (KE)
Petias (AP)
Phudgi (MR)
Pichari (KA)
Picharis (AP)
Pichasunta, Pichiguntala, Pichuguntala (KA)
Pichati (KA)
Pinganiya (BI)
Pirali (WB)
Pirna (JK)
Pita (OR)
Pitchiguntala (AP)
Pod (TR)
Poligars (AP)
Polli or Sachandi (KE)
Pomla (KA)
Pomla (RA)
Pondara (AP)
Poosala (AP)
Poraya (TP)
Porjas or Poraja-Boda, Bonda, Daruva, Didua, Jodia, Mundili, Parang, Pyadi, Salliya, Sanoand Sodia (TP)
Porjas-Bado, Bonda, Daruva, Didva, Jodia, Mundil, Sano, Pengu, Pydi, Saliya, Sodia and Pareng (OR)
Porogas Bodo, Prooja or sodia, Sano Poraja, Jadia Poroja and Pareng Proja (KE)
Poroja (KE)
Poroja-Bado, Perojaor Sodia, Jodia Peroja, Pareng Peroja and Sono Poroja (AP)
Powara (KA)
Powara (RA)
Proja-Boda, Nonda, Daruva, Didava, Jodia, Kundili, Pengll, Phdi and Saliya (KE)
Pulaya (KE)
Pulayan (AP)
Pulayan (KA)
Pulayan (OR)

Pullavan (KA)
Pulluvan, Pulluvar (TP)
Pusuale (TP)
Puthiraj Vannan (AP)
Putligar (MP)

Rabari, Sorthia Charalia, Charmta, Luni, Kushar, Tank Muchhal kadiyakumbhar (excluding the Nesses of the forest of Alech, Barada & Gir) (GU)
Rabha (ME)
Rabha (MR)
Rabha (TR)
Rachband (CH) (CH)
Rachband (HR)
Rachevar (MR)
Rachkoya (AP)
Rachkoya (MR)
Rai (SI)
Rai-Sikh (CH) (CH)
Raika (RA)
Raikari (MR)
Raj (UP)
Raj Pardhi, Gaon Pradhi, Haranshikari (MR)
Rajdhobi (BI)
Rajgir (MP)
Rajgond (MP)
Rajput Bhamta, Pardeshi, Bhamta, Pardesh Bhamti (MR)
Raju (TR)
Rajwar (OR)
Rajwar (TR)
Rakhal (WB)
Ramoshi (MR)
Raneyar (AP)
Raneyar (OR)
Rangwa (BI)
Raot, Rautia, Rawt (MR)
Rasali (WB)
Rathodia (GU)
Raulo (AP)
Rautia (MP)
Raval, Raval or Raval Yogi (MR)
Raval-Ravalia, Jati or Raval Yogi, Rawal Jati, Jagaria, Padat, Ravar Rawalia (GU)
Rawal (MP)
Rawal, Ravalia, Paul (KA)
Rawat (RA)
Rawat, Bedar, Gahira, Rast, Rawar, Thethwar (MP)
Rawat, Raya, Rewath (KA)
Rebbari (RA)
Rehar, Rehara, Rer, Rihar (CH) (CH)
Rehar, Rehara, Rihar, Rea (HR)
Reinudas (KA)
Relli Orachanji (KA)
Relli, Sachndi (TP)
Relse (MI)
Rhar (MP)
Rohade, Sujharia (MP)
Rohangia, Roshangia (WB)
Rohit (GU)
Rona (KA)
Rona (KE)
Rona (TP)
Ronas (OR)
Routia (OR)
Ruchbandhia (MP)
Rupai (TR)

Saara (KA)
Sacra (KE)
Sad-Sausi (Sehar) (RA)
Sadhumatha (KA)
Sagar (GD)
Sagarpasha (OR)
Sahora (AS)
Sahic (MR)
Sakaravar (Kavathi) (KE)
Sakka (RA)
Salat (GU)
Saloi (ME)
Sanai Thalavar (Elavaniar) (KE)
Sangare (KA)
Sangastrash (BI)
Sangheda (GU)
Sangtrash (JK)
Saniyar (KA)
Sanji (MR)
Sanjogi (MR)
Sankhari (OR)
Sansi (GU)
Sansi (JK)
Sansi (KA)
Sansi (WB)
Sansia (KA)

Santal (KA)
Santal (MR)
Santal (MR)
Santhal, Santal (AS)
Santhals (AS)
Saora (AP)
Sapari (AP)
Sapari (KE)
Sapera (JK)
Sapera (MR)
Sapera, Kalbedia (UP)
Sarabara (RA)
Sarania (GU)
Sarania (KA)
Sarania (MR)
Saranjia (MP)
Sarbhangi (MP)
Sare (AP)
Sare (KA)
Sargara (GU)
Saroa (TP)
Sarodi, Sarada (KA)
Satarkar (KA)
Saunsi (UP)
Sauria Paharia (OR)
Sauta (Sota) (BI)
Savara (KE)
Savara Kopu Savara, Khutto Savara & Maliya Savara (TP)
Savara, Kapusavara, Kuttusavara, Maliya Savara (KA)
Savara-Kapu Savaras, Khutto Savaras, Mallya Savaras (OR)
Savaras-Kapusavaras, Khutto Savaras and Maliya Devaras (KE)
Sayar (WB)
Semban (OR)
Semman (KA)
Semman (OR)
Senatal (AP)
Severas (AS)
Shagird Pesha (WB)
Sharia (MP)
Shikkaligar (KA)
Shikligar (GU)
Shingdev or Shingadhya (MR)
Shingdevor Shingadya (KA)
Sholaga (AP)
Sholaga (KE)
Sholagar (KA)
Sholagar (KE)
Sholagar (OR)
Sholager (AP)
Shorgir (HR)
Shorigir (CH) (CH)
Shorigir (PU)
Shypri, Wattal (excluding those in S.C.) (JK)
Sikkalgar, Katari (MR)
Sikliagr (JK)
Sikligar (MP)
Siklighar, Gadi Lohar (RA)
Sindhor (AP)
Sindli (MR)
Singalu (AP)
Singhiwala, Singhikaut (CH) (CH)
Singiwala (MP)
Singiwala (MR)
Singpho (MR)
Sinkes (OR)
Sirkiwala (RA)
Siyal (WB)
Siyane (MP)
Soir, Soyar (BI)
Soliga (KA)
Sondhiya, Chandel (MP)
Sonsi (RA)
Sore (AP)
Sore (MR)
Suba (SI)
Sud (OR)
Sudra Das, Dey (AS)
Sulia (OR)
Sumra (GU)
Sunar (SI)
Sundi (OR)
Sunna (AP)
Sunna, Sunnai (KA)
Sunri (BI)
Sunri (TR)
Surera (HP)
Suriman, Gunjamar (DE)
Surimar (JK)
Surva (KA)
Sut (ME)
Sut, Soot (AS)
Synteng (MR)

Tachavira (KA)
Tahkar (GU)
Takankar (KA)
Takankar (MR)
Talabia (GU)
Talavia (KA)
Taleyari (AP)
Talwar Kanade (MR)
Tamang (SI)
Tamang (WB)
Tamariya (BI)
Tans (OR)
Targala (MR)
Targala, Bhaviya, Bhojai, Nayak (GU)
Tausa (AS)
Telega, Pamula, Paddati Golla (TP)
Thakaroa, Baria, Dharala, Patanwadia. Thakore (GU)
Thami (MP)
Thandan (TP)
Thanta Pulayan (KE)
Thantapulayan (TP)
Thanu (OR)
Thanwar (MP)
Tharu (BI)
Tharu (WB)
Tharu (WB)
Thatari (OR)
Thathera (BI)
Thavar (TP)
Thawin (HP)
Thelari (MR)
Thettia Naick (KE)
Thetwar (MR)
Thiyaa (TP)
Thiyya (KE)
Thogra, Bholla baliga (AP)
Tholko Laus (KE)
Tholuva, Naicker and Vetalakara Naickar (TP)
Thondaman (TP)
Thontoman (KE)
Thori (MP)
Thori, Turi (CH) (CH)
Thoria (MR)
Thoriyar (TP)
Thotawadu (KA)
Thotewadu (MR)
Thoti (OR)
Thoti, Burud (MP)
Thotian (KE)
Thottai Naicka (TP)
Thottia Naicks (AP)
Thottia Naik (KA)
Thottiya Naicker (including Gollavar, Silavar, Rajakambalam, Thockalavar and Tholuva Naicker) (TP)
Thuria (MP)
Thuria (OR)
Tilari, Tirate (KA)
Timali (KA)
Timali (MR)
Timali (RA)
Tipara (ME)
Tipara (WB)
Tipara, Tipera (AS)
Tipera (MR)
Tippera (WB)
Tirgar (MP)
Tirmale (MP)
Tiruvalluvan (KA)
Tirwalli (MP)
Tiyar (BI)
Tiyar (OR)
Tiyar (TR)
Tiyar (WB)
Toda (KE)
Toda (OR)
Toda (TP)
Tonla Gaul (OR)
Tsong (SI)
Turha (MP)
Turha (WB)
Turha, Sao (BI)
Turi (AS)
Turi (KA)
Turi (UP)

Ulladan (TP)
Ullatan (TP)
Uppaliga, Uppara, Uppaliyan, Mannu-Upper, Gavandi, gavandi, Goundi, Veldar, Sagara, Chunar, Lonari, Melusakkare, Agri, Lama (KA)
Uppar, Sagar (AP)
Uppars (Upp lillia Segara) (TP)
Urali Gounders (TP)
Urao, Bandot, haro, Karkata, Luidu,

Shitheo, Tigga, Tirki (WB)

Vadder-Bevi, Upparilu (AP)
Vadi (KA)
Vaghari, Salat, Salat Vaghri (MR)
Vaghri (KA)
Vaghri (MR)
Vaghri-Gamicho, Vedva Churalia, Jakhudia (excluding Kutch Distt) (GU)
Vahivancha Charan Gadhvi or Harijan, Vankar and Chamar (GU)
Vaidu (KA)
Vaidu (MR)
Vaiti (MR)
Vala (GU)
Valaan (KE)
Valaiyar (TP)
Valan (TP)
Valand and Nai (Hindu) Hajjam, Khalipha (Muslims) (GU)
Valayar (KA)
Valiayar (TP)
Valluvan (AP)
Valluvan (OR)
Valmiki (AP)
Valmiki (KE)
Valmiki (TP)
Valmiki Boya (Boya, Bedar, Kirataka, Nishadi, Yellapi Pedda Boya) Talayari and Ghundu Vallu (AP)
Valuthadanayar, Valuthanathwanayar (TP)
Valvai (MR)
Valve (KA)
Vannan (Mannan, Bathiyan) (TP)
Vannar, Rajakula Valuthadar (where the community is a S.C. Agasa Madivala mali) (TP)
Vans-foda, Vansfodia or Vanza (GU)
Varli (RA)
Vathiriyan (KA)
Ved (RA)
Vedar (TP)
Vetan (TP)
Vettuvan (AP)
Vettuvan (OR)
Vilathethal Nair (Velakkithalavan) (KE)
Vina Tulavina (OR)
Vitholia (KA)
Voluthadathu Nai (Veluthedan and Vennathan) (KE)
Vottakkaran (KE)

Waddar or Kala Waddars or Pathrods (AP)
Waddar, Wadders (Kalawaders or Patharods) (MR)
Wadla (AP)
Wadwa Waghari (GU)
Waghari, Dataniya, Waghari, Vodu Waghari, Talapada, Waghari, Gamachia, Godalia Wgahari, Chibhadia Waghari, Morawad Waghari (GU)
Waghri (DE)
Waghri (RA)
Wanha (MP)
Warthi (MR)

Yadavan (Idayan) (KE)
Yakthungba (SI)
Yanadi (MR)
Yanadi (TP)
Yanady (TP)
Yandi (KA)
Yandi (OR)
Yanudi (KE)
Yaras (AP)
Yarukula (KE)
Yarukula (TP)
Yashkun (JK)
Yata (AP)
Yavana (TP)
Yeklar, Yeklar, Yekkali, Egalika (KA)
Yenadiwad (KA)
Yenadiwad (MR)
Yeragolawad or Thella Pamalawade (MR)
Yeralu (KA)
Yerasolawadorthella, Pamalwada (KA)
Yerkilwar, Yerkula (MP)
Yerna Golla (OR)
Yerukula (OR)
Yetla (AP)
Yoda (AP)
Yogi, Jogi, Nath (TR)
Yueruleu (AP)

Zemrol (RA)

Minute of Dissent by Shri L.R. Naik, Ex-M.P.

I have endeavoured to the best of my ability and understanding of the socio-economic problems of the backward classes of citizens of India to assit the Chairman and the other members of the Backward Classes Commission in carrying out the arduous task entrusted to them by President of India in terms of reference prescribed. I am happy that I received full co-operation and encouragement from them, especially Shri B. P. Mandal, Chairman of the Commission. It is, therefore, not without feelings of regret and reluctance that I write a separate minute of dissent only with reference to categorisation of socially and educationally backward classes of citizens, identified by the Commission in terms of reference made to them.

The Commission have, on certain criteria as delineated in Chapter XI prepared a common list of socially and educationally backward classes of citizens and I suggest its modification in the following manner:

> I held very sincerely that castes/classes mentioned in the common list, each having homogeneous and cohesive characteristics, are not at the same degree of level or social and educational backwardness and I fear that the safeguards recommended for their advancement will not percolate to less unfortunate sections among them and the constitutional objectives proclaming an establishment of an egalitarian society will remain a myth. Some of the communities in the common list who would be called hereinafter as 'Intermediate Backward Classes' on the lines delineated in the report of the Tata Institute of Social Studies (Volume IV) have made their presence felt in the caste hierachical society in India, either on their numerical strength or their age-old co-existence along with other advance communities in villages and towns. Given better opportunities and encouragement in future, I have, no doubt, in my mind they would integrate with the general populace sooner than

later. But there are number of castes and classes in the common list who are incapable of making such a dent, in the near future, being extremely backward, both socially and educationally and also economically. Their economical, backwardness is evidently the consequence of their age-old social and educational backwardness. By way of clarity they would be, hereinafter, called 'Depressed Backward Classes' as distinct from the 'Intermediate Backward Classes'. I am of the opinion that these unfortunate classes of people, i.e. 'Depressed Backward Classes' stepped as they are in massive backwardness would take time for their enlightment and advancement, unless, of course, concerted efforts, at national level, are made by way of sagacious inputs of safeguards the benefits of which should be precolated to them in a large measure. So there is a compelling need to shift them carefully from the main common list and create a separate entity of equals or near-equals to bring about a healthy competition among them for the benefits of the safeguard. The rest of the communities in the common list should then form a distinct category for the same reason of creating an atmosphere for competition among equals for the safeguards. This device is necessary in the interest of the nation as a whole.

The 'Intermediate Backward Classes', in my opinion, are those whose traditional occupation had been agriculture, market gardening, beatle-leaves growers, pastoral activities, village industries like artisans, tailors, dyers and weavers, petty bussiness-cum-agricultural activities, hearlding, temple service, toddy selling, oil mongering, combating, astrology etc. etc., who have co-existed since times immemorial with upper castes and had, therefore, some scope to embibe better association and what all it connotates than many unfortunate 'Depressed Backward Classes' whose intermingling with the Indian society was either denied, prohibited and even segregated obviously on account of stigma of their traditional occupations, stigma of criminality, stigma of nomadism resulting in their abysmally low social status. They, generally, are ex-criminal tribes, nomadic and wandering tribes, earth diggers, fishermen, boatmen and palanquin bearers, salt makers, washermen, shepherds, barbers, scavangers, basket makers, furriers and tanners, landless agricultural labourers, watermen, toddy tappers, camal-hardsmen, pig keepers, pack bullock carriers, collectors of forest produce, hunters and fowlers, corn parchers, premitive tribes (not specified as Scheduled Tribes), exterior classes (not specified as Scheduled Castes), and being communities etc. etc.

These very names amply connote their social and educational backwardness and, therefore, should have been postulated by the Founding Fathers of our Constitution as in the case of the Scheduled Castes and Scheduled Tribes for the purpose of specification. Things are obvious proof. I sincerely consider that this lapse on the part of our constitution-makers has resulted in a serious constraint in establishing an eqalitarian society based on justice: social, economical and political. These decades of Independence and the Drawn of Freedom is yet to bestow a willing smile on many of hamlet and slum of these unfortunate segments of the Indian Society. They continue to submit to the decrees of fate rather than have the benefits of the decrees of our basic laws. Liberty, Equality and Fraternity so richly enshrined in the Constitution of our country have still to acquire meaningful proposition for all of them. Most of these communities are either Scheduled Tribes, Scheduled Castes depending on their characteristics in relation to some States, but no so in other States.

During the couse of my extensive tours throughout the length and breath of India, I observed that a tendency is fast developing among 'Intermediate Backward Classes' to repeat the treatments or rather ill-treatments, they themselves have received from times immemorial at the hands of the upper castes, against their bretheren. I mean, the 'Depressed Backward Classes'. In an unequal society like ours, it is necessary that the Commission take all precuations so that the more helpless and needy segments are not deprived of the benefits of the various safeguards by avoiding cut-throat competition among unequals. The casteism is still very much in our nidest and this is assuming new forms without showing much loss of its original vitality. In fact, several observers feel that the logic of democratic politics and mass mobilisation has brought casteism to the centre of the stage. It is with regret, I affirm that political leaders belonging to 'Intermediate Backward Classes' are not immune from such aberration nor they are imaginative enough to bring about the advancement of the people who are at the bottom of our society, such as these 'Depressed Backward Classes'. All that they seem to be doing is to emulate some disgruntled upper castes in userping economic and political power in the name of backward classe. This is a mental aberration which deserves outright condemnation from whatever quarters it may emanate — whether from Upper Castes or Intermediate Backward Classes.

The ancient adage that 'if a big fish and a small fish are put together the former will swallow the latter', is still very apt in the context of the caste hierarchical society of India. Care should, therefore, be taken with all emphasis at our command that the benefits of safeguards are dispersed equitably and rationally, as far as possible, among all sections of the backward classes. This, I consider, can happen by avoiding competition for benefits among unequals or by bringing about competition among equals. I, therefore, propose that the common list should be categorised into two parts, 'A' and 'B'; 'A' consisting of those classes whom I have described as 'Depressed Backward Classes' and 'B' the rest of the communities in the list to be described as 'Intermediate Backward Classes'. The list of 'Depressed Backward Classes' in relation to States and Union Territories is given in *Annexure II*.

Quantum of Reservation

A percentage distribution of Indian population by castes and religious groups has been indicated in the body of the main report. It is seen therefrom that the percentage population of Other Backward Classes including non-Hindu communities is derived at 52. It is further seen that the population percentage of Hindu backward castes/groups is 43.70, whereas that of non-Hindu communities is 8.40. Now on categorisation of Other Backward Classes into 'Intermediate Backward Classes' and 'Depressed Backward Classes', a fresh statement of percentage distribution of Indian population is prepared and is at *Annexure I*.

It is seen therefrom that the percentage popualtion of 'Depressed Backward Classes' is 25.56 and that of 'Intermediate Backward Classes' is 26.44. It is undoubtedly safe to assume that these two categories are equal to each other from their population point of view.

After good deal of discussion with which I am in full agreement, the commission has recommended reservations to the extent of 27 per cent in all services under the Central Government. It has further recommended that seats should be reserved in all scientific, technical and professional institutions run by the Central as well as the State Governments and the quantum of reservation should be the same as in public services, i.e. 27 per cent.

In all fairness and in view of the fact that the 'Depressed Backward Classes' are comparable in matters of backwardness to those of the

Scheduled Castes and Scheduled Tribes, I recommend 15 per cent reservation them out of 27 per cent both in public services and educational institutions as mentioned above. For all other concessions they should be treated on par with SC/ST. I refrain from recommending political reservation. I however, urge them to unite and organise. They have nothing to lose except their chains of age-old degradation, social, economical and political. Hatred towards none and love and affection for all should be their motto. They should be recognise that an essential part of their battle against their social backwardness is to be fought in their own minds of their salvation. At the same time, I have a word of caution for the ruling elite in our country that there cannot be an egalitarian society unless the depressed are enable to be on par with them. They should, therefore, refrain from agitating against any reservation for the backwards and if they do so it is at their own peril and that of the nation.

Acknowledgement

I am quite aware that Shri B.P. Mandal, Chairmen of the Commission is Mainly responsible for my induction in the Commission. I am greatful to him. His encouragement and profound kindness that he showered on me will be ever cherished. I am also greatful to my other esteemed and distinguished colleagues for their co-operation.

I must put on record the invalueable co-operation and assitance I received from Dr. S. Bheemappa. Professor of Surgery, Bangalore Medical College, Bangalore (Karnataka) in identifying the 'Depressed Backward Classes' from all over India and in deriving their population figures. It has been his second habit to understand the problems of the underdog at their depth. His expert advice on the subject to the Commission deserves all appreciation.

I am also greatful to all Co-opted Members from all the States and Union Territory for their co-operation and advice.

Sd/-

(L.R. NAIK)

Percentage Distribution of Indian Population by Caste and Religious Groups

Sl. No.	Group Name	Percentage of total population
I. Scheduled Castes and Scheduled Tribes		
A-1	Scheduled Castes	15.05
A-2	Scheduled Tribes	7.51
	Total of 'A'	22.56
II. Non-Hindu Communities, Religious Groups, etc.		
B-1	Muslims (other than STs)	11.19 (0.02)*
B-2	Christians (other than STs)	2.16 (0.44)*
B-3	Sikhs (other than SC/ST)	1.67 (0.22)*
B-4	Budhists (other than STs)	0.67 (0.03)*
B-5	Jain	0.47
	Total of 'B'	16.16
III. Forward Hindu Castes & Communities		
C-1	Brahmins (including Bhumihars)	5.52
C-2	Rajputs	3.90
C-3	Marathas	2.21
C-4	Jats	1.00
C-5	Vaishyas-Bania, etc.	1.88
C-6	Kayasthas	1.07
C-7	Other forward Hindu/Castes/Groups	2.00
	Total of 'C'	17.58
	Total of 'A', 'B', 'C'	56.30

IV. *Backward Hindu Castes & Communities*

D.	Remaining Hindu castes/groups which comes in the category of OBCs	43.70@

V. *Backward Non-Hindu Communities*

E.	52 per cent of religious groups under Section 'B' may also be treated as OBCs	8.40
F.	The approximate derived population of OBCs including non-Hindu communities	52% (Aggregate of D & E rounded)

NB : It is proposed to divide the population percentage of OBCs mentioned in serials 'D' & "E' into--

(a) percentage of population of 'Intermediate Backward Classes' and
(b) percentage of population of the 'Depressed Backward Classes'.

VI. *'Intermediate backward Classes' including Non-Hindu communities*

G-1	Land owner and cultivating castes and communities excluding Marathas and Jats.	6.40
G-2	Marketing Gardeners	2.06
G-3	Pastoral Castes excluding shepherds Artisans, viz.—	2.50
G-4	(a) Vishwakarma	2.10
G-5	(b) Tailors and Dyers	0.18
G-6	(c) Weavers	1.40
G-7	(d) Potters	1.10
G-8	Petty business-cum-agricultural Castes	0.50
G-9	Oil Mongers	1.40
G-10	Combatants other than Rajputs	1.80
G-11	Heralders	0.10
G-12	Temples servants and Astrologers	0.10
G-13	Non-Hindu communities excluding Scavangers, Muslim ex-criminal tribes, Muslim nomadic tribes and Muslim Shepherds	6.80
	Total of 'G'	26.44

H.	Percentage population of 'Intermediate Backward Classes' + Backward Non-Hindu communities	26.44
I.	Percentsge of population of 'Depressed Backward Classes', i.e. 'F' minus 'H'	20.56@

* Figures in Brackets give the population of SC/ST among these non-Hindu communities.

@This is a derived figure.

APPENDIX III

Report of the Research Planning Team of the Sociologists (Mandal Commission)

The Research Planning Team consisting of the following members met at Delhi during 12th to 14th June, 1979 to draw up a plan of studies and researches which should be undertaken/sponsored by the Backward Classes Commission for determining in a scientific and objective manner the criteria for defining the socially and educationally backward classes.

Members

1. Prof. L.K. Mahapatra
2. Prof. N.S. Reddy
3. Prof. Leela Dube
4. Dr. A.K. Danda
5. Shri N.K. Banerjee
6. Shri S.S. Gill
7. Prof. B.K. Roy Burman

1. The Study Team after considering the context in which the provisions in respect of socially and educationally backward classes have been made in the Constitution as well as the actual wording of the Constitution felt that these relate to socially recognisable and persistent collectivities and not to individuals.
2. As a corollary to the foregoing it implies that, that type of social backwardness which is more relevant to the present enquiry pertains to ascriptive status and not achieved status.
3. The study Team felt it necessary to consider the problem of relationship between social backwardness and educational backwardness. While social backwardness refers to ascriptive status, educational backwardness refers to achieved status. It is obvious that the former can change only over a length of time, while faster change is possible in case of the later. Hence, while

determining the criteria of socially and educationally backward classes, social backwardness should be considered to be the critical element and educational backwardness to be the linked element, though not necessarily derived from the former.

4. In the Indian context of task of identifying collectivities with ascribed socially backward status, can be achieved from two vantage positions which, however, very frequently tend to overlap. The, first is to identify the castes of ethnic groups which are traditionally assigned a low status (Other than the Scheduled Castes). The second is to identifies the traditional occupations which are assigned a low status but which are also linked with specific castes or ethnic groups. These ethnic groups may belong to any religion. Once the collectivities are identified in terms of the traditional frame-work, one is to examine what changes have taken place in their social and educational status under the impact of the various forces in modern society.
5. As regards identification of castes with traditional low status, considerable amount of data are available in the Census Report up to 1931. Similarly, for ascriptive status of occupation also the earlier Census Reports Provide considerable information. Caste index of 1891 gives information about the distribution of the various castes in sixty occupational categories. 1901 Census gives a ranking of castes and also an indication of the social privileges and disabilities associated with them. The subsequent Censuses up to 1931 give an indication of the social mobility movements among the castes and process of change in their respective status. If a comparative statement is prepared indicating the baseline data available in 1891 and 1901 Censuses and the subsequent changes, the same will give a fairly clear picture of the pattern that had taken shape in the pre-independence period.
6. As regards educational status of the castes or ethnic groups of the population engaged in various traditional occupations in the pre-independence period, some information is available in the early Census reports. While it is recognised that a large number of people belonging to the different castes do not at present adhere to their traditional occupation or occupations, it is assumed that in most cases the bulk of the population engaged in the traditional occupations embodied in the pre-industrial

technological nexus still belong to the castes or ethnic groups which have been associated with such occupations for generations. Some information about the educational status of the persons practising the various traditional occupations is available in the earlier Census reports. This is required to be compiled.

7. (a) The Problems of determination of current social and educational status of collectivities that can be identified as backward on an examination of early source materials can be considered both at the conceptional and empirical and statistical levels.

(b) The Problems of approach at the conceptual level would be considered later. At the empirical and statistical level the following sources and procedures are noted:

(i) Cross-tabulation of occupation data of the Census;
(ii) Village and Town studies and craft studies of the Census Agro-economic Research Centres and a number of other institutions and scholars;
(iii) Studies specially conducted by Anthropological Survey of India on the Weaker Sections of the population;
(iv) Studies sponsored by ICSSR;
(v) Reports of Seminars organised by Backward Classes Federation and Other Agencies;
(vi) Sample surveys to be specially sponsored by Backward Classes Commission.

(c) (i) A special mention is to be made of the problems of cross-tabulation of census data and of the sample surveys to be sponsored by the Backward Classes Commission. As regards cross-tabulation of occupation and education data it is to be noted that currently such data are available only up to three digit code of the NCO. But most of the traditional occupations with low ascribed status would not come out in the three digit code. For this, it will be necessary to get special cross-tabulation done at the five digit code based on 1 per cent sample slips computerised at the national level; 10 per cent slips computerised in respect of Urban areas, and 5 per cent slips computerised for rural areas of some parts of the country.

8. As regards sample surveys to be sponsored by the Backward

Classes Commission, the important question is that of the unit. Rislay has listed more than 5,000 castes in India the first B.C.C. has listed more than 2,000 other backward classes. If a sample survey is conducted with reference to territorial units only, most of the numerically small castes which are likely to be more backward, may not be covered. If such surveys are to be be done with caste as the unit the sample frame will not be available without a time-consuming and costly operation of enumeration of all castes throughout the country.

9. It seems that it will not be possible to go in for a single dimension sample survey, it will be necessary to make multiprong approaches to gain an insight into the situation in a general way, rather than for identifying the actual conditions prevailing along all the specific collectivities that deserve to be treated as socially and educationally backward classes. The vantage points of multiprong approaches would be as follows:

   (a) From an analysis of the census data up to Taluk level, it will be possible to identify areas where SC/ST constitute insignificant proportion of the population and where at the same time level of literacy is low. Sample surveys will be carried out in such areas to examine the factors of educational backwardness and also to find out to what extent, social backwardness is associated with the same.

   (b) From and examination of the village survey monographs, it will be possible to prepare an inventory of communities which have been found to suffer from social disabilities and which are at the same time educationally backward. Sample surveys can be conducted in these areas on the basis of purposive sampling.

   (c) On examination of the traditional craft survey reports as well as in consultation with Handicrafts Board and Khadi and Village Industries Commission information can be obtained about social and economic conditions and mobility movements of the population engaged in these traditional crafts and industries which are graded as backward. The District Census hand books of 1961 Census also provide information about the distribution of different household industries at the village level. Studies may be conducted in respect of some of them on the basis of purposive sampling.

(d) Ex-criminal Tribes Enquiry Committee and Nomadic Tribes Inquiry Committee provided information about a good number of communities and about the areas were they are to be ordinarily found. Some of them should also be covered by the survey.

(e) LOKUR Committee set up by the Home Ministry has provided a list of communities who represented for being included in the list of SC and ST, but who had to be left out. The report gives some indication of the social status of many of these communities. Similar representations received from time to time by the Home Ministry and Commissioner for SC and ST and the Commission for SC and ST for being treated as SC and ST which have not been found to satisfy the criteria for inclusion in one of these categories of SC and ST, may be taken for examination about their social and educational status.

(f) The Communities already listed as OBCs in several States can also be studied on a sample basis to ascertain their actual social and educational status and also the impact of the various measures adopted for amelioration of their condition.

10. The team considered that the studies conducted by the Anthropological Survey of India on Weaker Sections would be very much helpful in gaining a conceptual insight about the process of generation of backwardness or of persistence and change of the same. The report of these studies may be carefully examined.

11. While empirical and statistical data collected in the foregoing manner will help in identifying the current social and educational status of a number of castes and communities and other collectivities (traditional occupation groups) a perspective about the long-range trend and the future will also be necessary. For this purpose as well a conceptual framework appears indispensable.

(a) It can be assumed that the factors and processes of generation, persistence and change of backwardness would differ in different historical formations and social situations. For instance, in the area, pre-dominantly inhabited by the tribals ritual disability may not be an important criterion for determination of backwardness for the non-tribal minorities residing there. In their case access to centres of political power may be a more important factor. Similar differences can be noticed in the enclaves of semi-feudal or capitalistic economy and society.

(b) Significances of some of the prevailing attributes of social and educational backwardness would be very much different in areas where social mobility movements have taken place among various castes and communities and traditional occupation groups, from the areas where no such movements have taken place.

12. While designing empirical studies extent of prevalence of the following variables may be taken into account:-

(a) Socio-ritual services extended by other ethnic groups.
(b) "Low" status of occupations of the category concern.
(c) "Low" self-evaluation compared to other ethnic groups in the region (Gram Panchayat/Block/Taluqa).
(d) Literacy rates in relation to other neighbouring groups in Gram Panchayat/Block/Taluqa.
(e) Occupations requiring investment of child-labour (Up to 15 years).
(f) Economic levels of castes and communities.
(g) Representation in public or private sector services or in professions.

Criteria for Identifying O.B.C. Employees (Both Hindu and Non-Hindu Communities) in Central Government Offices

In my D.O. letter under reference I had requested for the supply of information regarding the total number of employees belonging to Other Backward Classes working in your Ministry.

2. Though a number of State Governments have drawn up lists of Other Backward Classes, no such lists have been compiled by the Central Government. In fact, the first term of reference of Backward Classes Commission pertains to the defining of criteria for determining Backward Classes. As the desired criteria could be evolved only after extensive field surveys and examination of data called from various agencies, the Commission itself is also not in a position to indicate specific and well considered criteria for defining Backward Classes.

3. In view of the above difficulties and looking to the urgency of obtaining information regarding the employment of members of Backward Classes under the Central Government, the Commission, has decided to lay down the following rough and ready criteria on purely *ad hoc* basis.

4. Article 340 of the Constitution refers to "socially and educationally" backward classes. The following test may, therefore be applied to determine socially and educationally backward classes:

(a) In respect of employees belonging to the Hindu Communities

(i) an employee will be deemed to be socially backward if he does not belong to any of the three twice borne (Dvij) 'Varnas' i.e. he is neither a Brahmin, nor a Kshatriya/nor a Vaishya; and

(ii) he will be deemed to be educationally backward if neither his father nor his grandfather had studied beyond the primary level.

(b) Regarding the non-Hindu Communities

(i) an employee will be deemed to be socially backward if either

(1) he is a convert from those Hindu communities which have been defined as socially backward as per para 4(a)(i) above, or

(2) in case he is not such a convert, his parental income is below the prevalent poverty line, i.e. Rs. 71 per head per month.

(ii) he will be deemed to be educationally backward if neither his father nor his grandfather had studied beyond the primary level.

5. It may please be noted that an employee will qualify for membership of Other Backward Classes only if, both socially and educationally, he is found to be backward according to the above criteria.

D.O. letter No. 17020/5179 SC & BCD - I dated 19th March 1979, from Shri S.S. Gill, Secretary, Mandal Commission

APPENDIX V

Listing of Central and State Commissions/ Committees on Backward Classes

CENTRAL

Backward Classes Commission, 1953-1955.
Chairman: Shri Kakasaheb Kalelkar

Backward Classes Commission, 1979-1980.
Chairman: Shri B.P. Mandal

Study Team on Social Welfare and Welfare of Backward Classes, 1958-1959.
Chairman/Leader: Smt. Renuka Ray

STATES

Andhra Pradesh

Backward Classes Commission, 1968-1970.
Chairman: Shri Mandhai Pershad

Committee of the Fifth Legislature Assembly to Recommend Further Measurers for the Welfare of Backward Classes, 1977.
Chairman: Shri Agisam Veerappa

Bihar

Backward Classes Commission, 1971-1976.
Chairman: Shri Mungeri Lal

Bombay

Scavenger's Living Conditions Enquiry Committee, State of Bombay, 1954.

Gujarat

Backward Classes Commission, 1972-1976.
Chairman: Shri A.R. Bakshi

Jammu and Kashmir

Backward Classes Committee, February-November, 1969.
Chairman: Shri J.N. Wazir

Backward Classes Committee, 1976-1977.
Chairman: Justice (Dr.) Adarsh S. Anand

(Gajendragadkar) Commission, 1967-1978.
Chairman: Gajendragadkar

Karnataka

Backward Classes Committee, 1960-1961.
Chairman: Dr. R. Naganna Gowda

Backward Classes Commission, 1971-1975.
Chairman: Shri L.G. Havanur

Kerala

Evaluation Committee, 1961-1963.
Chairman: V.K. Vishwanathan

(Backward Classes) Commission, 1964-1965.
Chairman: Shri G. Kumara Pillai

Backward Classes Reservation Commission, 1967-1970.
Chairman: Shri M.P. Damodaran

Maharashtra

Committee to Report on Reservation of Backward Classes in the Services, 1961-1964.
Chairman: Shri B.D. Deshmukh

Mysore

Committee to Recommend Steps for Adequate Representation for Non-Brahmins in the Services of the State, 1918.
Chairman: Sir L.C. Miller

Punjab

Committee on Backward Classes, 1951.

Evaluation Committee, 1965-1966.
Chairman: Shri Brish Bhan

Vidhan Sabha Committee on Welfare of SC & ST and Backward Classes, 1975-1976.

Tamil Nadu

Backward Classes Commission, 1969-1970.
Chairman: Shri A.N. Sattanathan

Uttar Pradesh

Most Backward Classes Commission, 1975-1977
Chairman: Shri Chhedi Lal Sathi

West Bengal

Committee (on Backward Classes) to Find out Whether It was Necessary to Invoke the Powers Vested in the State Government under article 15(4), 16(4) and 29(2) Read with Article 15(4) of the Constitution, August 1-30, 1980.

PRE-INDEPENDENCE RELEVANT REFERENCES

1885

Madras Government, Grant-in-Aid Code to Regulate Financial Aid to Educational Institutions Providing Special Facilities for Students of Depressed Classes, 1985.

1871

Criminal Tribes Act, 1871.

1911

Criminal Tribes Act, 1911.

1919

Montague-Chelmsford Reforms of 1919.

1935

Government of India Act, 1935.

Nehru was Against Quota in Services

Jawaharlal Nehru was strongly against any kind of reservation, mainly in services and promotions, based on caste or group.

The first Prime Minister was in favour of providing opportunities for good education and "help" on economic considerations and not on caste, but opposed reservation in jobs which might kill efficiency.

Nehru's views on reservation are clearly recorded in the letter he wrote to the Chief Ministers way back on June 27, 1961. This is one of the 91 letters published in the fifth and last volume of Jawaharlal Nehru's letters to Chief Ministers, covering the years from 1958 to his death in 1964.

In this letter, Nehru put due emphasis on efficiency and the need to get out of "our traditional ruts".

This necessitates "our getting out of the old habit of reservations and particular privileges being given to this caste or that group," he wrote.

He referred to a meeting attended by the Chief Ministers to consider national integration, which laid down that help should be given on economic considerations and not on caste.

It is true that the country is tied up with certain rules and conventions about helping the Scheduled Castes and Tribes, Nehru wrote.

They deserve help but, even so, "I dislike any kind of reservation, more particularly in services. I react strongly against anything which leads to inefficiency and second-rate standards".

Nehru wanted the country to be a "first class" country in everything, and said the moment "we encourage the second-rate we are lost".

The only real way of helping a backward group, Nehru wrote, is to provide sufficient opportunities of good education. "This includes technical education which is becoming more and more important. Everything else is provision of some kind of crutches which do not add to the strength or health of the body".

In this context, he referred to two "very important" decisions by the Government. One was universal free elementary education which, Nehru said, is the base. The second was scholarships on a very wide scale at every grade of education to the bright students. This applies not merely to literary education, but to technical, scientific and medical training.

Nehru paid stress on the bright boys and girls because it is only they who will raise "our standards".

"I have no doubt that there is a vast reservoir of potential talent in this country if only we can give it opportunity".

But if the country goes in for reservations on communal and caste basis, "we swamp the bright and able people and remain second-rate or third-rate," he wrote.

Nehru was grieved to learn of how far this business of reservations had gone based on communal considerations.

(*Indian Express*, September 19, 1990)

Burman Questions 1931 Census

Mr. B.K. Roy Burman, associated with the Mandal Commission as *Chairman* of Research Planning Team and Technical Sub-Committee and also as the member of the Expert Committee, has questioned the findings of the report and also the basis of its recommendations.

Mounting a scathing attack on the very structure of the recommendations of the Mandal Commission, Mr. Burman stated at a Press conference today that the Government should forthwith release all information about the data-base as processed by the Mandal Commission.

Questioning the assertion of the Commission secretary that not a comma had been changed from the recommendation of the expert committee. Mr. Roy Burman said that the whole episode amounted to putting a question mark on the reputations of the experts associated with the Commission.

The Mandal Commission expert asserted that disagreement with the final recommendations could in no way be used to question our integrity.

"It has both a legal as well as moral dimension but I am more concerned with the moral aspects, "Mr Roy Burman said without ruling out the possibility of taking recourse to the legal action.

The Mandal expert also questioned the 1931 Census that formed the base of OBC-identification. "To begin with the very census needs scientific scrutiny," he said.

Mr Roy Burman while answering a question said that if proper procedures were made use of, not more than 20 per cent of the recommended OBCs come within the domain of the protection in jobs. "I stand for reservations for economically vulnerable sections of society particularly from the OBCs," he said.

Mr Roy Burman said that having, questioned the findings of the Mandal Commission immediately after its presentation to the President, he had been informed by the then Home Minister P.C. Sethi that the various date that formed the basis of the recommendations were not with the Home Ministry. "Till date, the Home Ministry has failed to retrieve the same," he charged.

Mr Roy Burman also wrote to Prime Minister V.P. Singh on August 20 this year regarding the objections of the experts to the Mandal Commission Report. However, he did not receive any reply.

(*Hindustan Times*, September 20, 1990)

Job Reservation in Railways and Accidents

Wanchoo Railway Accidents Inquiry Committee observed in 1968 that "failure of railway staff was responsible for 95 to 100 per cent of collisions and 67 per cent of derailments".

The Sikri Committee, which was set up for the same purpose, found that out of 7,957 consequential railway accidents between 1968 and 1979 in which the cause was established, a total of 5,648 of these mishaps were due to "failure of staff" (3,218 due to direct and 2,430 due to indirect failures)'. The Committee came to the conclusion that one of the "main factors" responsible for the staff failure was the "reservation of posts during promotion for Scheduled Castes and Scheduled Tribes". The Wanchoo panel earlier had also dealt with the effect of reservation for SCs and STs on the morale of the staff. It did not link it with the accidents. Nevertheless, it noted: "In the course of evidence tendered before us, it was pointed out that among the factors responsible for the discontent among supervisors, one was the present procedure of reservation of posts for Scheduled Castes and Scheduled Tribes. Such reservation, we were told adversely affects the enthusiasm, incentive for hard work and devotion to duty, and in turn the efficiency and morale of supervisory staff".

The Railway Reforms Committee, which was set up in 1981, to "examine and report on various aspects of railway working", took notice of reports of both the Wanchoo and Sikri panels. It conducted its own studies on the "morale and motivation" of the staff, and observed in its ninth report in 1983: "We have been struck in our meetings with various railway officers and staff bodies, by the extent to which promotional quotas for reserved groups has evoked resentment and protest. Time and again this has been quoted as the single biggest cause for low morale, lack of motivation and a pervasive sense of frustration especially among staff in Class III".

These three reports about just one Government department caution about the effect of reservation on morale of the staff. These concern only SCs and STs for whom the reservation quota is 22.5 per cent. The findings of these committees are all the more relevant in the present context when the reservations have been extended to an additional 27 per cent of population. These are warning enough about the effect on the morale and efficiency of the staff now that 49.5 per cent of jobs will be reserved. If the timing of the reports is taken into account, the obvious inference is that the situation has worsened over the years. The Wanchoo Committee noticed the malaise in 1968, the Sikri panel in 1978 and the Railway Reforms Committee in 1983.

Experience Must

The railway Reforms Committee was of the view that while implementing the reservation policy for promotions, "a minimum experience criterion" should be laid down and that "there should be a special emphasis on training of reserved categories".

One feature of the reports of these panels is that despite taking a sympathetic view of the plight of Scheduled Castes and Scheduled Tribes, these do not minimise the need for maintaining a certain level of efficiency of the administration. The Wanchoo Committee says: "We have given thought to the question of reservation of posts and weightage for Scheduled Castes and Scheduled Tribes in the promotion vacancies. It is true that Article 16(4) of the Constitution permits such reservation with a view to giving adequate representation to the relatively backward communities in the society: We are also aware that the principle of promotion vacancies was upheld by the Supreme Court. The provision in the Constitution and the pronouncement of the Supreme Court show the concern and sympathy for Scheduled Castes and Scheduled Tribes. These, however, have necessarily to be counter-balanced with the need for maintaining the efficiency of the administration at a reasonable level. It must be appreciated that reservations for a community or a group of people must not be at the cost of overall efficiency of the administration".

The Sikri Committee stated: "Special provisions for promotions of Scheduled Castes and Scheduled Tribes do not appear to consider the effect of such promotions on the persons who have been superseded and feel frustrated and disheartened. The depth and extent of frustration and its ill-effects and safety on railway working should be studied further".

The Railway Reforms Committee came to the conclusion: "Frequently competent persons have been overlooked and made to serve under their own juniors, who have been promoted on the quota system with a lowered qualifying standard. According to the evidence rendered to us, it is a moot point whether in practice, even the reduced qualifying marks are always achieved by persons selected from the reserved list owing to procedural problems. We are informed that in each case wherein the prescribed percentage of reserved candidates can- not be filled up in a promotion test, a detailed explanation has to be given and the selection committees are virtually put on the mat. Officers, therefore, prefer to push up requisite number of persons from the reserved list".

The Committee pointed out certain other anomalies as well. The pass marks for a general employee are 50 per cent whenever a promotion is on the basis of seniority-cum-suitability while for employees in the quota category these are 40 per cent. In the case of selections, the qualifying marks for general employees are 60 per cent of the professional portion of the selection test, while they are 50 per cent in the reserved quota. In the case of selections, if a suitable candidate is not available, "the zone of consideration can be enlarged up to two grades below the prescribed level, with the permission of the head of the department. Such permission," the Committee noted, "is invariably given in the absence of any guidelines on which discretion is to be exercised. This has frequently resulted in otherwise competent supervisors having to serve under their own subordinate staff and lose all enthusiasm for their work".

Quota Exceeds Limits

The Committee also referred to how the quota for SCs and STs exceeded the prescribed limit of 22.5 per cent. It stated: "The quota for reservation is at each promotion based on vacancies and not related to the communitywise incumbencies already existing. After successive promotions, in the higher grades the age-group of Scheduled Tribe and Scheduled Caste candidate tends to become lower than their colleagues owing to their having jumped seniorities in the earlier selection process. Retirements, therefore, become faster in the higher grades amongst the general employees, therefore, starts going beyond the prescribed percentage".

As a test case, the Committee examined a representation made by one of the recognised unions of the Northern Railway to the Railway Board, concerning the seniority list of parcel and booking clerks. It found out "that in a seniority list of 37 persons in the higher grade, 28 are from among the Scheduled Castes and Scheduled Tribes". Similarly "in one of the most vital safety categories of the railways, that of Controllers, we find that the representation of reserved categories on the Delhi Division is already 32 per cent in the case of those in the grade Rs.700-Rs.900, and based on ages of superannuation will rise to more than 50 per cent in the next five years".

"The important consideration of experience and competence," according to the Committee, "has not found expressions in the policy as it has been implemented even for those directly responsible for train running".

The Committee remarked: "In its anxiety, the Ministry of Railways have failed to take care of the interests of administrative efficiency, the general morale of its staff, and the pervasive implications on the safety of the vast body of the travelling public. Even the ground slightly retrieved in not applying the above policy to safety categories, has not helped very much".

The Committee expressed the opinion that the Railways had gone beyond even the Government guidelines "with deleterious repercussions" and had adopted certain features "which are neither mandatory nor desirable".

Expressing "in principle" the "greatest sympathy" with the reserved categories, the Committee made many suggestions about what the Railways should do to improve its functioning. It suggested that promotional aspects being dismal in the higher officer grades, "cadre reviews should be carried out strictly as per Government's decision, and a senior officer should be specially put on whole time for the job".

It suggested following steps with regard to the reservation policy of promotion:

(1) A minimum experience criterion be laid down for each promotion, equally applicable to all employees irrespective of whether they are in the reserved list or otherwise.

(2) The system of promotion on trial from amongst the best of failures be dispensed with (Under this system, in the case of suitability tests, if no suitable candidates are found, 'best out of the failures' are promoted for a period of six months, provided they do not belong to safety categories).

(3) The zone of consideration should be the same for all employees viz., that of the lower grade and the zone of consideration

should not be enlarged by including even lower categories in order to fill in a quota.

(4) There should be special emphasis on training of reserved categories.

(5) The reservation policy should not apply in any form to the safety categories, because no relaxation can be permitted in matters relating to safety, as the hazards would far outweigh any other consideration. In this context, the Railways should examine the safety implications of the work of all staff of the Railways, by taking into consideration responsibilities fixed in the past railway accidents and refix the coverage of this term on realistic and pragmatic considerations.

In particular it should be examined if the safety categories should include *inter alia*: all staff involved with train control; all staff involved in train formation and train passing; all driving crew and guards, all train examining staff and locomotive fitters and supervisors, all staff involved in permanent way maintenance and all staff involved in signalling work and communication.

(*Indian Express*, September 19, 1990)

Reservations and the Plight of Brahmins

The following extract from an article 'The Plight of Brahmins' by Meenakshi Jain (*Indian Express*, September 18, 1990) tries to focus attention on the other side of the coin:

> A study of the Brahmin Community in a district in Andhra Pradesh reveals that all purohits today live below the poverty line. Eighty per cent of those surveyed stated that their poverty and traditional style of dress and hair (tuft) had made them the butt of ridicule. Financial constraints coupled with the existing system of reservations for the "backward classes" prevented them from providing secular education to their children.

Overall Decline

> In fact, according to this study, there has been an overall decline in the number of Brahmin students. The average income of Brahmins being less than that of non-Brahmins, a high percentage of Brahmin students drop out at the intermediate level. In the 5-18 year age group, 44 per cent Brahmin students stopped education at the primary level and 36 per cent at the pre-matriculation level. The study also found that 55 per cent of all Brahmins lived below the poverty line, that is below a per capita income of Rs. 65 a month. Since 45 per cent of the total population of India is officially stated to be below the poverty line, it follows that the percentage of destitute Brahmins is 10 per cent higher than the all-India figures. There is no reason to believe that the condition of Brahmins in other parts of the country is any different.
>
> In this connection it would be revealing to quote the per capita income of various communities as stated by the Karnataka Finance Minister in the State Assembly on July 1, 1978: Christians Rs. 1,562, Vokkaligas Rs. 914, Muslims Rs. 794, Scheduled Castes Rs. 680, Scheduled tribes Rs. 577 and Brahmins Rs. 537.

Appalling poverty compelled many Brahmins to migrate to towns leading to spatial dispersal and consequent decline in their local influence and institutions. Brahmins initially turned to government jobs and modern occupations such as law and medicine. But preferential policies for the non-Brahmins have forced the Brahmins to retreat in these spheres as well. According to the Andhra Pradesh study, the largest percentage of Brahmins today are employed as clerks, followed by teachers. Over 15 per cent are employed as domestic servants. The unemployment rate among them is as high as 75 per cent.

Clearly it is time to sit up and see reality as it is before we complete the task the British began — the atomisation of Indian society and annihilation of Indian civilisation

Bibliographical Documentation*

Annuals, Bibliographies and General References

Agrawal, S.P., 1975, Castes, communities and tribes in India, *Contemporary Social Sciences* 4 (8) April-June, p 5-6; 4 (9) July-September, p 5-6.

Agrawal, S.P. and Aggrawal, J.C., 1990, *Information India 1989-90: Global View*, Concept Publishing Company, New Delhi, 530 p.

Anon, 1966, *Bibliography on scheduled castes, scheduled tribes and selected marginal communities of India*, Manager of Publication, Delhi, for Offices of the Registrar General of India.

———, 1972, *Social welfare and welfare of backward classes*, Planning Commission Library, New Delhi, 10 p, mimeographed, Planning bibliography series No. 92.

Business India (Periodical), September 3-16.

Business World (Periodical), 1990, September 12-28.

India, Planning Commission, 1990, *Annual Report, 1989-90*, Planning Commission, New Delhi, 100 p.

India, Ministry of Information and Broadcasting, 1988-89, *Reference Annual*, Publication Division, New Delhi, p 826.

India, Ministry of Welfare, 1990, *Annual Report, 1989-1990*, Ministry of Welfare, New Delhi, 129 p.

India Today (Periodical), 1990, September 15

Sunday (Periodical), 1990, September 9-15

Backward Communities

See

Backward Classes

---

* Includes Sources scanned (1947-1990).

Backward Classes Commission, 1953-55

Backward Classes Commission, 1953-1955, New Delhi, 1955, *Report*, Ministry of Home Affairs, New Delhi.
Chairman: Shri Kakasaheb Kalelkar

Vanyajati (Periodical), 1953, Backward Class Commission, *Vanyajati* 1(2) April, p 25-26, editorial..

Backward Classes Commission, 1979-80

Backward Classes Commission, 1979-1980, New Delhi, 1984, *Report*, Controller of Publications, New Delhi, 2 parts.
Chairman: Shri Bindhyeshwari Prasad Mandal

Backward Classes Commission, 1979-80 : News Analysis and Critique

Abraham, A.S., 1990, OBC forces in full cry: Bid for power in perpetuity, *Times of India*, September 4, p 8, col 2-4.

Amrik Singh, 1990, Mandal Commission : Educational impact, *Times of India*, August 18.

Badhwar, Inderjeet, 1990, Mandal Commission : Dividing to rule, *India Today*, September 15.

Bhatia, Prem, 1990, A mostly unread document, *Tribune*, September 7.

Business India (Periodical), 1990, Risking the Mandal Report, *Business India*, September 3-16, editorial

Chatterjee, Raj, 1990, First thing first, *Tribune*, September 7.

Datta Ray, Sunanda K., 1990, Class into caste : V.P. Singh's political insurence, *Statesman*, September 9.

Dhawan, Harmohan, 1990, Text of Harmohan Dhawan's letter to P.M., *National Herald*, September 9.

Dube, S.C., 1990, Against fratricidal caste war, *Mainstream* 28(46) September 8, p 4-5.

———, 1990, A retrograde fetish, *Hindustan Times*, September 3, p 11, Col. 2-5.

Gandhi, Rajiv, 1990, More politics than jobs, *Hindustan Times*, September 8, 1990.

Ganguli, Amulya, 1990, Divide and lose : Mandal in Shah Bano's wake, *Statesman*, September 5, p 6, col. 4-6.

Garg, R.K., 1990, For development sans divisions, *Patriot*, September 5.

Gill, M.S. and Singh, A.M., 1989, Reactionary dissent by caste Hindu employees, *Social Change* 19 (3) September, p 16-22.

Hindustan Times (Newspaper), 1990, The Mandal mess, *Hindustan Times*, September 19, editorial.

———, 1990, Time for second thoughts, *Hindustan Times*, September 13, editorial.

Hoshiar Singh and Malik, Jagdish Kumar, 1984, The Mandal Commission report : A plea for share in power, *Political Science Review* 23(3-4) July-December, p 250-268, bibliography, tables.

India Today (Periodical), 1990, Policy reservations, *India Today*, September. 15, editorial.

Jain, Meenakshi, 1990, The plight of Brahmins, *Indian Express*, September 18.

Karlekar, Hiranmay, 1990, Undermining India, *Indian Express*, August 25.

Khanna, H.R., 1990, Weakening the roots, *Hindustan Times*, September 13.

Khushwant Singh, 1990, Mandal mess, *Hindustan Times*, September 8.

Kothari, Rajni, 1990, Meaning of Mandal, *Hindustan Times*, September 24, p 13.

Madhok, Balraj, 1990, Creating new tensions, *Hindustan Times*.

Mishra, Sudhanshu, 1990, Most party leaders keep aloof, *Link* 33(4) September 2, p 6-7.

Muthamma, C.B., 1990, Change the system, *Hindustan Times*, September 21.

Puri, Rajinder, 1990, Mandal : A way out, *Hindustan Times*, September 11.

Rajappa, S., 1990, Tamil Nadu for it, rest of South quiet, *Statesman*, September 4.

Ramaiah, A., 1990, Mandal Commission's recommendations : A critical view, *Mainstream* 28 (43) August 18, p 19-20 +.

Ramanathan, K.V., 1990, Lessons from experience, *Indian Express*, September 7.

Roy Burman, B.K., 1990, Burman questions 1931 Census, *Hindustan Times*, September 18.

Sangal, P.S., 1990, Re-examination of criteria necessary, *National Herald*, September 9.

Sardesai, Rajdeep, 1990, Mandal fails to agitate Maharashtra, *Times of India*, September 1.

Sharma, K.L., 1990, A backward step, *Indian Express*, September 19.

Shourie, Arun, 1990, Three sets of facts on Mandal : Rank 413? So sorry. Rank 14246? But of course . . . *Indian Express*, September 2.

Shukla, Rajiv, 1990, Mandal Commission : Where does the Janata Dal stand? *Sunday*, September 9-15.

Srivastava, Manju, and Srivastava, Saraswati, 1983-84, The Mandal Commission report : A critique, *Journal of State Politics and Administration* 6 (2) July-December 7 (1) January-June, p 75-86, bibliography, footnote.

Tharyan, P., 1990, Attack caste, not Mandal, *Hindustan Times*, September 8, p 11, col. 2-5.

Verghese, B.G., 1990, Quake remedies, *Indian Express*, September 12.

Backward Classes Commission, 1979-80: News Items

Advani assails V.P. on minorities quota, *Hindustan Times*, September 2, 1990.

Advani assails V.P. on Muslim quota, *Times of India*, September 2, 1990.

Agreement on four point says Upendra, *National Herald*, September 4, 1990 , p. 1, col. 1.

Ahir and Gujjars 'left alone', *Statesman*, September 7, 1990.

All party meet not a failure : N.F., *Hindustan Times*, September 5, 1990, p. 24, col. 4.

All party meet to discuss reservations, *Hindustan Times*, August 31, 1990.

Anger of the elite? *Statesman*, September 7, 1990.

Anti Mandal stir : No decision on Delhi rally, *Times of India*, September 9, 1990.

Anti quota stir hits grain trade, *Times of India*, September 8, 1990.

Anti quota stir spreads: Four killed in Patna violence, *Times of India*, September 5, 1990, p 1, col. 1-2.

Anti quota stir toll rises to 7 in Orissa, *Statesman*, September 3, 1990, p 1, col. 3-5; p. 7, col. 5.

Anti reservation stir in Bihar: Situation needs mature handling, *Patriot*, September 1, 1990.

Anti reservation stir unabated: Four killed in Orissa police firing, *Times of India*, September 2, 1990.

Army alerted in Baroda : Curfew in three cities : *Hindustan Times*, September 6, 1990.

Army alerted in Shimla, *Hindustan Times*, September 8. 1990, p 1, col. 5-7+; *Tribune*, September 8, 1990.

Army called out in Kangra district: H.P. rejects Mandal report, *Times of India*, September 7.

B.J.P. against quota for minorities, says Advani, *Hindustan Times*, September 3, 1990, p 1, col. 4.

B.J.P., C.P.M. for talks with students, *Tribune*, September 7, 1990.

B.J.P. flays Government on job quota issue, *Hindustan Times*, September 8, 1990.

B.J.P. for 50 per cent as quota limit, *Hindustan Times*, September 1, 1990.

B.J.P. Left–call for economic criterion, *Times of India*, August 18, 1990.

Backward quota a forward step, *Hindustan Times*, September 7, 1990.

Backwardness won't go by playing petty politics: Rajiv: V.P.S. obstinacy will divide India: Plea for uplift of poorest of poor in marathon L.S. speech, *National Herald*, September 7, 1990.

Bandh no way to do it, say traders, *Hindustan Times*, September 7, 1990.

Basu calls for modifications, *Indian Express*, September 1, 1990.

Be your own light, *Tribune*, August 19, 1990.

Beyond mere palliatives, *Hindu*, September 9, 1990.

Bill on job quota for SC, ST on anvil, *Hindustan Times*, September 3, 1990, p 18, col. 1-2.

Bommai warns of bloodshed, *Tribune*, September 9, 1990.

C.P.M. favours Karpoori formula, *Hindustan Times*, August 31, 1990.

C.P.M. view on quota against its policy, *Times of India*, September 2, 1990.

Cabinet not split over quota: V.P., *Times of India*, September 5, 1990.

Carring the can, *Times of India*, September 5, 1990, p 8, col. 1.

Caste not basis, says V.P. Singh, *Hindu*, September 7, 1990.

Cauldron of caste tensions, *Hindu*, September 4, 1990, p 8.

Central order on job reservation, *Hindustan Times*, August 19, 1990, p 12., col. 5-8.

Centre accepts States plea, *Times of India*, September 3, 1990.

Chakka Jam plan washed away, *Hindustan Times*, September 8, 1990, p 5, col. 2-5.

A challenge to political parties, *National Herald*, September 2, 1990.

Congress I flays Government more on quota, *Indian Express*, September 5, 1990, p 9, col. 1-5.

Congress to boycott all-party meet, *Hindustan Times*, September 3, 1990, p 1, col. 1-3; p 18, col. 1-2.

Consensus eludes all party meet: Cong leaders attend, Govt. stand rigid, *Hindustan Times*, September 4, 1990, p 1, col. 1-4.

DUTA Chief's bid to scuttle discussion condemned, *Hindu*, September 2, 1990.

DUTA split over Mandal report, *Times of India*, September 2, 1990.

Dalit Christians allege bias, *Hindustan Times*, August 18, 1990, p 5, col. 5-8.

Dalit Christians demands SC status, *Times of India*, August 18, 1990.

Dalit Christians want SC status, privileges, *Hindu*, August 18, 1990.

Decision on Mandal report hasty: Dhawan, *Tribune*, September 9, 1990.

Delhi incident-free, but stir continues, *Hindu*, September 2, 1990.

Divided they stand, *Tribune*, September 5, 1990, p 6, col. 1-2.

Do not destroy country: Dinesh, *Hindustan Times*, September 6, 1990.

Don't take a hasty decision on quota, Left tells V.P., *National Herald*, September 5, 1990, p 1, col. 1.

Double talk on castes, *Hindustan Times*, September 7, 1990.

End the drift, *Hindustan Times*, September 7, 1990.

Expert disagrees with Mandal report, *Hindustan Times*, September 1, 1990.

Extend reservation to education, MPs, *Patriot*, September 17, 1990.

Farmers blast quota policy, *Hindustan Times*, September 9, 1990.

Fire spreads, *National Herald*, September 8, 1990, p 6, col. 1-2.

Firing in Bihar : Stir spreads to South, *Times of India*, August 19, 1990.

Five die in Bihar anti-quota stir, *Indian Express*, September 5, 1990, p 9, col. 1-4.

Five lakh likely to attend : Anti Mandal forum rally, *National Herald*, September 4, 1990, p 3, col. 2.

Forum asks students to go back to classes, *Hindustan Times*, September 1, 1990.

Fresh violence in Bihar, Haryana, *Hindustan Times*, September 6, 1990.

From crisis to crisis: The unmaking of the Singh Government, *Probe India*, 11 (7) September, 1990, p 8-12.

Full speed backwards by P.M., *Times of India*, September 4, 1990, p 8, col. 2-4.

Govt. has put students fate in jeopardy: Aiyer, *National Herald*, September 4, 1990, p 3-5.

Govt. pulled up for not tabling report, *Tribune*, September 7, 1990.

Govt. urged to seek apex courts advice, *Hindu*, September 8, 1990.

Gujarat coalition in fresh row, *Patriot*, September 8, 1990.

Gujarat 'no' to Mandal report, *Statesman*, September 3, 1990, p 1, col. 7-8.

Gujjar leader assails report, *Indian Express*, September 5, 1990, p 16, Col. 1-3.

Haryana observes complete bandh, *Times of India*, September 1, 1990.

Haryana panel on backward classes, *Hindustan Times*, September 9, 1990.

High living, plain thinking: Mandalised metropolitan mind, *Times of India*, September 5, 1990, p 8, col. 2-4.

How a tragedy is enacted, *Indian Express*, September 5, 1990, p 8, col. 1.

The impasse continues, *National Herald*, September 6, 1990.

In a bind of sports, *Hindu*, September 5, 1990, p 8, col. 1.

Injustice will be legalised, *Indian Express*, September 8, 1990, p 5, col. 6-7.

Irony of the Mandal, Meenakshi Jain, *Indian Express*, September 3, 1990, p 8, col. 3-6.

Is shoe-shining that shameful? *Times of India*, September 9, 1990.

JNU students join anti quota stir, *Times of India*, August 19, 1990.

Janata Party opposes, Mandal report, *National Herald*, September 3, 1990, p 11, col. 5.

Job quota ends Manus legacy, *Statesman*, September 8, 1990.

Job reservations for backward classes, *Patriot*, September 3, 1990.

Kanshi Ram assails V.P. on Mandal, *Hindustan Times*, September 6, 1990.

List of castes delayed, *Times of India*, September 9, 1990.

Lung power keeps pot boiling, *Hindustan Times*, September 7, 1990.

Mandal: Champion of backward classes? *Indian Express*, August 19, 1990, p 1, col. 1-5; p 9, col. 1.

Mandal: Myth of merit and equity, *Times of India*, September 4, 1990, p 8, Col. 6-7.

Mandal mania and social justice, *Indian Express*, September 5, 1990, p 8, col. 2-5.

Mandal not relevant to Orissa, says J.B. Patnaik, *National Herald*, September 3, 1990, p 12, col. 2.

Mandal panel report: Harvest of headcounts in caste politics, *Link*, 33 (4), September 2, 1990, p 4-5.

Mandal report not to be imposed on States: V.P., *Indian Express*, September 2, 1990.

Mandal report scientific: Gill, *Hindustan Times*, September 6, 1990.

The Mandal trap, *Hindustan Times*, September 1, 1990.

A messiah always in the news, *Times of India*, September 9, 1990.

Minority govt. arrogance, *Tribune*, September 4, 1990, p 6., col. 2-4.

Mishra Urges V.P. to accept Rajiv formula, *National Herald*, September 5, 1990, p 9, col. 8.

More politics than jobs, says Rajiv, *Hindustan Times*, September 8, 1990, p 9, col. 5-8.

NF allies may seek changes in Mandal, *National Herald*, September 2, 1990.

NF Parliamentary party backs implementation, *Indian Express*, September 4, 1990, p 1, col. 2-4; p 9, col. 5.

National debate on reservation imperative, *Statesman*, September 1, 1990.

Need for dialogue, *Indian Express*, September 6, 1990.

Need, not caste, *Times of India*, September 8, 1990.

Need to redefine backwardness, *National Herald*, September 1, 1990.

Nehru for Lohia? *National Herald*, August 24, 1990.

No compromises on Mandal: Mulayam, *National Herald*, September 3, 1990, p 11, col. 2-3.

No confrontation with States: V.P., *Times of India*, September 27, 1990.

No consensus on Mandal report, Cong, attends all party meet, *Times of India*, September 4, 1990, p 1, col. 3-4; p 16, col. 2.

No legal hurdles to job quota, *Hindustan Times*, August 19, 1990, p 1, col. 1.

No plan to change quota formula: Nayanar, *Indian Express*, September 8, 1990, p 14, col. 1-4.

No way to consensus, *Patriot*, September 5, 1990.

Not by closure, *Patriot*, September 3, 1990.

Not by violence, *Times of India*, August 18, 1990.

Not without a consensus, *Hindustan Times*, September 5, 1990, p 14, col. 1.

Now it is caste fanaticism: *Hindustan Times*, September 8, 1990, p 5, col. 1-3.

Omens in Gujarat, *Times of India*, September 6, 1990.

One killed in UP firing, *Times of India*, September 4, 1990, p 1, col. 5-7; p 16, col. 3.

Orissa asks for Central forces, *Hindustan Times*, September 2, 1990.

Orissa firing toll 6: Agitation continues in many States, *Indian Express*, September 3, 1990, p 1, col. 6-9; p 12, col. 3-5.

PM dividing nation on caste lines, Rajiv, *Times of India*, September 9, 1990.

PM urged to defuse crisis, *Hindustan Times*, September 7, 1990.

Patnaik orders probe into firing, *Patriot*, September 4, 1990.

Pointless polemics, *Patriot*, September 8, 1990.

Politicians view point, *Hindustan Times*, September 9, 1990.

The politics of Pell Mell, *Hindustan Times*, September 2, 1990.

Professors oppose job quota, *Hindustan Times*, August 18, 1990, p 1, col. 4; p 22, col. 1.

Pro-quota men set for rally, *Hindustan Times*, September 6, 1990.

Pro-quota rally a damp squid, *Indian Express*, September 8, 1990, p 1, col. 5-7; p 9, col. 1.

Pro-quota youth rally today, *National Herald*, September 4, 1990, p 3, col. 5-6.

Protest against Mandal report, *Tribune*, September 3, 1990, p 7, col. 2-5.

Quota a hasty step: NF leader, *Hindustan Times*, September 9, 1990.

Quota created caste divide in Muslims, says Mishra, *National Herald*, September 9, 1990.

Quota for OBC adhoc solution, *National Herald*, September 3, 1990, p 12, col. 3-4.

Quota for OBCs in education also sought, *Hindustan Times*, September 4, 1990, p 1, col. 5.

Quota should be availed of once only, *Indian Express*, September 8, 1990, p 3, col. 4-6.

Quota stir spreads to many areas, *Hindustan Times*, September 7, 1990.

Rain God is anti-Mandal, Paswan, *Hindustan Times*, September 8, 1990, p 1, col. 11+

Rajiv urges exhaustive paper, *Times of India*, September 4, 1990, p 16, col. 1

Reservations are necessary, *Tribune*, September 3, 1990, p 6, col. 3-5.

Reservation doesn't mean mediocrity, *Times of India*, September 3, 1990.

Reservation partisan, *Tribune*, August 8, 1990.

Reservation won't lead to mediocrity, Paswan, *Patriot*, September 3, 1990.

Rift in Bihar Cong-I over quota issue, *Indian Express*, September 7, 1990.

Right to work demand, *National Herald*, September 7, 1990, p 3, col. 2-4.

Road, rail traffic disrupted, *Times of India*, August 24, 1990.

70 injured in DU clash, *Times of India*, September 7, 1990.

Schools closed in three states, *Times of India*, September 9, 1990.

Shared warning on stir, *Hindustan Times*, September 3, 1990, p 18, col. 2-4.

Sikkim also rejects report, *Times of India*, September 8, 1990.

Sikkim to benefit by Mandal report, *Times of India*, September 7, 1990.

Slamming the doors, *Indian Express*, September 8, 1990, p 8, col. 1-2.

Society's supplements, *Hindustan Times*, September 2, 1990.

Statement on extension of reservation policy, *Mainstream*, 28 (46) September 8, 1990, p 2.

States of unrest, *Statesman*, September 8, 1990.

Storm round the corner, *Link*, 33 (4) September 2, 1990, p 7-8.

Students block roads in Haryana towns, *Hindustan Times*, September 1, 1990.

Students burn Mandal report, *Statesman*, August 18, 1990.

Students clear warning, *Hindustan Times*, September 2, 1990.

Students get farmer's support, *Hindustan Times*, September 5, 1990, p 1, col. 4-7.

Students must join talks, Bommai, *Times of India*, September 4, 1990, p 4-6.

27 per cent but for whom? Rajeev Dhavan, *Patriot*, September 7, 1990.

28 injured in clashes, *Hindustan Times*, September 4, 1990, p 1, col. 1-3, Back col. 1.

Talk to youth, Advani tells govt., *Indian Express*, September 5, 1990, p 9, col. 6.

The talks fail, *National Herald*, September 5, 1990, p 6, col. 1.

Teachers front back reservation, *National Herald*, September 4, 1990, p 3, col. 2-3.

This is not collectivism, *National Herald*, September 4, 1990, p 6, col. 1.

Tikait not to lead anti-quota agitation, *Times of India*, August 18, 1990.

Toll figure inflated, says Bihar C.M., *Hindu*, September 6, 1990, p 4, col. 2-5.

Top Cong. leaders held in Orissa, *Hindustan Times*, September 5, 1990, p 1, col. 1-2.

Troops patrol M.P. towns, *Times of India*, September 8, 1990.

U.P.C.C. Chief flays quota policy, *National Herald*, September 3, 1990, p 9, col. 4.

Uncharacteristic calm: political compulsions, *Hindu*, September 9, 1990.

Undertaking democracy right, *Hindu*, September 4, 1990.

The unmaking of the Indian Union, *Indian Express*, September 3, p 1, col. 1-4.

Upendra claim absurd, *National Herald*, September 5, 1990, p 1, col. 2.

V.P. No going back on rights of minorities, *Tribune*, September 3, 1990, p. 1, col. 7-8.

V.P. asks NF MPs to explain Mandal report to people, *Hindustan Times*, September 8, 1990, p 1, col. 2-3.

V.P. dares Cong. to reverse decision, *Hindustan Times*, September 6, 1990.

V.P. gets backing of state by J.D. chiefs, *National Herald*, September 3, 1990, p 1, col. 4-5+

V.P. revised agenda, *Tribune*, September 4, 1990, p 1, col. 2-5.

V.P. Singh in a blind, *Patriot*, September 4, 1990.

V.P. working to divide nation on caste lines, Rajiv, *Hindustan Times*, September 7, 1990.

V.P. wrote to CMs before decision, *Hindustan Times*, September 2, 1990.

V.P.'s bid to score over Devi, Mishra, *National Herald*, August 19, 1990, p 4, col. 3-8.

V.P.'s challenge to Cong-I, *Indian Express*, September 6, 1990.

V.P.'s other storm-trooper, *Tribune*, September 7, 1990.

Vajpayee hails all party meet on quota, *National Herald*, September 3, 1990, p 12, col. 1.

Violence in more States : Cuttack curfew extended, *Hindustan Times*, September 1, 1990.

Violence mars bandh in Delhi: 214 rounded up, *Hindustan Times*, September 7, 1990.

Violence unabated in Orissa, *Link* 33 (4) September 2, 1990, p 8-9.
Wages of silence, *Indian Express*, August 25, 1990.
Walkout by BJP, CPI, CPM, *Tribune*, September 3, 1990, p 6, col. 1-2.
Who is to do it? *Hindustan Times*, September 7, 1990.
Woes of Mandal beneficiaries, *Tribune*, September 6, 1990.

Benefits

Dushkin, Lelah, 1979, Backward class benefits and social class in India, 1920-1970, *Economic and Political Weekly*, 14, Annual Number, April, p 661-667.

Caste and Politics

Blair, Harry W., 1980, Rising kulaks and backward classes in Bihar : Social change in the late 1970's, *Economic and Political Weekly* 15 (2) January 12, p 64-74.
Dorairaj, S., 1985, AIADMK's balancing tactic, *Link* 27 (37) April 28, p 12-13.
Jain, Meenakshi, 1985, Failure of Indira strategy : Backward castes support not enough, *Times of India* 13 (8) July, p 3-5.
Mitra, Chandan, 1989, Moulded in caste : AJGAR versus the lessor OBCs, *Times of India*, August 23, p 6, col. 3-5.
Sheth, D.L., 1979, Politics in caste conflict, *Seminar*, 233, January.

Clubs and Societies

Bhattacharya, Biswanath : 1965, A short note on clubs and libraries of the backward communities, *Bulletin of Cultural Research Institute*, 4, p 53-57, tables.

Commissions/Committees : Centre State (including Pre-Independence)

See Appendix 3

Constitution of India

Constitution of India, as on the 1st February, 1990, Diglat edition, Ministry of Law and Justice, New Delhi, 1990, 299 p.

Criminal Tribes

Sher, Sher Singh, 1960, Ex-criminal tribes of Northern India need reclassification on more authentic and scientific ground, *Journal of Social Research* 3 (2) September, p 35-42, tables.

Criminal Tribes Act, 1911

Radhakrishna, Meena, 1989, The Criminal Tribes Act in Madras Presidency : Implications for intiterant trading communities, *Indian Economic and Social History Review* 26 (3) July-September, p 269-295.

Criteria for Recognition

See
Determinants

Dalits

Anon, 1986, Shiv sena enters rural politics : Campaign against Dalits in Marathwara villages, *Economic and Political Weekly* 21 (50) December 13, p 2166-2167.

Bhuskute, R.V., 1989, Tribals, Dalits and government lands, *Economic and Political Weekly* 24 (23) June 10, table.

Gani, H.A., 1990, Dalit unity, *Janata*, 45, Annual Number, p 41 +.

Times of India (Newspaper), 1988, An effective reposite, *Times of India* 9 (6) February, p 1-2, editorial.

Depressed Classes Institute, Bombay

Social Service Quarterly (Periodical), 1927, Depressed Classes Institute, *Social Service Quarterly* 12 (3) January, p 144-145, editorial.

Determinants

Parvathamma, C., 1986, Should caste be a basis for recognising backwardness, *Guru Nanak Journal of Sociology* 7 (2) October, p 89-101, bibliography, table.

Rama, Badri, 1990, Connotation of merit, *Hindustan Times*, September 4, p 11, col. 6-7.

Education

Aggarwal, J.C., 1989, *Education in India : Policies, programmes and development : Global View*, Doaba House, Delhi, 186 p.

———, 1989, *Year book of Indian education, 1988-1989, World overview*, Doaba House, Delhi, 798 p.

———, 1990, *Development and planning of modern education*, Vikas Publishing House, New Delhi, 424 p.

———, 1990, *Educational reforms in India : World perspective : A comparative study of education for all by 2000 A.D. and National Policy on Education*, Doaba House, Delhi, 136 p.

———, 1990, *Elementary education and teacher functions*, Doaba House, Delhi, 270 p.

———, 1990, *Theory and principles of education : Philosophical and sociological basis of education*, Vikas Publishing House, New Delhi, 361 p.

———, and Aggarwal Sarita, 1990, *Education in India : A comparative study of States and Union Territories*, Concept Publishing Company, New Delhi, 120 p.

———, and Agrawal, S.P., 1989, *National Policy on education Agenda for India 2001*, Concept Publishing Company, New Delhi, 153 p.

———, and Biswas, A., 1990, *Seven Indian educationists* (Including 35 other thinkers on education in modern India), Arya Book Depot, New Delhi, p 327.

Anon, 1987, (Book review), *Journal of Sociological Studies*, January 6, p 187-190.

Review of the book: Bag, Dulal Chandra, 1984, *Impact of education on some backward communities of West Bengal*, Calcutta, OPS Publishing, viii, 304 p.

Biswas A. and Agrawal, S.P. 1986, *Development of education in India: A historical survey of educational documents before and after independence*, Concept Publishing Company, New Delhi.

Chitnis, Suma, 1972, Education and equality, *Economic and Political Weekly*, 7, (31, 32 and 33), p 1975-1981.

Committee for Review of National Policy on Education (NPE), 1986-1990, New Delhi, 1990, *Towards an enlightened and humane society : A perspective paper on education*, Ministry of Human Resource Development, Department of Education, New Delhi, 45 p.

D'Souza, Claude, 1986, Weaker section of the Indian society and their education, *Social Action* 36 (1) January-March, p 13-25.

Education Commission, 1964-1966, *Report*, Manager of Publications, New Delhi, 692 p.

Educational India (Periodical), 1964, Backwardness, *Educational India* 30 (9) March, p 308-309, editorial.

Gupta, L.P., 1979, A study of personality syndromes and cognitive characteristics of scheduled castes, backward classes and non-scheduled caste students, *Journal of Higher Education* 4(3) Spring, p 381-87.

India, Government, 1968, *National Policy on Education*, Ministry of Education, New Delhi, 28 p.

India, Government, 1979, *Draft National Policy on Education*, Ministry of Education, New Delhi, 18 p.

India, Government, 1985, *Challenge of education: A policy perspective*, Ministry of Education, New Delhi, 119 p.

India, Government, 1986, *National policy on education*, Ministry of Human Resource Development, Department of Education, New Delhi, 32 p.

India, Government, 1986, *Programme of Action*, Ministry of Human Resource Development, Department of Education, New Delhi, 200 p.

Jain, S.P., 1989, Educating backward classes : Role of U.G.C., *Economic Trends* 18 (5) April, p 3-6.

Lele, T.P., 1967, A comparative study of the students from different communities, *Education and Psychology Review* 7 (3) July, p 117-24, tables.

Rao, T.S., 1972, Free education for all, *Social Welfare* 19 (9) December, p 18-20.

Sharma, R.S., 1985, Developing educational technology for deprived sections of the Indian society, *Bulletin of Non-Formal Education* 3 (3) December, p 1-17.

Varma, R.P., 1984, Educating the disadvantaged : A few suggestions, *National Journal of Education* 6 (2) May, p 1-6, references.

Verghese, Alexander V., 1984, Education, earning and occupation of weaker castes, *Journal of Higher Education* 9 (3) Spring, p 373-81, references.

Verma, B.P. and Sharma, Keshav, 1989, A comparative study of locus of control and self concept of higher, backward and scheduled caste students, *Progress of Education* 63(9) April, p 205-208.

Educational Status

Deshmukh, B.D., 1957, Educational status of the backward communities, *Progress of Education* 32 (3) October, p 97-98, letter to editor.

Empowerment

Jetley, Surinder, 1968, Transfer of power to a low caste, *Interdiscipline* 5 (3) Autumn, p 199-206

Equalisation

Aggarwal, Pratap, 1986, *Halfway to equality*, Manohar Publishing, New Delhi.

Anon, 1986, (Book review), *Journal of Indian Law Institute* 28 (1) January-March, p 117-121.
Review of the book : Galanter, Marc, 1984, *Competing equalities : Law and the backward classes in India*, Oxford University Press, New Delhi, 525 p.

Ramaswamy, Uma, 1986, Protection and inequality among backward groups, *Economic and Political Weekly* May 21, p 399-403.

Issues and Trends

Cheluva Raju, K.H., 1986, Backward classes in India : Issues and trends, *Indian Journal of Political Science* 47(4) October-December, p 473-485.

Land and Backward Classes

Galanter, Mare, 1985, *Law and the backward classes in India*, Oxford University Press, New Delhi, 625 p.

Libraries

Bhattacharya, Biswanath, 1965, A short note on clubs and libraries of the backward communities, *Bulletin of Cultural Research Institute* 4, p 53-57, tables.

Living Standards

Hanumantha Rao, K. and Sastry, K.V.S., 1990, Levels of living and poverty among social groups in Andhra Pradesh : A cross-section analysis, *Journal of Rural Development* 9 (1) January, p 91-105.

Mandal Commission

See

Backward Classes Commission, 1979-1980

Manifestoes of Political Parties

Agrawal, S.P. and Aggrawal, J.C., 1990, *Lok Sabha and Vidhan Sabha Elections in India, 1989-1990 : Process and results with comparative study of manifestoes*, Concept Publishing Company, New Delhi, 266 p.

Problems

Anon, 1985, (Book review), *Vision* 4 (3) January-March, p 67-69, Review of the book : Sahoo, B., 1985, *The problem of weaker sections*, New Era Publishing, Bhubaneshwar, 248 p.

Protest/Reform Movements

Aziz, Abdul, 1980, The backward class movement in Karnataka, 1918-1929, *Journal of Historical Studies* 16, p 50-62.

Irschick, Eugeno F., 1969, *Politics and social conflict in South India : The Non-Brahminic movement and Tamil separatism, 1916-1929*, Oxford University Press, Bombay

Kuppuswamy, B., 1978, *Backward classes movement in Karnataka*, Bangalore University, Bangalore.

Parvathamma, C., 1986, Role of protest movements in social transformation, *Guru Nanak Journal of Sociology* 7 (1) April, p 1-22.

Reclassification

Sher, Sher Singh, 1960, Ex-criminal tribes of Northern India need reclassification on more authentic and scientific grounds, *Journal of Social Research* 3 (2) September, p 35-42, tables.

Research

Roy Burman, B.K., 1961, A list of research projects with operative significance for welfare of the backward classes (with special reference to West Bengal) *Vanyajati* 9 (1) January, p 9-21.

Zutsi, G.L., 1959, Preliminaries regarding applied research among backward classes, *Vanyajati* 7 (3) July, p 84-93.

Reservation Issue

Abraham, A.S., 1985, Anti-reservation protest : Growing clout of backward classes, *Times of India*, March 1, p 8.

———, 1985, Caste war in Gujarat : Wider objectives of agitation, *Times of India*, 14, p 6.

———, 1985, Going beyond reservations : Framework for a wider policy, *Times of India*, April 20, p 8.

———, 1985, Turmoil over reservations : Backward classes in full cry, *Times of India*, April 12, p 8.

———, 1986, Backward class quota : Forming a national consensus, *Times of India*, 19 (8) September 19, p 8.

———, 1986, Goodbye to modernism : Warning over reservations, *Times of India*, August 1, p 8.

Anon, 1985, (Book review); *National Herald* 2(5) October 20, p 5; *Patriot* November 3, p 4.

Review of the book : Mehta, Haroobhai and Patel, Hasmukh, 1985, *Dynamics of reservation policy*, Patriot Publishing, New Delhi, 320 p.

———, 1985, (Book review), *Patriot*, May 12, p 4.

Review of the book : Desai, I.P., et al., 1985, *Caste, caste-conflict and reservations*, Janata Publication, Delhi, viii, 218 p.

——, 1985, A cynical ploy, *Times of India*, January 17, p 8.

——, 1985, Govt. staff in Gandhinagar strike work, *Times of India*, May 1, p 1 +.

——, 1985, Gujarat : Threat of fresh agitation, *New Age*, November 24, p 2.

——, 1985, Gujarat accord, *Times of India*, July 22, p 8.

——, 1985, Gujarat caste war, *Times of India*, April 17, p 8.

——, 1985, Gujarat government accepts agitators' demands, *Times of India*, April 20, p 1 +.

——, 1985, Reverse discrimination defended, *Link* 27 (36) April 21, p 12.

——, 1985, Statesmanship leads to disaster, *Times of India*, (Sunday Review) April 28, p 1 +.

——, 1985, A thorny problem, *Times of India*, March 7, p 8.

——, 1986, (Book review), *India Quarterly* 42 (1) January-March, p 103-105; *Link* 28 (25) January 26, p 109-111; *Patriot*, March 9, p 4; *Sunday Statesman*, March 11, p 11; *Tribune*, April 27, p 11.
Review of the book : Mehta, Haroobhai and Patel, Hasmukh, 1985, *Dynamics of reservation policy*, Patriot Publishing, New Delhi, 320 p.

——, 1986, (Book review), *Indian Express* (Magazine) August 31, p 5.
Review of the book : Anon, 1986, *Scenario of the 7 per cent*, Cenemart Foundation, New Delhi, 2 Vols.

——, 1986, Mr. Hegde surrenders, *Times of India*, October 9, p 8.

——, 1986, Policy of reservation : A symposium, *Parlance* 9 (11) August, p 10-21.

——, 1987, (Book review), *Times of India*, (Sunday review), March 8, p. 6.
Review of the book : Sandanshi, D.N., 1987, *Reservations for social justice*, Current Law Publishing.

——, 1990, All party meet to discuss reservations, *Hindustan Times*, August 31.

——, 1990, Extend reservation to education : MPs, *Patriot*, September 4.

——, 1990, Job reservations for backward classes, *Patriot*, September 3.

——, 1990, Nation debate an reservation imperative, *Statesman*, September 1.

——, 1990, Reservations are necessary, *Tribune*, September 3, p 6.

———, 1990, Reservation doesn't mean mediocrity, *Times of India*, September 3.

———, 1990, Reservation partisan, *Tribune*, August 18.

———, 1990, Teachers front back reservation, *National Herald*, September 4, p 3, col. 2-3.

Athre, H.V.R., 1980, Reservation policy, *Mysore Economic Review* 65 (1) January, p 1-3.

Bakshi, P.M., 1985, Reservations for backward classes : Some reflections, *Journal of Indian Law Institute* 27 (2) April-June, p 318-335.

Bakshi, Rajni, 1985, Will the movement spread? *Indian Express*, May 5, p 8.

Baxi, Upendra, 1985, Reflections on reservation crisis in Gujarat, *Mainstream* 23 (41) June 8, p 15-22; 23 (42) June 14, p 20-25; 23 (43) June 22, p 20-24.

Bhattacharjea, 1990, Anti-reservation stir : skirting the basic issue, *Mainstream* 28 (46) September 8, p 3 +.

Bommai, S.R., 1990, Quota for weaker sections must, *Indian Express*, September 9.

Chopra, Pran, 1989, Casting a deadly bait, *Indian Express*, August 1, p 1 +.

Desai, I.P., et al, 1985, *Caste, caste-conflict and reservations*, Janata Publication, Delhi, viii, 218 p.

Deshpande, Anjali, 1990, Reservations and Mandal report, *Mainstream* 28 (44) August 25, p 5 +.

Dhagamwar, Vasudha, 1985, Reservation : Missing the wood for the trees, *Mainstream* 23 (36) May 4, p 5-6.

Dhar, M.K., 1990, PM commitment to reservation total, *Hindustan Times*, September 1.

Dhawan, Shiv, 1985, Reservations : A critique of social justice, *Patriot* (Magazine), August 4, p 1.

Guru, Gopal, 1985, Politics of reservations : A class approach, *Social Change* 4 (3) April-June, p 131-139, bibliography.

Guru, Gopal, 1984, Reservations and the Sanskritisation of scheduled castes : Some theoretical aspects, *Sociological Bulletin* 33 (1-2) March-September, p 29-38, bibliography.

Hanumantha Rao, 1990, Job reservations for backward classes, *Mainstream* 28 (46) September 8, p 6.

Hasan, Shariful, 1985, Social-backwardness is the end result of poverty, *Organizer* 37 (1) May 19, p 8.

Hegde, Ramakrishna, 1986, Reservation policy in Karnataka, *Monthly Commentary on Indian Economic Conditions* 28 (2) September, p 10-13.

———, 1990, Hegde for economic criteria, *Indian Express*, September 19, p 9.

Heredia, Rudi, 1986, Minority rights and reservation policy : Towards coherence and consistence, *New Frontiers Education* 16 (2) April-June, p 60-63.

Hoshiar Singh and Malik, Jagdish Kumar, 1984, The Mandal Commission report: A plea for share in power, *Political Science Review* 23 (3-4) July-December, 250-268, bibliography, tables.

Jain, Deepa, 1985, Should reservation policy be continued? *Radical Humanist* 49 (1) April, p 25-28.

Karanalki, Jose, 1986, Secular state and religious criterion for reservation, *Social Action* 36 (2) April-June, p 137-148.

Khusro, A.M., 1990, Job reservations : Pro-side, con-side and inside, *Indian Express*, September 13.

Kothari, Milap, 1990, What price reservation, *Hindustan Times*, September 6.

Leela Singh, 1984, Job reservation : Political and legal perspective, *Modern Review* 148 (9-10) September-October, p 267-274, bibliography.

Limay, Madhu, 1990, Reservations, *Hindustan Times*, September 10.

Makwana, Yogendra,1985, Reservation : Does it promote class war, *Link* 27 (36) April 21, p 9-11.

Manohara Prasad N., 1986, The great reservation divide, *Social Action* 36 (2) April-June, p 212-219.

Mathew, P.M., 1988, Caste reservations : A critique, *Social Change*, 18 (2) June, p 93-99, bibliography.

Mehta, Dhawal, 1985, Anti-reservation agitation in Gujarat, *Radical Humanist* 49 (4) July, p 25-31.

Mehta, Haroobhai and Patel, Hasmukh, 1985, *Dynamics of reservation policy*, Patriot Publishing, New Delhi, 320 p.

Mishra, K.K., 1985, The Dalits reply back, *Link* 27 (36) April 21, p 13.

Nehru, B.K., 1988, Do we still need reservations, *Indian Express* April 17, p 1, col 1-6.

Nehru, Jawaharlal, 1990, Nehru was against quota in services, *Indian Express*, September 19.

Pandya, Dinakar, 1985, Defeated casteists on rampage, *Link* 27 (33) March 31, p 21-27.

Paranjape, H.K., 1985, New look at reservations : Other ways to better opportunities, *Times of India*, June 6, p 8; 7 (8) June, p 8.

Parmanand Singh, 1987, Preventing exploitative acquisition of reservation benefits through adoption strategem, *Journal of Indian Law Institute* 29 (1) January-March, p 100-109, footnote.

———, 1987, Reservations reality and the Constitution: Current crisis in India, *Cochin University Law Review* 11 (3-4) September-December, p 284-318.

Paswan, Ram Vilas, 1990, Reservation won't lead to mediocrity, *Patriot* September 3.

Patwardhan, Vidya and Palshikar, Vasant, 1990, Are educational reservations a waste? The results of a survey, *Janata*, 45, Annual Number, p 35-39.

Pinto, Marina, 1980-1981, Reservation policy in India, *Journal of the University of Bombay* 49 (53), p 65-82, table.

Rajaiah, B., 1982, Reservations in higher education and jobs, *Educational Review* 88 (3) March, p 55-58.

Ramnathan, K.V., 1990, Reservations: Lessons from experience, *Indian Express*, September 7.

Roy, Ashim K., 1985, Anti-reservation movement: A political assessment, *Economic and Political Weekly* 20 (32) August 10, p 1343-1344.

Saksena, N.S., 1985, The reservation issue: A possible basis for consensus, *Times of India*, May 3, p 3-5.

Seerval, H.M., 1985, Reservation is education and public service, *Monthly Commentary on Indian Economic Conditions* 27 (1) August, p 79-86.

Saraf, Pushp, 1990, Job reservation in Railways and accidents, *Indian Express*, September 19.

Shah, A.M., 1990, Reservations : Double talk on castes, *Hindustan Times*, September 7.

Shah, Ghan Shyam, 1985, Caste, class and reservation, *Economic and Political Weekly* 20 (3) January 19, p 132-136, footnotes.

———, 1987, Middle class politics : Case of anti-reservation agitation in Gujarat, *Economic and Political Weekly*, Annual Number, 22 (19-21) May, AN-155 - AN-172.

Sheth, D.L., 1985, The great reservation debate, *Indian Express* (Magazine) May 12, p 1 + ; *Sarvodaya* 33 (1-2) July-August, p 9-19.

———, 1986, The problem of reservations : Economic backwardness or social injustice? *Indian Journal of Adult Education* 47 (5) May, p 9-15; 47 (6) June, p 4-7 + ; 47 (7) July, p 14-21 ; 50 (1) April, p 9-14 ; 50 (2) May, p 13-19.

———, 1987, Reservation policy revisited, *Economic and Political Weekly* 22 (46) November 14, p 1957-1962, footnotes.

Shyama Nand Singh, 1986, Reservation controversy in Andhra Pradesh, *Mainstream* 25 (2) September 20, p 2-5 +, tables.

———, 1989, Politics of job reservation, *Mainstream* 27 (44) July 29, p 15-20, bibliography, tables.

Solanki, 1985, Only half of reserved jobs are filled, *Link* 27 (36) April 21, p 7-8.

Sundaresh, Aruna, 1989, Constitution law and reservations, *New Frontiers in Education* 16 (2) April-June, p 33-40.

Suri, Dona, 1985, Reservations : Are they still valid? *Tribune*, April 14, p 1.

Thirupati Rao, U., 1987, Job reservation policy in India, *Educational Review* 93 (2) February, p 29-31.

Vaid, Minnie, 1985, Gujarat is going the way of Assam, *Illustrated Weekly of India* 106 (8) June 30, p 36-37.

Verma, B.R., 1985, Rationale of reservations, *National Herald* (Sunday Herald) August 11, p 1 +.

Viswam, S., 1985, The reservation conundrum, *Mainstream* 23 (35) April 27, p 3-5 +.

Yagnik, Achyut and Desai, Harshad, 1985, The wages of populism, *Illustrated Weekly of India* 106 (8) June 30, p 38-39.

Social Change

Jetley, Surinder, 1968, Transfer of power to a low caste, *Interdiscipline* 5 (3) Autumn, p 199-206.

Social Classes

Aurora, G.S., 1968, Caste and backward classes. *Man in India* 48 (4) October-December, p 297-306, footnotes.

Blair, Harry, W., 1980, Rising kulaks and backward classes in Bihar : Social change in the late 1970s, *Economic and Political Weekly* 15 (2) January 12

Jetley, Surinder, 1968, Transfer of power to a low caste, *Interdiscipline* 5 (3) Autumn, p 199-216

Kothari, Rajni, 1970, *Caste in Indian politics*, Orient Longmans, New Delhi.

Kusumakar, H., 1986, To be "backward" is good, *Times of India* (Sunday Review), p 1-8.

Mallaradhyan, J.B., 1977, *Veerasaivas to be classified as Backward*, All India Veerasaivas Mahasabha, Bangalore.

Radhakrishnan, P., 1981, Tamil Nadu backward classes, *Voluntary Action* 27 (5-6) November-December, p 65-67 +.

Sinha, Surajit and Bhattacharya, Ranjit, 1969, Bhadralok and Chhotolok in a rural area of West Bengal, *Sociological Bulletin* 6 (2) January, p 104-106, references.

Welfare

Adibasi (Periodical), 1965, Defence-cum-production orientation of the programme of backward classes welfare, *Adibasi*, October, p 1-4, editorial.

Anon, 1947, Government drive for uplift of backward classes, *Social Service Quarterly* 33 (1) July, p 27-29.

———, 1953, Scheme of the Madras State Government for the welfare of the scheduled castes and scheduled tribes and other backward classes, included in the Five Year Plan, *Vanyajati*, 1 (2) April, p 42-43.

———, 1965, Welfare of backward classes : Planning Commission panel discussion, *Vanyajati*, 13 (2) April, p [illegible]-40 +.

Bajpai, Rajendra Kumari, 1986, National policy on upliftment of weaker sections, *Secular Democracy* 19 (1-2) January-February, p 51-52.

Biswas, Onell, 1985, *From justice to welfare*, Intellectual Publishing House, New Delhi, xix, 272 p.

Dava, P.C. 1966, Voluntary organisations and the welfare of backward classes, *Vanyajati* 14 (4) October, p 156-164.

Gopala Reddi, B., 1956, Welfare of tribals and other backward classes, *Indian Journal of Social Work* 16 (4) March, p 294-296.

Husain, Syed Khaja Mahboob, 1949, The rural uplift of tribes and backward classes in Hyderabad, Deccan, *Man in India*, 29 (3-4) July-December, p 185-198.

Nancharaiah, G., 1987, Land reforms and weaker sections : A case study, *Yojana* 31 (11) June 16, p 8-13, tables.

Index